LIFFEY
SHIPS
& SHIPBUILDING

PAT SWEENEY

LIFFEY SHIPS
& SHIPBUILDING

MERCIER PRESS

IRISH PUBLISHER – IRISH STORY

MERCIER PRESS

Cork

www.mercierpress.ie

Trade enquiries to CMD BookSource,

55a Spruce Avenue, Stillorgan Industrial Park,

Blackrock, County Dublin

ISBN: 978 1 85635 685 5

10 9 8 7 6 5 4 3 2 1

A CIP record for this title is available from the British Library

Printed and bound in the EU.

CONTENTS

ACKNOWLEDGEMENTS

This book has taken ten years to write and has been undertaken to tell the story of an all but unknown segment of the maritime history of Ireland and of Dublin in particular, in which I participated during my forty-five years as a professional photographer.

I wish to thank the following: the Marine Institute for financial support in travel; Niall Dardis of Dublin Port Archives; Rev. John Gordon, the last surviving director of the Liffey Dockyard, for permission to use photographs; Dr Maire Kennedy and the staff of the Dublin City Library & Archives, Pearse Street; Mr Terence Brownrigg for the photograph of his grandfather John Smellie and permission to quote from his book; Alan Twigg of Vancouver for permission to quote from his father's book Union Steamships Remembered; the authorities at the British National Archives, Kew, for permission to quote from British Admiralty records; Cambridge University Library for permission to quote from Vickers Archives held there; Penny Allen of Wanganui Archives and Rosemary Deane of Auckland Maritime Museum for permission to use photographs; and Terry Conlan for his encyclopaedic information on Irish coastal shipping companies.

To my family for all their encouragement and technical help from David, Paul, Roseanne and Niall. Finally to Rita my wife, who was always there when the seas got too rough. If I have left anyone out I apologise and all mistakes are mine.

Pat Sweeney, Stillorgan, Co. Dublin
June 2010

CHAPTER 1

THE STORY OF SHIPBUILDING ON THE LIFFEY

Recounting the story of iron and steel shipbuilding on the banks of the River Liffey, during the nineteenth and twentieth centuries, cannot be done in isolation because of the important part Ireland played in the naval defence of the British Empire. Indeed, even after the foundation of the Irish Free State, Britain felt Ireland was so vital to their naval interests that they held on to the Treaty Ports – Cobh, Berehaven and Lough Swilly – until 1938. Yet to the vast majority of people in Ireland, when shipbuilding is mentioned, they think only of Belfast, the Harland & Wolff shipyard and the tragic maiden voyage of the *Titanic* in 1912. However, the shipyards in Dublin were founded before Harland & Wolff and their story deserves to be told.

Pulling together information about early shipbuilding in Dublin is difficult, although there are references to vessels being built in the eighteenth century on the south bank of the river – roughly along the line of present-day Townsend Street, where the famous *Ouzel* galley, which disappeared for a number of years before turning up safely, is reputed to have been constructed in the late seventeenth century. The building of ships in those days was very different to modern times, as all that was needed was a sloping bank with a reasonable depth of water to launch a vessel and an open space to store the required timber, with a saw-pit and a hut for an office.

Dublin has the distinction of being the place where the first catamarans in the western world were constructed, designed by Sir William Petty.[1] Petty was a man of many talents, with an interest in ships and the sea, and well versed in navigation because of his knowledge of mathematics and astronomy. He was also secretary to Oliver Cromwell and is best known for the Down Survey of the lands confiscated by Cromwell. H. Gilligan notes that Petty's 'double bottom machine' as he termed his creation, was launched in 1662 and built on the banks of the Liffey 'above the old bridge', which possibly refers to the present-day Ellis or Wolf Tone Quays.[2] Her trials were so successful that the following year Petty challenged all the boats in the harbour to a sailing race and on 6 January 1663 three other boats were easily beaten by the *Invention,* which reached a speed of sixteen knots. The vessel, built with backing from the Royal Society in London, had twin hulls and measured 6 x 0.6 metres. Petty ordered a second catamaran in the same year from Arklow, County Wicklow, and she could carry thirteen men and ten cannon. In July 1663, this second ship -sailed the Holyhead packet to Howth by fifteen hours. A third craft was built in London and sailed to Portugal in 1665, but was lost in the Bay of Biscay on her return voyage. Undaunted Petty returned to Dublin and built a fourth vessel, the *St Michael,* in 1684 at Ringsend. However, this 50-foot vessel proved so unstable during trials that the crew refused to take her out, thus ending Petty's interest in double-hull vessels and catamarans.[3]

THE EIGHTEENTH CENTURY

There are references to shipbuilding in Dublin in the 1700s, when the Corporation for the Improvement of the Port of Dublin, or Ballast Office as it was known, ordered lighters, a type of flat-bottomed barge, in 1708 from shipbuilders James Adair, Nathaniel Dwyer and Francis Drake; unfortunately, the locations of their yards are unknown.[4] The next mention of shipbuilding comes from Faulkner's *Dublin Journal* of 18 March 1731, which records 'a large ship launched at the shipbuildings near the Strand, named the *Dorset of Ireland*, at which were present great numbers of nobility and gentry. The crowds were so great that three people had the misfortune of having a leg broke.'

The same paper reported twenty years later: 'On Saturday last was launched at George's Quay the *Goodman* brigantine, 80 tons, built by Adair and Smith ship carpenters, and is allowed by good judges to be compleat a vessel of her burthen as ever built in Dublin'.[5] Two years later the *Journal* again reports: 'Yesterday a Custom House vessel called *The Ponsonby*, was launched at the Point of Ringsend, which is to cruise against the smugglers on the coast of Galway'.

Finally, towards the end of the century a privateer was launched in Ringsend. *Exshaw's Magazine* noted: 'Wednesday at noon the *Fame* privateer was launched from King's boatyard at Ringsend in the sight of many thousands of spectators whom the curiosity of seeing so beautiful a vessel had drawn thither. It is thought by many experienced marines who have viewed her that she will be the fleetest sailer ever built at this place so celebrated for some years for constructing swift-going vessels. She is carvel-built from her bearing upwards, and is also to have at her head a large and noble figure of fame, resting her trumpet on the top of the prow or cutwater, which as well as the figure, is to be enriched with elegant carvings.'[6]

In 1786, Cardiff and Kehoe are recorded as operating at City Quay. Their partnership broke up when Matthew Cardiff moved further down river to Sir John Rogerson's Quay and set up his own premises which can be seen in the well-known painting, 'The Hibernian Marine School', by James Malton dated 1793 – to the right of the school is Cardiff's yard. This view, from across the river at Spencer Dock, shows timber floating in the Liffey for seasoning. An article in the *Dublin Historical Record* in the 1940s speaks of a Matthew Cardiff who operated a shipyard at 33 Sir John Rogerson's Quay on the south side of the Liffey from the late 1700s, where he built a 500 ton vessel towards the end of that century.[7]

THE NINETEENTH CENTURY

At the start of the 1800s the era of modern iron and later steel shipbuilding began. References in the almanacs for that time to sites in Dublin are not very clear and it is uncertain whether entries for shipwrights refer to their place of work or a home address used for business as well.

In 1804 the British Admiralty commissioned a survey to find out the numbers of men engaged in shipbuilding across the United Kingdom, including Ireland.[8] This included both the royal dockyards at places such as Chatham and Sheerness, which were building men of war for the Royal Navy, and private yards, which built merchant ships. The survey was carried out to discover what resources were available for the continuation of the war against France. The document, submitted to the House of Commons and published on 25 June 1805, gives a very informative picture of shipbuilding manpower throughout the UK.

The survey reported that there were 3,165 shipwrights, caulkers and apprentices in government dockyards and a further 9,630 men employed in the private sector. There were sixty-three ports listed in England and Wales, with another twenty-five in Scotland capable of building ships. In total there were some 500 yards recorded and the figures for Ireland reveal a surprising situation. There were 307 shipwrights, caulkers and apprentices on the island, sixty-one of whom were employed in two yards in Belfast, both with the name Ritchie, while in Dublin, there were 179 employed in nine yards on the River Liffey.[9] The survey also records that there were six employed in Derry, twenty-five in Limerick and twenty-six in Waterford including yards at Cheekpoint, Passage East and Ballyhack.[10] However, there is no mention of any shipbuilding in Cork which was very active later in that century. The survey reported no shipwrights and caulkers over fifty years of age, while there were eighty-seven under that age. There were eighty-three apprentices in Dublin. The reason for this is that by fifty a shipwright was 'burnt out' owing to the physically demanding work in handling the large pieces of timber. Many workers were forced to give up because of injuries rather than from age. The Admiralty needed to know the numbers of skilled and able-bodied men available to build merchant ships and men of war.

According to Joe Clarke, the size of the Irish yards at that time was typical of those in Britain, although the yard of Kehoe or Keough as recorded in the survey, would have been considered large by the standards of those outside London.[11] However, the percentage of apprentices in the Dublin yards, which he puts at 27%, is low compared with 47% in the other yards in the country.

Trying to identify the locations of the yards in the Dublin almanac of the day and match these to the names given in the survey is difficult, as the location of only two of the yards is known – Cardiff, Furlong & Company at 33 Sir John Rogerson's Quay and Anthony Hill at 61 Townsend Street. Hill's name appears in *The History of the Port of Dublin* by Harry Gilligan, who located the yard in Ringsend and Gilligan refers to Hill building the hull of the first steam dredge for the Ballast Board in 1814.[12]

IRON SHIPBUILDING ARRIVES

The first iron vessel constructed in Dublin was apparently not built on Liffeyside for sea-going service, but on the banks of the Grand

Canal for inland navigation at Rathmines Bridge. The Grand Canal Company had introduced passenger services in 1788, and the vessels they used were horse-drawn and known as passage boats. These were divided into two cabins with the first-class forward and second-class aft. While the forward passengers had a table between the two facing seats, the second class had an extra of rows of seats back to back in place of the first-class table. The forward or state cabin, as it was known, could accommodate forty-five gentlemen and ladies, while thirty-five persons occupied the common cabin – both of them must have been very cramped.

In 1814, the directors of the company became interested in steam propulsion. One of them, James Dawson, is understood to have taken out a patent for a steamboat, which he had constructed in the previous year. This vessel seems to have been a type of catamaran, which had a paddle-wheel mounted between the two hulls and was capable of speeds up to three miles per hour. However, nothing further is heard of him or his craft.

Dawson was not the only inventor offering ideas to the Canal Company for pulling barges on the waterway. Two years later, the company directors carried out towing trials on the river in December 1816 with the steamer, *Princess Charlotte*.

The Grand Canal Company attempted to produce a lighter vessel and in 1828, William Mallet of Portobello Harbour, Rathmines, built an iron passage boat.[13] Named the *Harty*, she was horse-drawn, but even after modifications, she proved to be very heavy when loaded, making her too slow for the job she was intended for and she was sold in 1843 to Robinson of Athlone for conversion into a steamer.

In 1830 another iron vessel, the *Lord Cloncurry*, was constructed for the company by John Marshall at Ringsend, while in 1832 the *Hibernia* was delivered by Courtney Clarke, Ringsend Iron Works, at a cost of £275. Like previous vessels these were too heavy. The following year, the most successful of the company's Irish-built craft, the *James*, was delivered by Marshall, but even she did not last long and was broken up in 1849. In 1834, Courtney Clarke built an experimental steamboat named the *Rocket*, for the Grand Canal Company, but she, too, was not a success.

At the end of the 1830s, the Grand Canal Company was coming under increasing competition from the newly established railways and in the 1840s, in a desperate attempt to regain traffic, the directors decided to order two new iron passage boats. These two vessels carried 100 passengers and the hulls were built at a cost of £230 each by Barrington's of Ringsend, who had taken a thirty-year lease on the dry docks there. Their oscillating engines were manufactured by Messrs Inshaw of Birmingham and cost £475 pounds each. The boats were completed in 1852, but were not successful and the Grand Canal Company closed its passenger service on 31 December of that year. The two craft were used as tugs for a while, after which their engines were removed and they became cargo vessels until sold seven years later.

In 1851 Barrington's constructed *Towing Steamer No. 2* at a cost of £250 for the hull and a further £200 for the twin engines, again manufactured by Messrs Inshaw of Birmingham. Two days of trials were carried out by Sir John McNeill with this vessel, which was 60 feet in length and had a 12-foot beam. The first trial was on 24 April 1851, when three runs were made over a quarter-mile course; with a boiler pressure of 50 lbs per square inch and loaded with 41 tons of cargo, a speed of 3.5 mph was reached. On the following day when towing another barge loaded with 53 tons, only 2.29 mph could be reached. For the last run of the day, a second barge with 30 tons of cargo was added, giving a total load of 124 tons, which further reduced the speed to 2.05 mph. Two days later, on 26 April, *Towing Steamer No. 2*, this time loaded with only 20 tons, clocked 4 mph on her first run. For the second run, she pulled the barge loaded with the 30 tons and reached 2.43 mph. On the last trial that day, with the 50-ton loaded barge added, giving a total of

100 tons, a speed of 2.31 mph was reached. Following these tests, Sir John concluded that the barges in use, which had a hull similar to the Thames sailing barges, were too heavy and were unsuitable for canal navigation.[14]

To return to Liffeyside, the yard on Sir John Rogerson's Quay owned by Cardiff remained under his name until 1826. The following year he was replaced by Patrick Brady, a shipwright. The only vessel that is known to have been constructed by Brady is the *Brilliant*. Built in 1832, she was a lightship, costing £1,983 and was ordered by the lighthouse authority of the day, the Ballast Office. The ship was of 140 tons gross and was constructed of teak frames, with oak, teak and elm planking. It measured 67 feet in length and had a beam of 20 feet.[15] In 1833, the port's chief engineer, George Halpin Senior, gave evidence to the Commission on Tidal Harbours that there were then only four persons in Dublin building or repairing boats – Clements, Hill, Marshall and Brady. Strangely no mention is made of Courtney Clarke who built the ships for the Grand Canal Company. Just twenty-two years later, in 1855, the last mention of the Brady name on Sir John Rogerson's Quay is recorded.[16]

Also in 1855, an iron steamer called the *Sea Flower* (Official Number (ON) 26051), of 23 tons gross, 58 feet 3 inches in length, with a beam of 11 feet 4 inches and propelled by a 20 horsepower (HP) engine driving a screw, was registered in Dublin, owned by A.W. Lawe of Glanmire, Cork.[17] However, her builder is not identified and the almanac for that year gives a number of names in Thorncastle Street on the River Dodder, any one of which could have constructed this vessel. They were William Clements, shipbuilder; Henry Teal, shipbuilder and surveyor of steamers; the Dublin Dockyard Company; and Richard Weldrick, shipwright.

By 1855 there was an upsurge of trade into Dublin. This was caused by two factors: one was the increase in world commerce and the second was the increase in the depth of water on the Liffey bar. This was the result of the building of the North Bull Wall by George Halpin Senior, which together with the earlier Great South Wall, scoured the channel, allowing larger vessels to use the port and leading to an increased demand for better berths in the harbour. Timber wharves were constructed in front of the existing quays on the north side of the Liffey, to allow ships to lie afloat in the deeper water. Existing repair facilities and slips were not considered adequate for the larger ships now using the port, and plans were drawn up for a large graving dock, which could be drained of water to allow repairs to ships below the waterline. It was agreed that, to accommodate the latest mail steamers of that time, the new dock should be 400 feet long and 70 feet wide. The contract to build the dock went to the famous Irish railway engineer William Dargan and construction commenced in 1853. The dock took seven years to complete, at a cost of £116,704 pounds, and when complete was actually 80 feet wide. The first dock gates were constructed in Dublin by J.R. Mallet at their Victoria foundry and remained in service until 1881. These were replaced by another pair, which were in use until 1931.

This graving dock was opened on 9 February 1860 and remained in continuous service until 1989, when it had to be closed owing to the unsafe condition of the final pair of gates. Plans by the Port & Docks Board to fill in the dock to create more quay space for containers were not carried out and after a gap of some five years the gates were repaired and the facility was back in use until 2002, when the graving dock was permanently taken out of service. It was finally filled in in 2008.

THE ESTABLISHMENT OF THE NORTH WALL SHIPYARD

After the completion of the new graving dock, plans were put in hand to establish a yard to build large vessels in iron. Iron shipbuilding, which commenced in the early 1820s, accounted for some 50% of all vessels constructed in the United Kingdom by 1860. The 1863 Dublin street directory records for the first time, 'Walpole and Webb, Port of Dublin Shipyard, Iron and Wooden Shipbuilders'. This was the first of the operating firms at the new yard. The entry was changed the following year to read: 'Walpole, Webb and Bewley' to signal a new member of the partnership. This company was located at the then eastern extremity of the North Wall on reclaimed land leased from the Ballast Office, and alongside the new dry dock.

Before the establishment of this new yard, there was no tradition of iron-working on the Liffey, other than the few examples mentioned. Although there were four main employers of ironworkers at that time in the city – the Great Southern & Western Railway at Inchicore; the Midland Great Western Railway at the Broadstone; the Dublin & Drogheda Railway at Amiens Street; and the Dublin & Kingstown Company at Grand Canal Street – their workers, most of whom were boilermakers, would have been reluctant to leave the railway shops, as employment there was considered very secure. The first craftsmen had to be brought in from 'across the water' to build ships and get the yard up and running.

In nineteenth-century Ireland, most development was funded by cross-channel investors, as the conservative Irish preferred to put money into property. In 1854, Edward Harland came to Belfast to manage the shipyard of Edward Hickson, which the previous year had converted from building ships out of timber to using iron for construction. The owner had iron mines in Antrim and was seeking an outlet for iron plates. In 1859, Harland took over the yard and with the help of Gustavus Wolff, his partner, established the Harland & Wolff name. A Prussian financier in Liverpool provided capital and Harland's relationship with the Bibby shipping family in Liverpool ensured building orders for his yard.

An interesting aspect of the new North Wall shipyard is who the men behind the establishment of this yard were. Unlike Harland &

Wolff, the founders of the Dublin shipyard were all members of the Society of Friends, better known as the Quakers. The forefathers of the Quakers came to Ireland as part of Cromwell's army and in those days soldiers were paid at the end of a campaign with the spoils of war and land. Arriving in Ireland between 1650 and 1680, they settled first in Ulster, at Lisburn and Lurgan, and were then given land grants in the Suir valley. Later they spread to Cork and Waterford. A number of these soldiers turned their backs on war and became Quakers, a religious group who were opposed to war. They also refused to pay tithes or swear an oath of allegiance to the British monarchy and as a result were treated as second-class citizens similar to Catholics and regarded with hostility by the authorities. They were also excluded from university education and the professions. However, the Quakers themselves considered risk-taking a virtue when using their own money and they did not have an aversion 'to being in trade', which was looked down upon by the aristocracy (an attitude which lasted in some quarters in England right up to the Second World War). The Quakers became involved in milling and shipping, and also prospered as grain and wool merchants, and tea and coffee importers before 1800. Quaker families such as the Pims, Jacobs and Bewleys became household names in Dublin for their shopping, biscuits, and tea and coffee respectively.

The family with the longest involvement in the new shipyard was the Bewleys, who lived at Rockville House, Blackrock. Samuel Bewley (1767–1845) was in sugar refining and was also a shipowner trading in the Far East. His brother, Charles Bewley, made the first direct shipment of tea from China to Dublin, and Samuel's two sons, John Frederick Bewley (1841–1890) and Thomas Arthur (1841–1889), worked in the new yard. The other two men behind the yard were Thomas Walpole of Windsor Lodge, Monkstown, County Dublin and William Henry Webb of 7 Palmerstown Road, Rathmines. Thomas Walpole (1826–1901) was without doubt the most important man in the new enterprise with his experience in shipbuilding from his time in Waterford, where he had been the technical head of the White shipyard, which had started building wooden ships in 1820s. The Bewleys also had an association going back years with the White yard. In 1825 the fourth vessel launched there, the *Eblana*, was built for the Bewleys. The *Hellas* was also constructed for them by Whites in 1832 – she was the vessel that brought the first direct shipment of 2,099 chests of tea from Canton to Dublin on 1 March 1835.

Many of the men who populated the new Dublin yard had served their apprenticeships in shipbuilding yards in other parts of Ireland. The White shipyard was laid out in the 1820s and commenced building wooden vessels. The workforce at the Ferrybank yard was trained thoroughly by the yard superintendent Stephen Smith, who was considered to be a gifted builder and designer. Both Stephen Smith and his son Charles insisted on the highest standards and instilled into their trainees the need to have a great pride in their craft. Walpole was responsible for the design of the vessels *Pathfinder* in 1858 and *Mohican* in 1859, both built for Bath & Company of Swansea, which carried copper ore from Chile to England. In 1856 White's yard had constructed the largest sailing ship in Ireland, the 201-foot long *Merrie England*. However, the company went into decline in the 1860s and closed because of the advent of iron as a stronger building material.

The shining star of Waterford shipbuilding was the Neptune yard, which was owned by Joseph Malcomson, also a Quaker. The yard was only part of the family's industrial empire, which included shipping lines, the cotton mills at Portlaw and coal mining in the Ruhr valley. The Neptune yard built the *Neptune*, a 172-foot iron hull screw-propelled steamer in 1846. This yard, according to Bill Irish, gave Waterford the dominant role in iron shipbuilding in Ireland between 1850 and 1865.[18] The yard was a leader in the innovation of water-tight compartments, which were introduced on the *Leda* of 1854. Four iron vessels of over 300 feet in length were constructed in the 1860s. However, the Neptune facility built only for the Malcomson shipping companies group and outside orders were not solicited. This led to the yard's closure when it was sold to pay debts incurred by other companies in the group which were in difficulties.

In the middle of the nineteenth century there were three shipyards in Cork. Messrs Lecky & Beale launched an iron ship in March 1846 and continued to build large vessels up to 150 feet in length until they merged with the Cork Steamship Company in 1856. That yard had also commenced building iron ships in 1846. They continued building large vessels up to 220 feet in length until 1868 when the yard closed after a fire. The third iron shipyard on the Lee was Robinsons, which existed from the mid 1850s to the late 1860s, and became the leading yard, obtaining orders for tonnage from overseas as well as Irish owners, including the Malcomsons for whom they completed nine vessels. The largest, the *Lara*, was launched in 1863. The company went into decline in the early 1870s.

The River Lee has the distinction of being the river on which the first steamer in Ireland was constructed. This was the *City of Cork*, launched at Passage West from Andrew Hennessy's yard on 15 June 1815, for Captain Michael O'Brien of Cork and Christopher Owens of Cove (Cobh). The event was reported in the *Cork Mercantile Chronicle* of 12 June 1815. A number of other builders existed at Passage and later in the century a thriving ship repair business was carried on there. Also many vessels part-discharged cargoes there to reduce their draft to be able to proceed upriver to Cork city.

EARLY DAYS AT THE NORTH WALL

In 1860 it was recorded that a Mr Walpole became supervisor of

White's yard in Waterford and designed the last three vessels built there. He left the yard, which was in decline, in 1862. This Mr Walpole was without doubt Thomas Walpole, as archives in the Quaker library in Dublin disclose that he went to Waterford in 1851 and returned to the capital in 1862. His background at White's yard must have induced the Bewley family to become involved with him in his new venture, as he clearly had the skills necessary to build ships. This background also accounted for the new yard being entrusted with initial orders from Liverpool. Hard-headed Mersey shipowners would certainly not have come to a new and untried yard unless completely satisfied that the workmanship and standard of the ships to be built would be of a sufficient standard. Thomas Walpole is listed as living in Monkstown from 1864 until 1869.

The third person involved in the setting up of the North Dublin yard, Henry Webb, also appears to have had shipbuilding experience. A reference in the library of the Institution of Civil Engineers in Dublin credits him with serving his time in Liverpool along with Edward Harland, but this cannot be correct as Harland served his apprenticeship on the north-east coast of England, which he completed in 1850, while Webb is recorded by the Quakers' archives as going to Hull much later, in 1859.

The new yard's first launching was the *Knight Commander* (ON 48802, with the signal letters VWHK). Her owners were Messrs Carlyle and Company, the principal of which was T.H. Ismay, who four years later founded the White Star Line when he purchased the company and house-flag of Messrs Pilkington and Wilson for £1,000. We have two accounts of this first launch of an iron steamship in Dublin. The first, from *The Illustrated London News* of 1864, described:

Launch of the *Knight Commander* Iron Steamship at Dublin. The launch of the first large iron vessel ever built in the Port of Dublin is a noteworthy event in the progress of Irish industry and commerce. We have therefore engraved on this page a sketch of the *Knight Commander*, as she glided off her cradle into the high tide waters of the Liffey, on the morning of Wednesday week. The Lord Lieutenant of Ireland, with a large company of distinguished guests, visited on the occasion the building yard of Messrs Walpole, Webb and Bewley, North Wall. The Marchioness of Kildare performed the ladylike office of 'christening' the young ship by breaking a bottle of wine upon the bows. Next moment the 'dog shores' or props by which the vessel was upheld, were knocked away, and she gracefully descended into the river, saluted by the guns of HMS *Ajax* and by the cheers of the 20,000 spectators. The *Knight Commander* belongs to Messrs Carlyle and Gedes of Liverpool and is intended for the Calcutta trade. Her keel was laid down in January 1863, but it was necessary to go to work several months before that time, in order to firm the ground upon which her building was to take place, for which purpose, by driving in piles for an embankment, a space was reclaimed from the swampy bottom formerly covered by every tide. Sheds and workshops were erected on the artificial shore, where about 300 Irish workmen have been busy for the last twelvemonth, under skilled English and Scottish shipwrights or engineers, in building this fine iron steam vessel. Her length overall is 230 feet; between perpendiculars 210 feet; keel 200 feet; breadth of beam (moulded), 36 feet 6 inches; depth of hold 25 feet 3 inches to 26 feet 8 inches. Registered tonnage 1,450 tons, burden 2,500 tons. Her lower masts, bowsprit, and some of the yards are steel manufactured by Messrs Cato, Miller & Co., and the standing rigging is of steel wire. The same Dublin shipbuilders are now constructing a very swift passenger steamer to ply between Dublin and Kingstown, besides a ship 1,200 tons and several smaller craft.[19]

The London report is interesting on two counts. The first is its inaccuracy: the vessel is described as an iron steamer, when in fact she was a full-rigged sailing ship (square sails on three masts). Secondly the report confirms that skilled English and Scottish craftsmen had to be brought from the other side of the Irish Sea to the yard.

A local account of this event is found in *The Irish Times* and remarks made by the owner of the ship, James Carlyle, in reply to the toast of the ship are worth noting. The paper recorded his claim that 'the order had come to Dublin because of a visit by a young man to Liverpool, where they had twelve shipyards looking for work. He told him that he had set up shipbuilding in Dublin at the end of the North Wall where there was a lighthouse.' Carlyle concluded that 'it was a bold stroke for him, but a bold stroke always gained the day and the contract was signed.'[20] The young man who made the visit was Thomas Walpole.

According to Ernest B. Anderson, this vessel 'was a beautiful ship and might be termed a clipper ... she nearly came to disaster on her maiden voyage, while at anchor in Calcutta, when she was caught in the 1864 cyclone [and] was stranded and badly damaged. However she was re-floated repaired and stayed in the Calcutta and Australian trades until 1883 when she was sold.'[21] The next owners that we know of for the *Knight Commander* were Henry Ferne & Sons, also of Liverpool and she remained with them for seven years, until she passed into the hands of other Mersey owners Lowden & Company of Liverpool, who converted her in 1892 to barque rig. She was still in the general cargo trade at the end of the nineteenth century.

There is a certain amount of difficulty regarding the names and actual number of vessels built at the new yard. Harry Gilligan, who was secretary of the Dublin Port & Docks Board for many years, recorded in the *History of the Port of Dublin* that 'the yard's first customer was the board itself, which ordered an iron float [hopper] and that the order appeared to have been satisfactorily carried out, since the following year three further floats were ordered from the yard'.[22] However, no other information on this hopper is known, as no record has been discovered of any steam-propelled hoppers owned by the Port Board in the Mercantile & Navy List issued by the Board of Trade in London at that time. The only vessel recorded was the *Number One*, built Drogheda in 1866 and registered in Dublin in 1867. At that time many ships were not registered with the Board of Trade, but if the Drogheda-built ship was, it would be expected that a vessel built on the Liffey would also be officially entered on the register.

The second known vessel produced by the yard was the *Caldback* (ON 50284, with signal letters WHMF), of 807 tons gross and launched on 16 July 1864 for Messrs R. Nicholson of Liverpool. *The Irish Times* reported on the event on Monday 18 July and commented that 550 men were employed in the yard. Little is known about this second vessel, although a letter from the Rev. Harold Jones, printed in *Sea Breezes* magazine, recorded that he saw her hull beached 50 feet above the high water mark at Praia Grande in 1900.[23] He was seeking information as to how she ended up there.

In 1865 came another full-rigged ship and the last sailing vessel from the yard. She was the *British Nation* (ON 51477 with letters JTRH), a somewhat larger ship of 1,302 tons built for the British Shipowners Company of Liverpool. Ernest Anderson described her as one of the fastest in their fleet and she remained in the Calcutta trade until 1880, when she was sold to Messrs Sandbach, Tinne & Co. Ltd of Liverpool. The *British Nation*, which was the first iron ship in that owner's fleet, continued in the Indian trade. Her new owners had a contract to transport Indian labourers from Calcutta to the West Indies to work in the sugar plantations. There is a reference in *Sea Breezes* magazine for June 1936, about an event aboard the *British Nation* while she was in West Indian waters under the heading 'A Marvellous Boat Race'. The letter, written by H. Noyes Lewis, is worth quoting:

> The death of King George has brought to my mind an unbelievable boat race. HMS *Bacchante*, in which King George and the Duke of Clarence were then midshipmen, was anchored in Port of Spain

(Trinidad) when the coolie ship *British Nation,* in which I was third mate, arrived there.

The Harbour Master's had beaten the man-o-war's boat and the jubilation of the coloured population was hysterical. One day the Harbour Master came aboard, and was closeted in the saloon with our captain, while on deck the five splendid negroes who manned his boat were telling of their conquest. 'Bah,' said our chief mate, pointing to our gig, he said, 'I'd beat you with that boat any day.'

'Ga way massa mate, you talk too fooleesh,' replied the coxswain.

However when the Captain and the Harbour Master came from the cabin a race was arranged, and I believe that each of them wagered £5 on their respective boats. A day a fortnight ahead was fixed for it. The coloured men wanted a two mile course, but our mate (relying on the staying power of his crew) refused to start unless a four mile one was agreed and he won the day.

Noyes Lewis went on:

Now John Pierce was the finest seaman and chief officer that I have ever known. He was of Plymouth and had spent his spare time when a boy with the trawlers, and was an expert boat sailor and racer. The gig was got on deck and upturned. Her bottom was scraped bright and french polished, and the crew, who were very keen, practised every evening under Pierce's training, and a fine lot they were, for we had sailed from London on that voyage and a finer lot of quite efficient seamen I believe never trod a deck than they; Forrest, Yates, Matthews and Easom were chosen by Pierce for the boat.

A lighter was anchored two miles down the coast, and on the Saturday of the race the gulf was like a sheet of looking glass; a calm that only Trinidad knows and the entire population of the port was on the pier or sea-front, excited to frenzy. The crews of every ship then at anchor were in the rigging or lining the bulwarks. The boats were lined up opposite the pier end, and at gunfire off they went. To our horror the Harbour Master's boat, which was longer than ours and painted white; ours for the occasion being blue (upper strakes); jumped ahead on the first stroke. But we were puzzled because, having started so well, she did not increase her lead by one inch; and so they jogged along till we lost sight of them as they rounded the lighter; the blue boat nearly touching the stern of the white one all the way. But to our astonishment the blue boat came clear well ahead, and it appeared to us watchers that from that moment she just jumped a boat's length to the good at every stroke, and … the unbelievable part is that she finished one mile ahead, one out of four!

The secret of it was that Pierce had, with difficulty, restrained the enthusiasm of his crew on the way down, and, keeping close to the stern of the white boat he was being towed by it. But the Negroes had put all out on the way down and were fagged when they rounded the lighter, whereas our men were fresh; and the white boat being longer than ours, had made a wide sweep to round the mark, when Pierce making his men shorten in their port oars, slipped in between his antagonists and the lighter, and so came out a length ahead.

This was quite a story of fine boat handling.

In 1902 the ship was sold to German owners and renamed the *H. Hackfield*, while three years later in 1905, she hoisted the Norwegian flag as the *Australia*, but nothing is known about her ultimate fate.

THE FIRST STEAMSHIP OF THE NORTH DUBLIN YARD

In 1864, as noted in the *Illustrated London News*, Walpole, Webb and Bewley laid down the keel of their first steamship: 'The iron saloon paddle vessel, the *Anna Liffey*, for excursion traffic between Dublin and Kingstown'. Her owners were the Dublin and Kingstown Steam Packet Company, which was set up in 1861 in response to the poor service and high fares charged to the public by the Dublin & Wicklow Railway. The packet company was formed to run steamers between Dublin, Kingstown and Wicklow, and in July of that year, they took delivery of two steamers. The *Anna Liffey* (ON 49516) was handed over in 1865 and operated between Kingstown and Wicklow. The ships provided a good service, but the company closed in 1867, as traffic had declined because of competition from the London North Western Railway Company. The *Anna Liffey* is understood to have been sold to a company in South America.

The next steamship, and the first screw vessel built by the yard, was the *Lady Wodehouse* (ON 49527), built to the order of the British & Irish Steam Packet Company of Dublin and launched on 5 December 1865. In the following day's issue of *The Irish Times* it was noted that the 851-ton vessel was launched a day late because of the weather. The report continued: 'The ship was named by Miss Egan daughter of the secretary of her owners. She would carry fifty first class, sixty second class and steerage passengers. That she was the eleventh vessel by the yard and that a large screw collier was on the stocks for a UK Steam Collier Company'. This report that the *Lady Wodehouse* was the eleventh ship built by Walpole, Webb & Bewley raises the question of the number of vessels built by the yard, and one must ask if the reporter intended to convey the number of all the ships built and ordered in the yard up to that time?

We know that three small vessels were built by the yard in 1866. The only way to trace these is through their official numbers from the registers of the Board of Trade, the British government department responsible for merchant shipping. However, those registers are not an exact guide to the date of a ship's completion, as many small vessels were not officially registered until a number of years after they were built. All three ships were registered in Dublin in 1867 under the ownership of the Irish Sea Fishing Company of 179 Great Brunswick Street, in that city. The first recorded was the *Herring* (ON 55226), a screw steamer, 54 feet 4 inches in length and with a 14-foot beam, of 31 tons and propelled by a 60 HP engine. She was next registered at Belfast in 1877 as owned by James Douglas. Two years later she took her second name *Belfast*, when she was lengthened. In the next century, she became the *Moorcock*, and in 1919 was registered in Middlesbrough as the *Lily Duncan*, where she was also rebuilt.

The next vessel, the slightly smaller *Turbot* (ON 55228), had a length of 48 feet and a beam of 13 feet, of 28 tons gross and was propelled by a 67 HP engine driving a screw. By 1875, she was owned by William Williams, 115 Bridge Street, Birkenhead and registered in Liverpool.

The third ship, the *Pilchard* (ON 55234), was 45 feet 8 inches in length, with a beam of 13 feet 7 inches, and was propelled by a 20 HP engine driving a single screw. Her tonnage was 21. Five years later, she crossed the Irish Sea when bought by Robert Johnson Moss of Liverpool. In 1880, she was registered at Alexandria in Egypt, under the same owner. The type of these vessels is not known and they could have been fishing craft or towing vessels.

The two largest ships recorded as leaving the yard in 1866 were colliers, the first being the *Shark* (ON 55240). The Mercantile & Maritime Directory for 1871 shows her as owned by W.L. Moore of London. She was a ship of 163 tons, with dimensions of 119 feet 4 inches long and 19 feet 9 inches beam and propelled by a two cylinder 40 HP engine supplied by McNab of Greenock, Scotland. The *Shark* was sold for the first time in her thirty-four-year career in 1868, to the Berwick & London SS Company in the town of Berwick on the north-east coast of England and was renamed the *Tweed*. The following year she was recorded as being resold to a William Johnston of Liverpool and resumed her original name, which she kept until the end of her days. The *Shark* was sold a number of times and then in 1879 she was again Irish-owned when she was bought by Martin L. Moore of Dublin, who then sold her to Stephen B. Walsh of Kilmallock, County Limerick. In 1880, she returned to Dublin, owned once again by W.L. Moore, and later that year crossed the Irish Sea once more into the hands of Welsh owners. She came back to Ireland for the last time in 1888 with the Newry Steamship Co. Her last sale was in 1892 to the Boston and Hull Steamshipping Co. Ltd. On 6 December 1899, she left North Queens Ferry in the Firth of Forth with a cargo of granite for the port of Hull and disappeared without trace.[24]

The second collier completed in 1866 by the yard, was the vessel *Dublin* (ON 55293), of 494 tons. She was the first steamship ordered by Robert Tedcastle of Great Brunswick (now Pearse) Street for his coal importing business. Robert Tedcastle had come originally from Annan in Dumfriesshire in Scotland about twenty years before to act as the agent for a Cumberland colliery. Later he started his own coal importing business. He prospered and went into shipping, bought his first vessel, a sailing collier in 1856, and eventually owned a number of ships. The *Dublin* was placed on the Liverpool service in 1872. In 1885, Tedcastle took over the Whitehaven Steam Navigation Company and in 1897 merged with another firm, John McCormack, under the name of Tedcastle McCormack. They shared the Liverpool trade with the City of Dublin Steam Packet Company. While the *Dublin* was scrapped in 1890, Tedcastle McCormack continued to operate until 1919, when the six remaining steamers were sold to their City of Dublin partners.

The next ship launched was in 1867. It was the steamer *Dodder* (ON 55237), a paddle vessel 148 feet in length with a 17-foot beam, ordered by the London North Western Railway Company. This ship was intended to provide a link from Warrenpoint, the nearest railhead to Belfast on the County Down side of Carlingford Lough, and the new cross-channel port at Greenore in County Louth, the first railway-owned harbour in Ireland. However, since the Holyhead to Greenore route had not yet opened, the *Dodder* sailed between Dublin and Kingstown as an excursion vessel until 1873. Perhaps it was this competition which led to the closure of the Dublin & Kingstown Company. When the Greenore service began, she sank in July 1873, after a collision with the *Countess of Erne* another of the railway-owned fleet, which had come from the Dublin yard in 1868. The paddle steamer was raised in 1874, but the Warrenpoint to Greenore feeder service closed in August 1876, as by that time Greenore was connected by railway to Dundalk, and later the line was extended to Newry in 1876. The *Dodder* was withdrawn and converted into a coaling stage at Holyhead and broken up in 1890.

In 1867 the yard also built the first lightship ordered by the Commissioners of Irish Lights, the new lighthouse authority for Ireland, which had just been established to take over responsibility for all the navigation marks round the coast. Named *Shamrock*, she was constructed of oak frames, teak and elm planking sheathed with yellow metal and carrying a day mark and mast. She had the dimensions of 96 feet by 21 feet by 10 feet and cost £5,125 to build. 1867 also saw the completion of another vessel, with an interesting history. She was the *Boulogne* (ON 58400), of 257 tons gross, first recorded as owned by J.F. Bewley and registered in Gloucester, England. She was registered back in Dublin two years later as the *Tolka*, with her owner given as Michael Murphy, 17 Eden Quay, Dublin. She had dimensions of length 144 feet and beam 21 feet, and was propelled by a 50 HP engine. In 1874 her port of registry changed to Liverpool and her ownership changed to John Miller Junior, 3 York Buildings, still with the name *Tolka*. In 1878 Belfast became her port of registry and she was then owned by William A. Grainger. In the Lloyd's Register of Shipping for 1894 she surfaces in Norway as the *Thor*.

The following year, 1868, another lightship, the *Osprey*, was built for the Commissioners, which was sold out of the service in 1916. The yard also constructed three passenger vessels, two for the Irish Sea trade and the third for use on Lough Erne. The first to be constructed was the *Countess of Erne* (ON 58409), which was completed in September. This was the second vessel ordered by the London North Western Railway Company, but was intended for the Holyhead to Dublin service. A paddle steamer of 800 tons she could achieve a speed of thirteen knots and when the Greenore Service opened in 1873, she was transferred to the new route and inaugurated the first west-bound sailing from Holyhead on

2 May 1873. It was during her time on the Greenore run that she collided with and sank the *Dodder*. She was also involved in another collision with a steamer in 1883, the collier *Captain Parry*. The *Countess* was repaired and sold in 1889 to the Bristol Steam Navigation Company, but operated on their services to Cork and Waterford for only a year. She became a coaling hulk at Weymouth in Dorset, and was wrecked there in a storm in 1935.

The yard's next ship was the *Knockinny* of 70 tons, completed in the autumn of 1868, the first screw steamer to operate on Lough Erne for carrying passengers. She was built for J.G.V. Porter, Lisbellaw, County Fermanagh. She travelled to the lake via the River Shannon and was reputed to have taken three weeks to make the forty-mile passage on the Shannon Erne Canal which had fallen into disuse at that time. She made her maiden voyage in November and at first undertook a single weekly sailing to Belturbet and to Belleek from Enniskillen. In the 1870s her owner opened a hotel on the lough and used the vessel to carry guests there from Enniskillen. There does not seem to have been enough regular passenger or cargo traffic on the lakes to make her a paying proposition and she spent the remainder of her life running excursions. In 1903, she was laid up and sometime during the Great War she was scrapped.

The final passenger ship built in 1868 was the *Mullingar* (ON 58401). Completed in December for the City of Dublin Steam Packet Company, this was a paddle steamer of 761 tons, with a length of 261 feet and a beam of 27 feet. She served on the Liverpool to Dublin service and seems to have had an uneventful career until she was broken up in 1890.

There was also a cargo ship completed in 1868, which was a collier named the *Little Mountain* (ON 58404), a vessel of 169 tons, 111 feet long and with a 21-foot beam, propelled by a 25 HP engine driving a single screw. It was registered in Dublin that year to J. Shaw Campbell, a coal merchant of No. 1 Great Brunswick Street.

Before we leave this year, a vessel mentioned in a 1901 *Evening Mail* article should be included: 'A steamer of 120 tons, named the *Faugh-A-Ballagh* (Clear the Way), was built in 1868 for exploration purposes in Africa.' Although a ship of that name could not be found in the registers of British ships or in Lloyd's, she did exist, although not of the tonnage given. In its 8 August 1868 issue, the *Illustrated London News* carried an excellent drawing of the vessel with the caption: 'The *Faugh-A-Ballagh*, an iron Steamboat for African exploration.' The details set out there are best appreciated by being quoted in full:

> We present an illustration of the little steamboat called *Faugh-A-Ballagh* built by Messrs Walpole, Webb and Bewley of Dublin for exploration on Lake Nyassa in Central Africa. This boat was constructed by the order of Captain Faulkner, late of the Livingstone expeditions; and the requirements he set were peculiar. A vessel had to be built which could readily be taken to pieces and be re-erected at will, without the need for skilled labour and which would sail well and steam easy against a 4 knot current carrying about 20 tons, with a 3-foot draught of water. No part of the boat when taken asunder was to be so heavy that two men could not easily carry it over mountainous country or through thick jungle and undergrowth of the country. This rule was to be observed in every part of the boat and boilers. The vessel is 50 feet long, 11 feet broad and 6 feet deep. It is made of 80 pieces held together by 800 screw bolts. The expedition left by the Cape Mail of last June, and expects before return to explore thoroughly the shores of Lake Nyassa, and possibly carry the steamer to Lake Tanganyika and so pass to Albert Nyanza and down the Nile.

While the construction of this small vessel would appear to be a triumph for the newly established yard, to expect this craft to be assembled by unskilled labour in a hostile environment far from the yard seems a little far-fetched as surely one skilled man must have accompanied the vessel. The Livingstone expedition referred to had a similar vessel, built in Scotland in 1858, called the *Ma Roberts*.

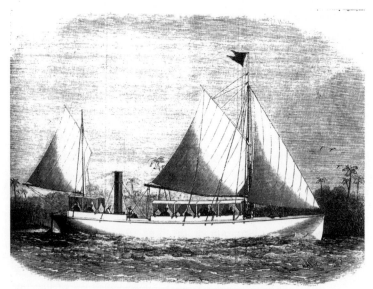

Faugh-A-Ballagh. Iron Steamboat built for river exploration in Africa.

THE FIRST EXPORT ORDER

As 1869 opened, the keel of the first export order, destined for the Philippines, was on the stocks. Launched in the first half of the year and named *Manila,* she was a paddle steamer 115 feet in length and 20 feet in beam and propelled by a 45 HP engine. According to a *Dublin Evening Mail* article in 1901: 'She was designed to operate in Manila Bay and the shallow waters of rivers and lagoons in the trade of her owners Ynchaust & Company.' The article continued: 'After trials in Dublin Bay she was dismantled and rigged as a sailing schooner, in which garb she made a good passage under canvas alone.' One assumes that what the journalist intended to convey here was that her paddle wheels had been unshipped for the outward passage. This article, which should be taken with a pinch of salt, went on to say: 'Her Master was Captain Thomas John Rochefort of Dublin who was Assistant Harbour Master for many years. She was the smallest vessel that ever made the passage out round the Cape of Good Hope. She continued up the China Sea at the tail end of a typhoon in which four other ships were lost.' This ship was first registered in Dublin with the official number 58414, as owned by John Frederick Bewley, the North Wall, Dublin, presumably because the contract stipulated that the ship was to be delivered by the Dublin yard to Manila.

The next ship built by the yard was the *Countess of Dublin* (ON 58415), launched in July 1869. She was a single screw steamer of 760 tons, ordered by the British and Irish Steam Packet Company of Dublin for their London service. She had a length of 220 feet and a beam of 28 feet. This route had been inaugurated in 1816, when the paddle steamer *Thames*, formerly the *Argyle*, called to Dublin on her first voyage. The *Thames* may have been the first cross-channel steamer in the world, although the Holyhead to Howth steam packet service, which had commenced that same year, also claimed this distinction. The London route lasted for 150 years, with the only interruptions caused by the two world wars. Before 1914 there were four ships a week, but by the 1930s sailings had been reduced to a single weekly vessel. After the war the route was operated by Coast Lines Ltd, the parent company of the B & I line, which had taken over the Irish firm in the 1920s. The two motor vessels which ran the route post-war, the *Caledonian Coast* and *Hibernian Coast*, were constructed by Hall Russell in Aberdeen in 1947 and 1948. Each carried eleven passengers, most of whom made a round trip. The Dublin-bound ship sailed from London late on a Friday and arrived on Sunday evening or early Monday and moored on the south side of the Liffey at Sir John Rogerson's Quay. The London-bound ship left the Liffey on Monday evenings headed for Liverpool for the return trip, which also included calls to the English south coast ports of Falmouth, Plymouth and Southampton, before arriving back in the Thames. This service ended in the 1960s.

October 1869 saw the construction of the *Killiney* (ON 5847), a ship of 285 tons with dimensions of 145 feet by 22 feet 4 inches, propelled by a 60 HP engine driving a screw. She was first registered at Dublin in 1870 as owned by Thomas F. Bewley. In 1874 she is recorded as being owned by James Shaw Campbell, No. 1 Great Brunswick Street, who was also the owner of the *Little Mountain*. In November of this year Thomas Walpole left the yard and the company was restyled Bewley, Webb & Company.

In 1870, four vessels were built. The *Alabama* (ON 58424), was launched on 30 July and, although a yacht, she was registered as a merchant vessel. The following day's newspaper reported her naming by 'Lady Blanche Sibyl King, about ten years old'. The vessel had a length of 110 feet, a beam of 16 feet 6 inches and a draft of 8 feet, with a tonnage of 79. She was propelled by a 35 HP engine driving a screw, giving a speed of twelve knots. Her cost was £8,000 and she carried a 20-foot steam launch also constructed by Bewley, Webb & Company. Her owner, the Earl of Kingston, had his seat at Rockingham in County Roscommon. However, he did not keep her long as in 1873 she changed her name to *Ceres* and her port of registry to Glasgow, with her owner given as George Robert Stewart.

The first ship completed in the yard that year was the *Calcium* (ON 58241) in April. She was an iron vessel of 179 tons, 119 feet in length, with a 20-foot 1-inch beam, and was propelled by a 45 HP engine driving a screw. Her first port of registry was Dublin and her owner is given as Thomas Bewley of Brunswick Street. In 1872 she was owned by William Greenfield of Drum House, Drumbey, County Down. The following year, 1873, her ownership and registry changed to Scotland, with her owners given as the Kirkcaldy & London Steamship Co. Ltd, 511 High Street, Kirkcaldy, with that town as her port of registry.

The next ship, built in May, was the *Rio Bento* (ON 58422), a steamer for Peter Stewart, 66 Bridgewater Street, Liverpool. A vessel of 206 tons, she had dimensions of 119 feet 6 inches in length and a beam of 20 feet, and was propelled by a 45 HP engine. She was registered in the Mersey port that year, although between 1873 and 1874 she hoisted a foreign ensign, as in 1875 when re-registered in London, there was a footnote that her 'foreign name was *Pomor*'. Her owner is recorded as John MacArthur of Roseneath on the River Clyde in Scotland.

Finally there was a steam tug built during 1870, named the *Grand Canal* (ON 99744), owned by the Grand Canal Company. This vessel only first appears in the Mercantile Navy List in 1892. She had dimensions of 58 feet in length, with a beam of 10 feet 4 inches beam, a gross tonnage of 25 tons with a 16 HP engine. However, Ruth Delaney states that 'there were two vessels of this name. The first was used for towing in the Liffey until 1874, when it was sold and replaced by a Barrow [shipyard] navigation craft which took the same name.'[25] The official government merchant marine list seems only to record the 1870-built ship.

In May 1870 Henry Webb was drowned in a canoeing accident in Lough Neagh. *The Irish Times* later reported the presentation of an address of condolence to his parents by the men employed in the yard.[26] The paper noted: 'The address, which is enclosed in a handsome frame, has been beautifully and artistically illuminated by Mr Hopkins of Great Brunswick Street, who has obtained for himself celebrity in this particular line of art.' Later in the year *The Irish Times* carried a report:

> The firm of Bewley, Webb and Co. That a meeting of the creditors of Messrs Bewley, Webb and Co. was held yesterday at the shipyard, North Wall. There was a large attendance of creditors. Mr Smith, of the firm of Messrs Thomas, James and Co., of Liverpool, presided. Mr Brown, the accountant read the statement of account, and the report of the gains and losses sustained during the past eight years, in which the following passage appeared: We may, in a few words, sum up the history of the financial results of this concern – of nearly fifty vessels of all kinds, large and small, built during the last eight years – seventeen

to twenty show a gross loss of £22,000, and depreciation between the present estimated value of the premises, concern, and plant and the cost thereof, exhibits a loss of £8,000, which, with the special losses sustained by the cost of experiments, raising sunken vessels under the Australian patent, and interest payable in consequence of borrowed capital, raises the total loss to about £40,000.

The present firm of Bewley, Webb and Company commenced in November 1869 on dissolution of the partnership of Walpole, Webb and Bewley by the usual Gazette at that date, when Mr Walpole retired, and the new firm was joined by Mr T.A. Bewley, who placed £6,000 of capital against the existing deficit, which may be seen on the sheet. One of the partners, Mr W.H. Webb was unhappily drowned on 28th of May last. For the satisfaction of all parties we give the enclosed abstract of the gains and losses throughout the three firms Walpole & Webb; Walpole, Webb and Bewley; and lastly Bewley, Webb and Company. (Signed) Brown, Reid and Co., Accountants. 26 Eustace Street, Nov. 18, 1870.[27]

After a lengthy examination, it was resolved to appoint three gentlemen representing the largest creditors to act for the interest of the whole body, who would have a full valuation of all the assets made and report to an adjourned sitting. Mr Molloy, of the firm of Messrs Molloy and Watson, attended on the part of the traders. At the close of the meeting Mr Simpson of Manchester, one of the largest English creditors, said 'he took the opportunity of expressing, on his own part and that of several large creditors, their most friendly feelings towards Messrs Bewley, who had equally with themselves lost so heavily in this enterprise, and they cordially hoped an amicable and satisfactory settlement would be arrived at by all parties, when their committee had completed their labours'. Mr Molloy, solicitor, stated 'the only wish of the traders was to give the highest possible dividend the estate, on careful valuation, could afford'.

It is assumed that as a result of the work of this committee of three that a resolution of this financial crisis was arrived at as no liquidation of the company took place and the firm continued to trade. There was no indication that the retirement of Thomas Walpole in late 1869 was connected to or brought about by these financial problems. However, perhaps because of his departure the yard had no technical head, which would have been a problem – the few ships completed after his departure were, in all probability, to his design. The firm's problems could have been added to by the shipping slump and the continued need to bring in skilled men from England and Scotland. Building costs were greater than other yards in the United Kingdom because of the expense of importing iron and coal. Mr Walpole resurfaces in a Dublin iron-working company on the North Wall a few years later.

An interesting aspect of the financial account is that the number of vessels built is quoted as 'nearly fifty'. There must have been a number of launches that were not large enough to be worthy of mention in the newspapers.

THE CLOSING YEARS

Harry Gilligan, records that in 1868 the new Dublin Port & Docks Board decided to grant the North Wall yard further land to expand their business. He adds: '… in March 1870 the board ordered three steam screw barges for carrying spoil out to sea from the dredging plant for dumping. However, late that year the yard got into further difficulty and could not complete the contract … a shipbuilder named Brassy from Liverpool was then invited to take over the work on the partially built hull of the first barge and complete the contract, which he did.' It is clear that the remaining two barges of this order were not built in Dublin. There is no record of any steam hopper vessels owned by the Dublin Port Board from 1863, other than *Number One*, already mentioned as built at Drogheda. However, in 1897 two steam hoppers were registered in Dublin by the Port & Docks Board, named *No. 1* and *No. 2*, and constructed at Birkenhead in 1873. Could these have been two of the three vessels ordered by the Port Board in 1870? Sir James Purser Griffith, the former chief engineer of the Dublin Port & Docks Board, writing fifty years later in 1924, said the difficulties besetting the shipbuilding industry in Dublin at that time were caused by having to import craftsmen.

The last year the North Wall yard built a seagoing ship was in 1871, when one vessel was launched. She was the *Washi* (ON 65574), of 336 tons with dimensions of 152 feet by 21 feet 2 inches and was screw propelled. She is described in one account as a 'composite vessel', meaning a wooden hull ship with iron frames. However, the 1872 Mercantile List records her as an iron ship, while another composite ship built and registered in Dublin is recorded that year. Although built for Khawjoo Gee, a firm in Penang, Malaya, for their China trade, she was registered at Dublin in 1871 as owned by John Rossi Hopper, 33 St Helens, London. In 1875 her registry was changed to Hong Kong, with Alex Levy of that colony as her owner.

While the Bewley & Webb yard ceased to build seagoing vessels after 1871, the firm still appeared to be building craft for the inland waterways of Ireland. Gerald D'Arcy records five barges built for the Grand Canal Company between 1876 and 1894.[28] The first was the *Fly*, which was motorised in 1913 and renamed *24M* later becoming *115M*. Then, two years later, came the *Owl*, which on being motorised in 1912 became *14M*, and later *120B*. D'Arcy states that there was a gap of sixteen years before the next three vessels, built in 1894. These were the *Old Art*, which was designated *8M* and later became the boat *76E*. *Horse Boat No. 53* took the number *25M* in 1913, when she received her motor. The third craft was the steam tug *Bee*, used for towage on the Shannon. When she also went over to diesel propulsion in 1912, apart from being renumbered *18M*, she was converted into a 'trade boat', and the space formerly occupied by the steam machinery and boilers became a cargo hold. However, it is not certain that the Bewley & Webb yard actually built these three vessels, because by that time the yard was in decline.

The management of Bewley and Webb in the aftermath of the financial troubles in 1870 seemed to be very wary of undertaking any new building work, which is evident from an item in *The Irish Times* of 24 August 1872, which stated:

> The Brazilian government at present are in want of 30 small steamers for canal and river traffic and have offered the contract for constructing them to Messrs Walpole of this city. Messrs Walpole are unable to take the contract as this would raise the number of men employed from 200 to 400. They hesitate to take work as they would bind themselves to its execution. Their profits would be converted into a loss by any advance on wages. The same firm lately declined to construct a large steamer for Holyhead. Whether shipbuilding will assume an important dimension in Dublin or remain in its present undeveloped position is a matter for the Dublin operatives, they can make or mar the business as they see fit.

The yard was still referred to as Messrs Walpole's, despite the fact that the company had been restyled as Bewley and Webb from 1869. After Henry Webb died, the shipyard continued to trade as Bewley and Webb and carried out repairs until the end of the century. Apart from the problem of having an erratic workforce, the firm had an ongoing battle with the Dublin Port & Docks Board over such matters as harbour dues charged on ships coming in for repairs, and the high cost of hiring both the dry dock and graving slips. The Dublin Port charges were considered excessive compared with similar facilities in other United Kingdom ports.

The Port Board, which as we have seen was constituted under the Act of 1867, was very short-sighted and even blinkered in the matter of giving practical help to ship repair on the Liffey. A *Dublin Evening Mail* article from June 1901 gave examples of the port authority's attitude and the punitive rates charged. It instanced that dry docks in Leith, Liverpool and Sunderland would charge £28 for a 1,000-ton vessel over twelve days, while only an extra £5 for the same length of time was levied in Falmouth, Portsmouth and Plymouth. Dublin on the other hand charged £70. In addition, those other ports exempted vessels under repair from dues on Saturdays, Sundays and public holidays when no work was being carried out aboard, but this was not the case in Dublin.

The *Evening Mail* article also spoke of the Drogheda Steam Packet Company sending their ships to the Liffey yard for repairs until 1882, when they stopped. The final straw was the Port & Docks Board's refusal to give a Drogheda vessel preference to use the graving dock over one of the board's own dredgers. This was despite the fact that the County Louth vessel would have paid £40 for three days and the yard would have benefited by £500 in revenue. This type of conduct by the Port Board seems to have been well known and was the result of the narrow base of board membership and the ability of self re-election by members. It appears that they were very much out of touch with the reality of the shipping world on the Liffey.

LABOUR IN EARLY IRISH SHIPBUILDING

According to labour archives in Britain, shipyard workers in Dublin were involved in union activity from very early days. The main iron-working union in the nineteenth century was the Boilermakers Society, which was formed in 1834 to cater for the men that made boilers in the railway workshops. The English historian Cummins notes the Dublin members of the society meeting in the 'Old Globe in Christmas Street in 1836', although there is no Christmas Street listed in Dublin then or later.[29] The Good Samaritan Lodge met in Belfast on 14 February 1841, and this Belfast Lodge was described as the first trade union representatives of Irish Boilermakers.[30] By 1840, there was movement across the Irish Sea in the search for jobs, as the union had an arrangement in place for travelling benefits, which allowed a member crossing to or from Ireland or England, the sum of five shillings.[31]

While the majority of the union members were boilermakers from the locomotive workshops, clearly the ironworkers who formed the key black squads (heavy iron-working squads) in the shipbuilding yards had to be considered. So the union extended its name and became the Boilermakers and Iron Shipbuilders Society in 1852. However, that society did not accept the drillers and hole cutters who were employed in shipyards. After a while as separate bodies this union amalgamated with the Shipwrights' Society. The general secretary of the new union from 1857 to 1871 was John Allen, who was born in Cork, but whose parents moved to Bristol shortly after his birth in 1804. By the time that Bewley & Webb ceased the building of seagoing vessels, the Dublin branch of the union had 110 members. Thirteen of these were on sickness benefit at a total cost of £35 10s 4d. Two had been on this benefit for almost a year (313 days and 312 days). Four Dublin members received travel benefit compared with twenty in Belfast.

In 1872 the Dublin members met in Mrs Moran's Tavern at No. 10 Cork Hill (Lord Edward Street) with a new secretary, T. Pennie. That same year the Boilermakers' annual report named ten works in Dublin where members were employed. Four of these were the railway shops already mentioned, two others were in Blackhall Place and Parkgate Street, while four firms were located on the Liffey. These were Webb & Bewley, Lower Sheriff Street; D. Donefield, Creighton Street; F. Barrington, Ringsend; and Ross, Stephens & Walpole on the North Wall. However, the Dublin Street Directory for 1872 lists no less than eight shipbuilders in the city, and yet the name of Donefield does not appear in this list. The names given, but missing from the Boilermakers' report, are the Dublin Dockyard Company, Matthew Good, Henry Marshall, Murphy & Hozier and Michael Scallon.

The other union involved in the shipbuilding industry in Britain and Ireland was the United Society of Shipwrights, although there is less information available about that body. The main reason is that before the late 1880s these craftsmen were organised in completely separate branches in each port. In the 1880s Belfast recorded 108 members, which figure had increased by six by April 1915. However, these separate groups came together once a year in June or July to discuss common problems. If a port was unable to send a delegate they simply posted a report to the gathering. Dublin was the venue for the 1857 annual general meeting, but there is no record of any further AGMs being held on Liffeyside. For the Glasgow meeting in 1876, the Dublin Society of Shipwrights sent a report stating they had 130 members, although this number dropped to ninety for the next two years. Dublin did not attend the 1880 and 1881 meetings. By 1894 the branch in Dublin had only 98 members, while Belfast, with its booming shipbuilding industry, had no less than 609 members. In March 1914, before the outbreak of the First World War, Dublin recorded 1,123 members and in 1915 1,337 men in the four different branches in the city. There were then 78 members in Passage West, Cork, and a further 82 members registered at Queenstown (Admiralty Dockyard at Haulbowline).

A Tragic Explosion

The year 1888 was the last that John Frederick Bewley and Thomas Arthur Bewley were both together in the North Wall yard. By that time the shipyard had diversified and the company had become engaged in the business of the manufacture and supply of hydrogen gas using a patented process. They also distributed oxygen, which was obtained from the Brin's Oxygen Company in London. These gases were supplied in metal cylinders to a variety of customers at a rate of some thirty bottles per week and this part of the business was apparently reasonably successful. It was overseen by a Francis Scarr, a book-keeper and cashier, who kept records of the movements of the gas cylinders, showing the dates filled, the customer's name, together with the dispatch and return dates from and to the premises. However, this part of the business led to tragedy.

On 27 December 1888, Mr Chancellor ordered a cylinder of oxygen, but was told by Thomas Bewley that he did not have any oxygen bottles in stock. However, in an attempt to help out his customer, Mr Bewley took an empty hydrogen cylinder, marked it with a red label and filled it with oxygen on the understanding that Mr Chancellor would use it that night. However, the customer returned the gas unused. When the cylinder came back, Mr Bewley either forgot or overlooked the fact that the red-marked bottle contained oxygen. He topped up the bottle with hydrogen gas and returned it to stock, now containing a highly explosive mixture of hydrogen and oxygen.

This lethal bottle, together with another oxygen cylinder, was issued to a Mr Lawrence, who gave magic lantern shows. When his assistant Mr Long was setting up in Naas, County Kildare, a slight explosion occurred when he connected the lethal bottle, but happily without causing any injury. The defective bottle was returned to the Bewley yard on 10 January with the notation 'mixed gases'.

At this stage the proper course of action would have been to release the contents of the bottle into the open air, but this did not happen and Mr Bewley took this cylinder into his own office, where it remained. The next time that the dangerous cylinder comes to notice was on Saturday 26 January 1889, when John Ruthvan, a foreman, drew Mr Bewley's attention to it and said it would be safer to discharge it in the open air, but again nothing was done. Two days later, on Monday 28 January, Foreman Ruthvan, presumably still concerned, reminded Mr Bewley about the bottle and asked how it had come to be filled with 'mixed gases'. At first Mr Bewley said he could not remember, but later that day recounted what had happened and concluded that he believed it was full of hydrogen and did not pose a risk to anyone.

At 4.25 p.m. that same evening Mr Bewley decided to remove the 'mixed gases' cylinder from his office and had just reached the top of the stairs when there was an explosion which killed him instantly. As a result of the blast, windows were blown out and furniture damaged. Mr Bewley's brother John was one of the first on the scene and he telephoned Dr Moore of Fitzwilliam Square, who pronounced Thomas Bewley dead when he arrived. The local C division of the Dublin Metropolitan Police was notified and sent a sergeant and a constable to guard the body until the city coroner Dr Whyte arrived.

An inquest into the tragedy was opened the next day with a fifteen-man jury. The attendance included a number of eminent personages, professors and Thomas Mayne, an MP. The coroner, in opening the inquest, said an explosion could occur in many ways and the jury was taken to the dockyard to view the accident scene where the remains of Mr Bewley still lay. On his return to the coroners' court Dr Whyte said he had intended to call Sir Howard Grubb FRS and some others to assist him, but he had learned that since the premises were being used to manufacture gas, he had to inform Her Majesty's Inspector of Explosives so that a government official would be present to ask any relevant questions. Also he was obliged to give four days notice to the Inspector in London to allow time for him or a representative to be present. He therefore adjourned the inquest until the following Monday at noon in the city morgue.

The inquest only resumed on Wednesday 8 February 1889, in the corners' court in Marlborough Street. The Bewley family was represented by a barrister and the Brins Oxygen Company of London by a solicitor. Dr Whyte explained that the delay was due to communications with HM's Inspector of Explosives. The Inspector had informed him that the death did not come within his remit and he would not be sending a representative. Meanwhile Dr Whyte had assembled a large amount of information from Mr Semple and Sir Howard Grubb about the explosion.

The Queen's Council, Mr Meldon, appeared for the firm and outlined how the business operated and the types of customers supplied. The first witness called was John Bewley, brother of the deceased, who explained the circumstances surrounding the tragedy and answered questions put to him about the pressures at which the gases were kept in bottles. There was no sign of any flaw in the remains of the bottle that had exploded. Bewley was followed by Francis Scarr and possibly the most important witness who could provide vital information, Foreman John Ruthvan, who outlined his concerns as expressed to Thomas Bewley.

Among the attendance were a number of academics from TCD, who gave 'expert' evidence. Professor Barrett stated that the cause of the explosion was the ignition of the hydrogen and oxygen mixture. He proposed that the government (1) should have an official to inspect gas compressing operations; (2) should certify that all cylinders were tested to twice their operating pressure; (3) should ensure that a distinct indelible colour or mark be placed on hydrogen or oxygen bottles; (4) should pass an act making it an offence for bottles not to carry such markings. Sir Howard Grubb and Professor Harty also put forward their theories. The coroner, Dr Whyte, summed up the evidence given and said no blame could be attached to anyone and the jury retired to consider its verdict.

When the jury returned after a short time they declared:

> We find that Thomas Arthur Bewley was killed instantly on 28 January 1889 at the yard of Messrs Bewley, Webb and Co., East Wall, by the accidental explosion of a gas cylinder used for the purpose of lime light; and we are of the opinion that the accident was caused by the mixing of two gases, oxygen and hydrogen; how it exploded we have not sufficient evidence to show. We are further of the opinion that the authorities should take steps to protect the public against similar

accidents by affixing a government stamp upon all cylinders used for such purposes.

Dr Whyte then closed the proceedings with a proposal that as a precaution against the mixing of these two gases in the same cylinder, the screws (pipe fittings) should be of different sizes.[32]

Sir Howard Grubb had been knighted in 1886 and was involved in the family company which manufactured optical measuring instruments. He invented sophisticated mechanisms for the precise control of telescopes. In 1900 his firm commenced supplying periscopes to the British navy from their factory in Rathmines. The firm must have been highly regarded to be entrusted by the Admiralty to manufacture optics for this new weapon of undersea warfare from the outset. The factory continued manufacturing for the first two years of the Great War, but following the 1916 Easter Rising, the facility was moved to southern England because of the fear of sabotage. Grubb died in 1931.

In 1890, in *Thom's Directory*, Joseph Bewley is the only person named at the North Wall yard. *The Irish Times* on 13 March that year carried a report that 'the Dublin shipyard is to be sold on the death of John Bewley. A question with the public is at this juncture if shipbuilding is to be revived at Dublin or are we to revert to a 6 rate port?'[33] The report noted that 'apathy has fallen on the business'. This arrangement was the end of Bewley family involvement in Dublin shipbuilding and repair.

THE ROSS ENTERPRISE AT WAPPING STREET

Although the Bewley and Webb company ceased building seagoing ships after 1871, it was not the only yard building iron vessels on the Liffey in the last quarter of the nineteenth century. For the origins and history of the other facility, we must go back to the same year that the Quaker firm laid the keel of their first ship at what became Alexandra Basin. In the year 1863, the name of the North Wall Foundry, proprietors Ross & Murray, first appears in *Thom's Directory* as operating at No. 53 North Wall. In 1869 their title was changed to Ross & Robinson, Iron & Brass Founders, Engineers & Mill-Wrights, while two years later in 1871 the company moved to Nos 65/67 North Wall. The owners were then given as Ross, Stephens & Walpole, and the enterprise was described as 'Iron & Brass Founders, Engineers & Boilermakers'. This was Thomas Walpole who had left Walpole, Webb and Bewley in 1869. In 1874, Ross is no longer listed as a director of the company. However, in 1878 the firm is still called Ross & Walpole, under which name it traded until 1897.

For the next part of the story of this company, we move up-river to the famous Guinness Brewery. In 1873 the St James' Gate Company constructed a jetty on Victoria Quay, just downriver from Kingsbridge (now Heuston) station, the terminus of the Great Southern Railway. This was to be used by barges loading casks of Guinness for transport to the port for export. In 1877, four years after the jetty was built, Guinness ordered their first steam-propelled river barge, called the *Lagan (No. 10)*, which was constructed at the Harland & Wolff shipyard in Belfast. In 1883 they obtained their second, named the *Shannon (No. 11)*, from Preston in England. Five years later in 1888 they took delivery of their first vessel built in Dublin from the Messrs Ross & Walpole facility on the North Wall.

The first Guinness steam barge from the Ross yard was appropriately named the *Liffey (No. 12)* and built at a cost of £2,544 which was £220 cheaper than the Belfast craft eleven years earlier! An iron vessel of 59 tons, she had dimensions of 80.3 feet by 15.5 feet. She was still listed as being in service in 1928. The following year two more craft came from Ross & Walpole. These were another steamer for Guinness named *Lee*, designated *No. 13* and the *Horse Boat No. 5*, built for the Grand Canal Company and apparently their first from this yard. She was fitted for motor propulsion in 1911 and became *26M*, although her engine was later removed and she was then used as a gravel barge.

The following year, 1891, the *Boyne* was completed and designated *No. 14* by the brewery. The next two vessels, built in 1892, were named *Slaney* (*No. 15)* and *Suir* (*No. 16)*. While the former was constructed of iron, the latter was built of steel, as were most of the later vessels. Another pair of steam barges were launched in 1897 and these were the *Foyle* (*No. 17)*, and the *Moy* (*No. 18)*. The *Moy* was built of iron according to the Mercantile Navy List for 1911, which lists the Guinness vessels for the first time. It is interesting that all these craft were only officially registered with the Board of Trade for the first time in 1910; while all had the same dimensions, their tonnages varied very slightly.

The firm of Ross & Walpole lasted as a partnership until 1897, when in August a dissolution of partnership agreement was signed by the different parties, ending their association. A copy of this document in the archives of the Dublin Port & Docks Board is stamped as being received in the secretary's office on 31 August that year:

> Notice is hereby given that the Partnership hitherto subsisting between William Ross and Thomas Walpole, and carried on by them at the North Wall in the City of Dublin, under the style and firm of Ross & Walpole, has been dissolved by mutual consent as and from the first day of August, 1897. The liabilities and obligations of the said firm will be discharged by the said William Ross, who will continue to carry on under the same name the business heretofore carried on by the said firm, and to whom all sums due to the late partnership are to be paid. Dated this 24 day of August 1897.

The agreement was signed by the two men and witnessed by their solicitors.

On 10 February 1898, the Companies Office in Dublin records

the incorporation of Messrs Ross & Walpole Ltd, and the allocation of the registration number of 2191. The directors listed were William Ross, Frederick Warren and David Telford. The company went on to construct three more barges for the Guinness Brewery in the twentieth century. In 1902, the *Vartry* was delivered as *No. 19*. She was followed nine years later in 1911 by the *Dodder*, which was given the designation *No. 20*.

In the Guinness archives there is some very interesting internal correspondence regarding this vessel, concerning her name and performance. The first is a memo dated 5 August 1911, from the engineering department, which appears to be addressed to the company secretary and which lists the existing fleet. The writer asks: 'Would be glad to know if the board approve of the new barge *No. 20* being given the name *Nore*, as suggested by the Forwarding Department. It might be mentioned that the contractors are now ready for having the name affixed to the boat.' However, the directors thought otherwise, as the terse one line written at the bottom of the page stated: 'The board think *Dodder*, would be more suitable' – short and to the point.

The second internal document dated to that year is from 30 November. It contains more interesting information and indeed some misgivings regarding the vessel. Headed *Dodder* it stated: 'This was given up [delivered] 16/10/11. She went down on eight occasions up to 11/11/1911, but owing to the hoist not working satisfactorily did not return on the right tide [on] these occasions with empties … That the engine was taken apart on 16/11/11 and found that the exhaust cam shaft was badly twisted and bent, also the timing was out of order.' In the next paragraph the much more serious allegation is made that 'her ballasting is not satisfactory as she does not appear to draw sufficient water when empty, also has decided tendency to be cranky when being swung. Even with empty casks aboard she is not satisfactory for swinging with the fore and aft tanks full. Also she is not self-propelling and is not safe to take down the river with a good flush on, as a good speed is needed.'

In the second last paragraph of the same memo there is an indication of the company's concern for their employees: 'There is no cabin fitted on the barge, and there was an objection to sending down the barge in the early morning, as the men are unable to get their breakfast aboard when left by themselves at a station discharging ... That it was proposed only to work the boat in fine weather, when there was no flush [*sic*] in the river. As the cost of installing fixed ballast and fitting a cabin is over one hundred pounds, this should not be done ...'

However, all these problems with the *Dodder* must have been rectified to the Guinness Company's satisfaction, since in 1913 the yard delivered another barge, their last to the brewery. She was the *Tolka* (*No. 21*), and her cost was double that of the *Dodder,* at £5,176 compared with £2,676.

Eleven years later, in 1924, the directors of the small yard named in the companies office were, in addition to William Ross and Frederick Warren, Richard Wilson Booth, Frederick Woods of Ranelagh and Joseph Mitchell of Ballybrack. The last craft believed to be constructed by the firm was the motor barge number *32M* for the Grand Canal Company, which was completed in 1926. She later became *32E*, an engineering department barge. Five years later, in 1931, the firm of Ross & Walpole Ltd was wound up and the premises sold. In the 1935 *Thom's Directory*, the site is listed as part of the adjoining Brooks Thomas Company Ltd timber complex.

By the end of the nineteenth century shipbuilding and ship repair were in serious decline in Dublin. The success of any business in a port is dependent on the measure of goodwill and co-operation between the users and the harbour authority, but relations had been poor between the Dublin Port & Docks Board since it was first established in 1867, and the firms working on the Liffey, particularly with regard to ship repair businesses. The board's attitude to the use of facilities in the port and their excessive charges made it extremely difficult for the various companies to run a profitable business. However, at the end of the century new legislation called the Dublin Port Act 1898 was passed through the House of Commons at Westminster and this act extended membership of the board to be more representative of all the various interests and traders using the port, a move it was hoped would reverse the trend.

CHAPTER 2

THE TWENTIETH-CENTURY REVIVAL

When writing about Irish shipbuilding at this time we must look at the wider scene at the start of the twentieth century, when there were about 100 yards around the coasts of the United Kingdom. There were the big companies such as Harland & Wolff and Workman Clark in Belfast. In Scotland on the Clyde were Scotts of Greenock, Dennys of Dumbarton, Barclay Curle and William Beardmore in Glasgow. On the west coast of England were Vickers of Barrow-in-Furness and Cammell Laird on the River Mersey. In the English Channel were Thornycroft and J. Samuel White at Cowes, while on the north-east coast were the yards of Swan Hunter, Wigham Richardson, Hawthorn Leslie, Doxfords and Armstrong Whitworth with two dockyards. These yards were building passenger ships, liners and naval vessels including battleships, cruisers and destroyers for the British fleet and foreign governments. There were also the Royal Dockyards at Chatham, Sheerness, Portsmouth and Pembroke in south Wales, which constructed warships for the British navy.

Apart from these major yards, the industry was made up of many smaller firms turning out the 'Bread and Butter' vessels of the mercantile marine, such as tramps and short sea traders, mainly colliers. These yards were most numerous on the Rivers Clyde, Tyne and Wear. Many undertook the construction of ships when demand was good and continued with ship-repair work when a slump came. Very few builders survived for any great length of time, as the workhorse steam coaster was a sturdily built ship which lasted up to forty years, with the result that shipowners were not interested in building new ships every year. It was into this world that Dublin shipbuilding was to relaunch itself.

The new Dublin Port & Docks Board met for the first time in 1901 and was made up of six members elected from Dublin Corporation plus twelve persons elected by the Dublin Chamber of Commerce and nine nominated by the shipping interests using the port. This board decided, as a matter of urgency, to get an operational shipyard on its feet, to terminate the old Bewley's lease and to advertise for a new tenant to occupy the site and make it a viable project. Apart from the new Port Board, other important groups in the city were anxious to see a shipbuilding industry re-established, including the Corporation of Dublin, the Chamber of Commerce and the labour unions. On the workers' side the main umbrella body was the Dublin Trades Council, although it only had an advisory role, as all the unions in Ireland at that time were branches of British unions and the local secretary reported directly to the head office in England which controlled all its branches. The Trades Council, which was headed by Alderman William Doyle as president, seemed to be very aware of the benefits that shipbuilding would bring to the city. At a meeting early in February 1901, Alderman Doyle proposed that 'the various public bodies be invited to meet to consider the question of reviving the shipbuilding and repairing industry and devise means to have same established'. Delegates were also appointed to attend any such conference when it would be held.

The following month Dublin Corporation nominated members for a committee to consider these proposals. The Port & Docks Board were also discussing this matter and terms of the lease currently held by Messrs Bewley from their predecessors in 1863. At this point, the sequence of what happened in the revival of shipbuilding is not clear. John Smellie later wrote that, after Bewley's closed down, private approaches and visits were made to Newcastle upon Tyne, to the headquarters of the Boilermakers (Iron Workers) Union and Shipwrights' Union to sound out their support to a revival of the industry in Dublin. This was 'on the definite understanding that Clyde Conditions [conditions for workers in the Clyde shipyards] as to labour matters including piece work would be observed, and Clyde rates of wages for piece and time work accepted'. These approaches were well received and promises of support given, which were honoured by the Unions.[1] However, Smellie did not spell out how or to whom these approaches were made: the Port Board, as a new body, would not have had the technical and commercial knowledge needed to be able to meet with unions and seek their assurances on crucial questions.

On 4 June 1901, there was a public meeting at the Mansion House, Dublin, which according to *The Irish Times* was 'to support the revival of shipbuilding in the city', at which the Lord Mayor of Dublin presided. The newspaper carried a full report of the proceedings and the attendance, but only recorded the names of important personages. The Lord Mayor, Tim Harrington, MP, opened the proceedings and a number of speakers took part, with another Member of Parliament, James MacCann, proposing that a committee be appointed to report as to what should be done. His resolution was seconded by William Ross of the firm of Ross & Walpole Ltd. It was also stated in the course of the meeting that Mr Bewley, who held the lease of the existing yard, had no problem in surrendering that document.

Following the passing of this resolution, a committee was formed to act in conjunction with the existing Corporation committee. The members were Alderman William Doyle, Councillor T. Byrne, William Ross, John Simmonds, Maurice Dockrell, James McCann, MP, Michael Murphy, William Field, MP, William Martin Murphy, Michael Hearne, Messrs C.P. Coote-Cummings, J. Lambert-Jones,

Richard Strong, MP, Lord James Dignam and Edward Bulger. The special Dublin Corporation body, with which the Mansion House committee was to work, was presided over by Lord Mayor Harrington and included the High Sheriff and Aldermen Hennessy, MacCarthy, Downes, Cotton and Lenehan, as well as Councillors Beatty, Broker, Tallon, Jones and Sir Thomas Pile. The publicity created by these events made shipbuilding a topic of discussion in the city and beyond. What would have impressed those in British shipbuilding was the total support of the public authorities and the calibre of the men behind the project, as well as the assistance being offered to any shipbuilding persons who undertook to meet the Dublin Port & Docks Board's requirements.

In August 1901, Lord Mayor Harrington invited two Scotsmen to come to Dublin and inspect the facilities available: Walter Scott and John Smellie. The former was the managing director of the S. McKnight shipyard at Ayr on the Clyde coast, while the latter was head of the design department at the Leven shipyard of William Denny & Company, at Dumbarton near Glasgow. John Smellie recounted that this invitation was the result of a letter sent by them to the Dublin Port & Docks Board in midsummer 1901 seeking information which was passed on to the Lord Mayor. Both men were very aware of the situation in Dublin, Smellie through the London North Western Railway Company for whom his yard had built fast cross-channel ships for their services between Holyhead and Ireland, and Scott through his good business contacts with coasting shipowners, whose colliers traded into Dublin and Irish ports mainly carrying coal and which came into his Ayrshire yard for repairs.

These two men knew each other well, as Scott had worked with Smellie at the Denny yard from 1888 to 1897, before he went to Ayr. Smellie wrote that his first interest in the Port of Dublin went back to his time as an engineering student at Glasgow University, when one of his teachers, Professor Dr James Thompson devoted considerable time to the engineering works carried out in Dublin. Thompson 'had an admiration for the far-seeing harbour engineers, who had transformed the River Liffey from little more than a ditch into a first class and well lighted waterway'.

The Lord Mayor brought the two Scotsmen into the port to see the Alexandra Basin and explained the provisions of the new parliamentary bill in the course of preparation, which had the object of improving the port. However, the two shipbuilders were not enamoured with their first impressions of the facilities, which as Smellie recalled were a distinct disappointment, as it was thirty years since shipbuilding operations. The buildings and machinery such as existed, were in 'a deplorable state, the yard was overgrown with grass and underwood, the fitting-out wharf a total wreck and [there was] an obstruction at the mouth of the graving dock'.[2]

While in Dublin, Smellie and Scott went to the Gresham Hotel to meet with the local trade union officials, where, according to Smellie 'the Lord Mayor's tact and understanding ensured a profitable discussion and wise decisions', but he noted that while the officers at the headquarters of the more important unions in Britain had given their support, 'it was equally if not more important to have this support confirmed by the Dublin officials of the respective unions'. Having thanked the president of the Trades Council for the meeting, the shipbuilder's case was put by John Smellie: 'The Clyde is a very old shipbuilding and repairing centre with small and large yards, building all kinds of vessels from the tiny tug to the largest liners and battleships, and as districts like Belfast, Barrow and Birkenhead concentrate on large vessels only, it is with the Clyde that we must of necessity in a humble way compete. Whatever type and size of vessel we build or repair, the Clyde price, and certainly not more, would be the measure of the value of our work'.

He went on to say that they would adopt Clyde practices and methods, and he invited the unions to come to a definite understanding: 'Clyde conditions regarding labour matters including piece work shall be observed and Clyde rates of wages for piece and time work be accepted.' He pointed out that this would simplify matters for both sides, as the shipbuilders would get information from the Clyde Shipbuilding Employers Federation 'as to rates of wages and conditions of employment', while the unions could check such by wire or letter to their society officials in the Clyde district. He was realistic as to the financial implications of such a new venture, noting that Liffeyside work would in certain respects cost more than similar operations on the Clyde. This was because all the materials needed had to be imported, including coal and gas for heating and power. It was also agreed that any change in Clydeside conditions would follow one month later in Dublin. Smellie concluded that since they could not expect to get the necessary highly skilled craftsmen in Dublin, they would need liberty of action in selection and freedom to import such people when needed. His summing up of the encounter ends by saying that all matters were fully discussed and agreed.[3]

The two main people in the Irish capital, who according to Smellie played important if not crucial parts in bringing shipbuilding back to Dublin, were Alderman Vincent Doyle, president of the Dublin Trades Council and the Lord Mayor, Tim Harrington, MP. Alderman Doyle saw the advantages of employment for workers in Dublin. While his council did not have the same authority as a modern-day labour congress, Alderman Doyle was a very influential figure in the workers' movement and held a moral sway over his fellow trade unionists. The Lord Mayor was an even more intriguing figure. He was a member of the Parnell wing of the Irish Parliamentary Party. He was from Castletownbere, County Cork, and was the Member of Parliament for the Harbour Ward electoral area, Dublin, in the House of Commons at Westminster – a seat he had held since 1885. He seems to have been a very remarkable man, as he had started his career as a teacher, founded the *Kerry Sentinel* newspaper and went on to study law at Trinity College Dublin. He was imprisoned in the 1880s for his support of John Mitchel's land proposals and was first elected as MP for Westmeath in 1883, before standing for a city seat. Called to the bar in 1887, he refused to meet King Edward VII during the royal visit to Dublin in 1903 and also declined a knighthood. He was re-elected Lord Mayor in 1902 and 1903 and held his Dublin seat in parliament until his death in 1910.

At the time there were plenty of shipping companies who would need the services of a repair and building facility in Ireland. A very detailed picture is given by John Smellie in his book, where he listed 106 vessels owned in Dublin in 1901, totalling 82,490 tons gross. Twenty-three ships were in the foreign trade with 36,639 tons gross. Palgrave Murphy had sixteen ships, John Wetherall owned four. There were three sailing vessels belonging to Messrs C.E. Martin. The cross-channel and coasting traders numbered forty-seven steamers with a gross of 43,072 tons, plus four sailing vessels adding another 1,081 tons to the Dublin register. In addition the Congested Districts Board had two ships, while Dublin Corporation owned one vessel. The Commissioners of Irish Lights operated four lighthouse tenders. The Dublin Port & Docks Board had thirteen harbour craft, while four trawlers or drifters were owned by the Dublin Steam Trawling Company and the Irish Fisheries Board had one vessel. In addition Messrs Guinness owned ten steam barges amounting to 5,900 gross tons. The main cross-channel shipowners were the City of Dublin Steam Packet Company with a fleet of fourteen vessels; the British & Irish Steam Packet Company had five ships and the Dublin Glasgow Line had four vessels; Tedcastle McCormack owned six ships and Michael Murphy owned six. Incidentally the latter's head office at No. 3 Beresford Place behind the Customs House is the current Stella Maris Seafarers Club (2009). Messrs Thomas Heiton, coal importers, owned three ships. There were four sailing ship owners each with one vessel: Messrs Betson & Company, W. Robinson, John Kearon and George Wood. Smellie lists separately the ships of the London North Western Railway Company, who had no less than eighteen steamers with a total tonnage of 20,860 gross. Although registered in the Irish capital they were operated from the Welsh port of Holyhead from where they traded to Greenore and Dublin.[4] (This was before the London North Western Railway Company gained access Kingstown, early in the first decade of the twentieth century).

SETTING UP THE NEW YARD

One of the disadvantages in the re-establishment of shipbuilding in Dublin was that while the new operators were starting on an existing site, all the machinery was thirty years out of date and had to be replaced. The new facility officially got off the ground on 8 November 1901, when a new lease for the yard was signed in the office of the law agent for the Dublin Port & Docks Board, which followed the partnership agreement drawn up between the two Scots.

Negotiations were quickly concluded for improved conditions in the new lease and for works to be carried out by the board, which included the reconstruction of the fitting-out wharf at the graving dock, the dredging out of that berth to accommodate vessels in safety, and the renewal of the carriage and winding gear at No. 2 slipway beside the yard. The board also agreed to carry out alterations to the floor of the dry dock to suit the modern vessels of the time and to provide a heavy lift crane at the North Wall Extension to discharge marine boilers and other ship equipment. The partners obtained the granting of preferential harbour dues for ships entering the port for repairs and reduced rates for material used in shipbuilding or repair being imported through the port. The two Scotsmen asked that the yard would have preferential use of the dry dock and slipways when not required by the port. However, this was refused as under the existing regulations, anyone on payment of a small fee could reserve these facilities for one or more ships, without having actually to occupy either. Once these ships were inscribed in the harbour register, they were entitled to priority. In spite of the initial concerns expressed by the builders about this arrangement, experience over the following twenty years showed that the harbour master did everything possible to facilitate the yard.

The clearance of old machinery and debris began in December 1901 and the construction of a new building to house a plate and angle-bending furnace was completed within a number of weeks. New plate rollers, punching and shearing machines, counter sinking and planning machines were purchased and erected, together with piping for hydraulic power and wiring for electricity to operate the equipment. In February 1902 a start was made on laying the keel and construction of the dockyard's first ship. The Dublin Trades Council and Alderman Doyle, who knew the value of publicity even in those days, proposed that a march should take place from the city centre at Sackville (now O'Connell) Street to the yard to mark the keel laying. However, according to Smellie 'the builders thought the occasion hardly of sufficient importance to justify such an honour.'[5]

Both Scott and Smellie had very clear ideas of what they wanted to achieve, but they were also very well aware of both the strength and weakness of their new enterprise, because of the yard's geographical situation. Their evaluation of the economic and industrial conditions pertaining to Dublin at that time made it apparent that ship repairs would be the mainstay of the yard. However, from necessity, a certain amount of shipbuilding needed to be undertaken from two points of view – to attract skilled craftsmen and to ensure steady employment when the volume of repair work fell. They realised that while Dublin was well placed to carry out work economically, it was not in close proximity to the main ports in England and Scotland.

The main orders would come from shipowners in Britain and the new yard must win these orders by executing ship repair both economically and with the highest standard of craftsmanship. To maintain such a high level meant that sufficient engineers, boilermakers, platers, riveters and carpenters must be available. The two Scotsmen were very much aware of the value of good labour relations with a contented workforce and Smellie paid tribute to the people in the yard. He recorded that while in the beginning it was necessary to bring in foremen and craftsmen for some of the departments, the many excellent men, local and otherwise, who were later taken on, were possessed of initiative, ability and loyalty to whom credit for the success of the yard must go.[6]

The partners were made aware very early on of the difficulty encountered by the new workers coming into Dublin of obtaining suitable lodgings. The first initiative to meet this need was to reconstruct an existing building on site and install a dining-room, a social hall and sleeping cubicles. This makeshift building became a 'non-sectarian and non-political social club'.[7] It is not very clear when this building was opened, but it must have been very soon after the establishment of the yard if they hoped to retain their new workers. The next step, as Smellie recounted, was the formation of a subsidiary limited company called The Economical Housing Company Ltd, which obtained a plot of land nearby to build housing. Their action was followed by other house building 'on a considerable scale', which solved the accommodation problem.[8] The plot purchased was at Church Road on the East Wall, and Fairfield Avenue soon came into existence. This appears for the first time in *Thom's Directory* in 1905, where 'twenty small houses' are recorded.

Today there is a two-storey block containing twenty apartment dwellings on the left-hand side of the street, as one turns into

Fairfield Avenue from Church Road. This building is known locally as the 'Scotch building' and its construction is completely different to later houses in this street, which was extended towards the railway embankment as Moy Alto Road. The building work was overseen by Alexander Maclean from Govan, Glasgow, who was later the foreman carpenter in the yard.[9]

Other steps were taken to encourage workers to stay. The new firm, apart from training apprentices within the yard, also encouraged them to attend evening classes at the City of Dublin Technical Schools for their particular trades. Some afternoon classes were also held on site and the firm paid all class and course fees, 'except where there was a poor take-up'. An accident fund was established in 1911, supported by the workers, and voluntary weekly deductions were taken from wage packets. An annual financial presentation was made to the various hospitals which treated the employees, in proportion to the numbers they looked after. Towards the end of the company's existence, in 1919, the hospital fund endowed two beds, one each in the Drumcondra and Mater Hospitals, for use by wives and children, again supported by weekly deductions. An annual dinner around Christmas-time was held for all staff and their principal assistants, when all departments and employees would do their party pieces.[10] The final initiative taken was a bonus system, introduced very early on in 1906, which lasted until the closure of the yard, and Smellie recorded that some £2,000 pounds per annum was distributed and that the yard was singularly free from serious accidents. In these steps the two principals were very forward-looking for their time.

The size of the facility when it opened in 1902 was similar to that of 1864 and it occupied the area between the No. 2 Graving Slipway on the west side and the dry dock to the east of the yard. The proximity of both of these to the yard premises made for easy access for carrying out repairs. When the yard opened, three building berths were laid out. The two outside berths, numbered 1 and 3, could accommodate vessels up to 280 feet in length, while the centre berth, number 2, was suitable for a 300-foot vessel. During the First World War extra ground was leased from the Port & Docks Board on the west side of the graving slipway, when two more berths, numbered 4 and 5, were laid out. These could build ships of up to 420 feet long.

In his very detailed account of the yard and the various departments, Smellie lists no less than ninety separate classes of tradesmen who needed to be employed. He also outlined the work undertaken by each section and his book could almost be taken as a text of how to establish a shipyard at that time.

The First Launch

While work commenced on the construction of the first ship, the partners lost no time in taking on ship repairs and tendered in February 1902 for collision damage repairs to the trawler *Curlew*, owned by the Dublin Steam Trawling Co. The yard's quotation was accepted and the trawler was docked on 4 February. The work required the fitting of a new stem, new shell plates and other structural items. At the end of the month they also docked the steamer *Bengore Head*, owned by the Head Line of Belfast and managed by G. Heyn & Sons Ltd, which initiated a twenty-year-long business relationship between these two companies.

The first vessel to be launched was the steamer *Gertie*, which took to the water at noon on Saturday 4 October 1902, from the most westerly or No. 3 berth in the yard. Her owner was Captain William Rowland, 9 Canning Place, Liverpool. 'The new vessel was christened by Miss Gertie Rowland, the owner's daughter and was named for her', according to the *Evening Telegraph* of 6 October, which printed a full account of the event: 'The launching party led by the Lord Mayor was then entertained to luncheon in the engine house, which was neatly decorated with flags.' The attendance included members of the Port & Docks Board and others associated with the construction of the vessel. In his opening speech Walter Scott, who presided said: 'He was pleased to have so many friends present and when he looked around it was calculated to make them very hopeful for the future having come to Dublin a few months ago practically strangers.' He went on to say that: 'He had met Captain Rowland four or five years ago and the *Gertie* had been designed especially for him. In her construction the firm had been much indebted to his wide experience and accurate knowledge of the trade for which she was intended. The yard hoped in a future time to provide in Dublin steam machinery.' This was a reference to the ship proceeding in a few days to Glasgow for the installation of her boilers and engines. In reply to a further toast to the Lloyd's and Board of Trade surveyors proposed by John Smellie, Lloyd's surveyor John McWilliams said that 'the duty of the surveyors had been easy. They had found very little difficulty – none at all – in having their requirements fully and faithfully carried out.'

In the final toast to the visitors Walter Scott paid particular tribute to the Lord Mayor (Tim Harrington, MP) for all his help in setting up the enterprise: 'They had been employing between 250 to 270 hands, who otherwise would have no employment and otherwise would have gone to the other side.' The Lord Mayor in replying thanked the other persons involved and spoke very highly of the two principals, Messrs Scott and Smellie, and J.L. Clerk. While this name does not appear in the attendance list, it must be presumed that Clerk was the yard manager. This was seemingly a very good start for the new yard, without the teething troubles usually connected with a new business.

The *Gertie* was a raised quarterdeck type coaster, with an exceptionally long single hatchway serving a single hold. She had a gross tonnage of 380, with a length of 150 feet and a beam of 24 feet and was propelled by a steam compound engine. While the crew were accommodated in the forecastle, the captain and other officers were aft, having 'a nice saloon artistically finished in polished hardwood with comfortable cabins adjoining'. It would appear that her owner, Captain Rowland, was engaged to carry long items of cargo, perhaps railway rails, to warrant such a long hatchway. In 1911 the ship passed into the ownership of James Henry Monks (Preston) Ltd of Preston Lancashire and later of Liverpool. She continued trading for the next thirty years, surviving the First World War. She sank on 23 November 1941 off the Tuskar Rock, having struck a British mine which had broken loose, while on a voyage from Port Talbot to Waterford with coal.

After the completion of their first vessel in November 1902 the Dublin Dockyard Company continued with the construction of their second ship on the middle berth of the yard.

THE YARD 'RECEIVES' ROYAL APPROVAL

The yard was 'graced and honoured', when the Viceroy George Henry, the Earl of Cadogan, visited on Wednesday 15 May 1903. As the *Freeman's Journal* of the following day reported: 'Yesterday His Excellency the Lord Lieutenant, accompanied by Leonard Earle, private secretary, and Major the Honourable Gerald Ward, ADC, paid a visit to the new shipbuilding yard at the North Wall, and made an inspection of the premises. His Excellency was shown over the yard by Mr Scott the manager, who pointed out how the industry could be developed and extended ...' The journalist's report is very interesting, as it was obviously more important to give the proper names and titles of the Lord Lieutenant's staff than the first name of Walter Scott, one of the two principals of the dockyard. Also the article made no mention of the senior officers of the Port Board or of the first citizen of the city, the Lord Mayor, who were also present on that occasion. The attendance of these other worthies only becomes apparent in a report in the 18 May edition of *The Irish Times* about a meeting of the Dublin Port &

Docks Board, which took place two days later: 'The Lord Mayor of Dublin, Mr T.C. Harrington, MP, the Chairman and Vice-Chairman of the Port & Docks Board, Mr J.M. Murphy and Mr John Moloney, JP, respectively, were present on the invitation of Mr Walter Scott, according to the chairman, who merely mentioned the matter because he thought it would be gratifying to every member of the board, to see that His Excellency took such a lively interest in the business of the port.' The report concluded that: 'His Excellency seemed greatly pleased with what he saw.' This visit to the new enterprise, would have confirmed to the partners that they had 'arrived' so to speak.

That same board meeting considered a letter from the Dublin Dockyard Company on the subject of the shipyard lease and suggested modifications, but what these were is not reported. However, the Lord Mayor's thoughts on the matter were reported: 'The board should facilitate the leasees in the matter, as it might mean the development of a great industry in Dublin. He pointed out that there were three boats now in the course of construction, one of 400 tons, a large vessel, which is to be launched in a few days. The LNWR had given an order for a barge to be used in Holyhead and the Grand Canal Company had placed an order for a steam tug. If alterations on the slip suggested by Mr Scott were carried out it would be possible to launch a vessel of 5,000 tons there.' The Lord Mayor then proposed that the law agent be empowered to organise such alterations. Alderman D.L. Bergin seconded the motion. However, one attendee, William Wallace, 'regarded this as a large principal, as it would give power of absolute assignment to their present tenants. After some further discussion it was agreed to refer the matter to a committee of the whole board to be held the following Thursday.'

A week before the viceroy's visit, the Dublin Port & Docks Board had published a notice in the local press to shipbuilders that they were prepared to receive tenders for a tug steamer. It detailed how to obtain specification and drawings, who to apply to and the closing date, and was signed by the secretary of the Dublin Port & Docks Board, N. Proud.[11] The new dockyard was awarded the contract to construct the tug, for a price of £5,000.

Also that year the yard's second vessel, the steam collier *Lagan* (ON 116004), was launched in July. She was of the raised quarterdeck type and built for Messrs Macpherson & Todd of Belfast, a firm of coal importers in that city, with a gross tonnage of 393.

The Grand Canal Company's order for a steam tug was completed before the end of the year. She was the tugboat *Barrow*, registered in the port of Waterford (ON 102004). She was 64 feet 5 inches in length and 14 feet 6 inches in beam, of 45 tons gross and propelled by a 16 HP engine. Twenty years later she was registered in Hull in Yorkshire as owned by Foster Tugs Ltd. Perhaps the Waterford trade had decreased on the canal system and there was no longer need for her.

There was also the order for the London & North Western Railway Company. This was the *Nancy*, a coaling barge with a single elevator, also completed in 1903 with a length of 77 feet and a beam of 27 feet. Information about this vessel only came to light in late 2007. She was used at Holyhead by the railway company to provide coal to their cross-channel steamers and operated until 1952.

The first vessel constructed in 1904 was the tug for the Dublin Port & Docks Board, which was launched in June. Named *Anna Liffey*, she was a ship of 174 tons gross (ON 117317). No report of her launch seems to have been made in the newspapers. The tug commenced her career with a mishap. On Thursday morning, 11 August, at 11.30 a.m., the *Anna Liffey* was coming into Alexandra Basin towing a grab hopper dredger, when she struck the schooner *T. and E.F.*, registered in Barrow, which was outward bound. According to a report submitted to the secretary of the Port Board on 16 August by Harbour Master Captain Hartford: 'The Schooner sustained considerable damage – carrying away her jib boom, stem and headgear and breaking some planks. She has had to put back [to port], and it will be necessary to discharge her cargo of native timber before docking for repairs.' He goes on to say: 'I investigated the matter along with the Engineer [Mr Griffith] and having examined the crews of the vessels, I consider it best to come to terms with the owner of the Schooner, as if brought to court the evidence would undoubtedly go against the steamer.' He continued that he had seen the ship's agent, Mr Doyle of 21 Eden Quay, to try to settle the matter 'subject to the approval of the board' and that after a good deal of consideration they agreed to settle in full for £150 pounds. In his report of the incident dated 13 August, John P. Griffith, the chief engineer, concurs with the harbour master that the matter should be dealt with out of court. The owners of the vessel, the Hodbarrow Mining Company Ltd, of Millom in Cumberland, did not agree and in a letter of 17 August to Doyle & Company, they stated that this figure would not compensate them for six weeks' loss of trading. However, they were prepared to close the matter for £175, which they considered 'a fair and reasonable spirit'. The matter was concluded for this sum, and the Port & Docks Board agreed to the owner's figure, as confirmed by the letter dated 22 August from Doyle & Company to the board. The port authority had no option but to settle, as their tug was obviously in the wrong.

The fifth vessel definitely constructed by the yard, again for cross-channel owners, was the *Bay Fisher* (ON 114228), which was launched on October 1904. She had dimensions of 168 feet 7 inches in length with a beam of 25 feet 8 inches, and was of 478 tons gross. It was built to the order of James Fisher of Barrow-in-Furness, a company with a long history in shipping. This vessel was later sold and as the *Madame Alice* sank on 16 February 1918, having been a in collision with the Admiralty steam yacht *Iolaire* near Oban while on a voyage from Fleetwood to Stornaway with a cargo of empty barrels.

The year 1905 was only nine days old when the yard launched their next ship and the largest to date, which merited a mention in the *Dublin Evening Telegraph* of Monday 9 January: 'Today at ten minutes after one o'clock the iron steamer *Lillabonne* which has just been built by the Dublin Dockyard Company, was christened and successfully launched.' However, the reporter got the name wrong – the correct spelling of her name was *Lillebonne* (ON 117525) and she was registered in Dublin. This vessel, built for John Harrison Ltd, 11 & 12 Great Tower Street, London, was of the raised quarterdeck type, built of steel and had a gross of 1,017 tons and dimensions of 220 feet in length and a beam of 34 feet 1 inch. Named by the wife of the former Lord Mayor, Tim Harrington, she would be the first of four vessels delivered to this owner over the next ten years. The newspaper goes into some detail about the ship: 'Apart from carrying 1,400 tons of cargo [she] has a strong double bottom, suitably adapted for loading aground and sub-divided into a number of compartments capable of containing upwards of 360 tons of water ballast, enabling her to proceed to sea in any weather when light, a most important quality these days when vessels very often have to shift port unexpectedly.' The newspaper continued: 'The ship has been constructed to the order of Mr John Harrison of London to meet the special requirements of his increasing trade and also to fill the direct service recently opened between Dublin and Treport in France.' The French Vice-Consul M. Bounet was present at the launch and it is of interest to note that the report states: 'Guests were entertained at a luncheon by Mr Walter Scott senior partner.' Again there was no public mention of John Smellie and one has the impression that he preferred to avoid the limelight.

In 1905 the Port & Docks Board fulfilled the agreement made four years earlier with the shipbuilders for the provision of a heavy lift crane for the port, to allow machinery for new vessels to be discharged, work which previously had to be done at Belfast. The

Hundred Ton Crane as it came to be known to generations of port workers, was erected at the end of the North Wall Extension on a massive foundation of 3,400 tons of concrete supported on 110 piles driven 40 feet into the ground. The crane, manufactured by Maschinenfabrik Augsburg Nürnberg AG, was capable of lifting 100 tons at 75 feet radius, while a secondary hoist handled loads up to 20 tons at a radius of 80 feet. The hoisting speeds of the electric crane were 5 feet per minute for 100 ton lifts and 20 feet per minute for 20 ton loads. This crane, a port feature until 1987, was eventually dismantled and cut up to clear the North Wall Extension for development.

The Dublin Port archives contain an interesting letter from John Purser Griffith, the engineer-in-chief, to the secretary of the Port & Docks Board, requesting payment of £10 covering wages and lodgings to one of two German engineers sent by the manufacturers to Dublin for one year to train local staff in the operation of the crane. The other German with the authority to draw this money weekly had left. Purser Griffith's comment on the missing man in a postscript was: 'Probably gone to America.'

The next vessel from the yard did not take to the water until October. She was the *Shellie* (ON 107004), built for the County Louth firm of Samuel Lockington & Co. Ltd, Quay Street, Dundalk. She was 145 feet long, with a 24-foot beam and had a gross tonnage of 358.

The First Twin-Screw Vessel

The first twin-screw ship constructed in the new yard was the *Shamrock* (ON 123121), launched in December 1905 and registered in Dublin early in 1906. Built for the Corporation of Dublin, she was a vessel of 148 feet 5 inches in length, with a beam of 31 feet and a gross of 468 tons. She was designed for the carriage of sewerage sludge from the Corporation's new settling tanks on the south side of the Liffey, beside the new Pigeon House Electric Generating Station, also operated by the Corporation. It is interesting to read what Smellie wrote about their first twin-screw ship: 'The contract for the building of this vessel was awarded to the Dublin Dockyard Co., in keen competition with many eminent British shipbuilders, on account of the satisfactory nature of the designs and specifications submitted with their tender, and as the *Shamrock* has proved herself very well suited to the work in which she is engaged it is thought that Dublin Corporation has not regretted the confidence they bestowed on the builders.'[12] This statement was endorsed by time, as she served the citizens of the capital city for fifty-three years, until replaced by another from the same slipways.

It would be the late summer 1906 before the next ship built by the yard would enter the water. This was the *Berne* (ON 123126), a steamer of 1,016 tons gross, the second built for John Harrison of London, which was launched on 22 August 1906. Once again we are faced with the question of the exact number of vessels completed by the yard. The *Shipbuilder* magazine for September 1906, reporting on this launch states: 'This is the nineteenth vessel built by the Dublin Dockyard Co. since their yard was opened.' A small motor yacht was completed in 1906, called the *Jewel*, only 27 feet in length with a beam of 9 feet 3 inches and a 5 HP engine. She was built for William Tihar of Falmouth. John Smellie has a section in his book under the heading of 'Yacht and Motor-Boat Building', where he wrote: 'The proximity of Kingstown as a yachting centre induced the Company to embark upon yacht and motor-boat building, and a considerable number of interesting and highly finished small craft were built. This department, however, had to be discontinued as the there was not enough local business to justify its existence, and searching for orders elsewhere was found to require an unjustifiable amount of the personal attention of the management.'[13] It would appear that small boat building ceased after that year. It was more profitable to build big ships.

The same *Shipbuilder* publication threw into sharp comparison, the output at Dublin compared with the rest of Ireland in their statistics for 1906. These showed the Belfast yards of Harland & Wolff Ltd completing 82,238 gross tons of shipping and Workman, Clark & Co. Ltd contributing another 65,478 gross tons, making a total of 148,716 tons for the northern city, while Dublin came next with 1,024 tons gross, followed by Larne, County Antrim, with 120 tons.

A very interesting event occurred in the middle of the following year, when the *Evening Telegraph* of 11 July 1907 ran a short report under the heading 'Harland and Wolff and Dublin Shipbuilding – Questions at Port & Docks Board'. The report stated: 'Today the weekly meeting of the Port & Docks Board was held in the offices at Westmoreland Street, the chair was occupied by Mr George Machine, JP' and listed those present. The news item continued:

The Assistant Secretary (Mr Dean) read the following letter from the Dublin Industrial Development Association forwarded by Mr Field, MP, with reference to the establishment of a dockyard or shipbuilding yard in Dublin:

Dear Mr Field – Mr Mulligan brought on some scheme in reference to getting Harland & Wolff, Belfast, to establish a dockyard or shipyard in the Dublin Port. The matter will again come up on Monday at four o'clock. What is suggested is that a deputation should wait on Lord Pirrie in reference to the matter and see if he would entertain a proposal to start a yard on the north side below where the Dublin Dockyard Company have their place. Of course the crux of the question is to know how the Port & Docks Board view the matter, or what are their feelings about it, and I would like to know for my council how best to get at the preliminary steps and see what the Port Authority is prepared to give, how much space etc., before approaching Lord Pirrie, or whether it would be better to know what he would require before meeting the Port & Docks Board. If you could spare a few moments to let me know how best to approach the matter or write your views I shall be glad to lay them before the council on Monday and see what can be done to prevent this important industry from being shipped to Scotland.

Yours etc. W.J. Brannigan.

Lord Pirrie was the chairman of Harland & Wolff Ltd. The published report concluded: 'Sir James Murphy said it would be better to get all the information from Lord Pirrie and it would receive most favourable consideration. This course was agreed, the secretary to inform the association. The meeting terminated.' No follow-up to this report has been found and no meeting with his Lordship ever seems to have taken place. However, the explanation for this approach and others by Lord Pirrie could be a dispute that Pirrie was having with the Belfast Harbour Commissioners. His Lordship was well known for getting his own way. In 1899, when an application by Harland & Wolff to the Harbour Commissioners in Belfast to lease all the land at their Alexandra Dock Works and the Musgrave channel for a large repair works was refused:

> Pirrie immediately began to look for a new location ... He made overtures to the recently reconstructed Dublin Port & Docks Board and visited possible sites in England and Wales. These manoeuvres were clearly designed to frighten the Commissioners into giving way, and the tactic succeeded. Speaking in Montreal in September 1899, Pirrie said, 'We have a great deal of correspondence with corporations in England and Scotland. Indeed the correspondence has pressured me, as you may see (holding up bulky documents) asking us not [to] remove any portion of our works to another part of Ireland, but to use the facilities, which they [the Belfast Harbour Commissioners] are ready to place at our disposal.[14]

Pirrie repeated these tactics in 1903 and again in 1911, by once again opening negotiations with the Dublin Port & Docks Board to site a yard on the Liffey when the company sought further land in Belfast and was refused. It is likely that Lord Pirrie's earlier approaches to the Dublin Industrial Development Association was what prompted them to consider approaching him in return.

The year 1907 was the start of a three-year slump in British shipbuilding, but it saw the Dublin yard complete two vessels for Irish harbour authorities, both of which were launched towards the end of the year. The first was the *Portlairge* (ON 102006), built for the Waterford Harbour Commissioners. This was a grab hopper dredger, 140 feet between perpendiculars, with a beam of 29 feet and a load draught of 11 feet when carrying 500 tons of spoil. The shipping magazine *Syren & Shipping* devoted two-thirds of a page to details of the ship, part of which stated: 'On Tuesday morning the 10th inst. the new grab dredger *Portlairge* left the hands of builders, the Dublin Dockyard Company, for Waterford.' A very full description of the ship was given, including the following:

> After filling up with dredgings to her load draught, the *Portlairge* proceeded to Skermorlie [in the lower River Clyde between the Isle of Bute and Renfrewshire], where progressive trials were made on the measured mile and thereafter a six-hour continuous trial was accomplished, when a mean speed of 8.6 knots was obtained, or fully half a knot over the guarantee. The dredging trials were likewise most successful, it being found possible for each dredger to make two complete cycles in one and a half minutes when operating at a depth of 40 feet, and it was particularly noticeable that when both dredges were operating over the same side of the vessel that the angle of heel was quite inappreciable … On taking delivery of the vessel, Mr Allingham, Secretary of the Waterford Harbour Commissioners, and Mr Friel, harbour engineer, under whose superintendence the vessel had been built, expressed themselves thoroughly satisfied in the vessel and all its details and in the manner in which the contract had been carried out.[15]

The *Portlairge* continued working in the port of Waterford for the next seventy-five years, until the early 1980s, when she was taken out of service and laid up. Plans by the Waterford Harbour

Commissioners to sell her to a Maritime Museum being established at Maryport in Cumbria fell through and in 1987 she was sold for £3,000 to Seán Finn of Saltmills, County Wexford. At the end of August that year the *Portlairge* left Waterford crewed by her new owner, a mechanic from New Ross and her former fireman, with a steam enthusiast priest as supercargo. The *Waterford News and Star* on Friday 4 September 1987, quoted her new owner as saying: 'There will be more voyages in the future, the ship is a fine example of Irish workmanship and I am glad she did not go abroad.' Regrettably nothing has happened since then and the vessel remains at the mercy of the elements on the mud flats at Saltmills.

The second vessel of 1907 was also a grab hopper dredger, built at a cost of £3,000 for the Tralee & Fenit Pier Harbour Commissioners. The *Samphire* (ON 128352), named after a small island on which Fenit pier is built, was a smaller version of the Waterford ship of only 158 tons gross. She was engaged in keeping navigation open in the Kerry ports, in particular dredging the canal between Blennerville and the Tralee town quays. However, in the 1930s trade declined owing to the economic tariffs imposed on imports from Britain. During the Second World War no ships berthed there and in 1945 the gates to the canal were closed and the waterway to the town quays silted up.

In February 1951 the *Samphire* caused concern when she went missing for two days while on a return passage from Rushbrook Dockyard. As a result the lifeboats at Valentia and Fenit were launched, but she was spotted off Brandon Head by the Fenit lifeboat, having been delayed by bad weather, which included fog and a storm, causing her master to spend twenty-two hours at the wheel. Seventeen years later she made another sea passage to Rushbrook for repairs costing £17,000. She was sold in the mid 1970s, as she had become too expensive to run as a coal-burning vessel.

In 1907 the yard also built a steel tug for the Grand Canal Company, named the *Killaloe*. She was 57 feet in length, with a 12-foot 8 inch beam and a gross of 31 tons, and was propelled by a 16 HP engine.

The following year the yard completed three ships for owners in Ireland, two of which were cargo vessels, while the third was the yard's first government order. The first ship for that year was the *Carlingford* (ON 126961), which was launched in January. A collier of 371 tons gross, she was built for the Dundalk coal importers, Samuel Lockington Ltd, of Quay Street, and was a sister ship of the *Shellie*, delivered to the same owners three years earlier in 1905. The second cargo vessel, completed in December 1908, was the *Rosaleen* (ON 128485) built for Michael Murphy Ltd, 3 Beresford Place, Dublin, and registered in Cardiff, where most of the company's ships were entered on the books. A vessel of 409 tons gross, she was the first of seven built for Michael Murphy's general cargo trade over the next decade. The *Shipbuilder* end of year tonnage returns mention the construction of a barge of 157 tons.[16]

THE *HELGA*

The third and most famous vessel built in 1908 was the *Helga*, described by John Smellie in his book as:

> This graceful and useful cruiser built in 1908 to the order of the Department of Agriculture and Technical Instruction for Ireland (Fisheries Branch) is probably the fastest vessel of her type on these coasts. Built to Lloyd's A1 Class, her dimensions were: Length 155 feet BP [between perpendiculars], breadth 24 feet 6 inches, depth 13 feet 6 inches. She was specially fitted out for patrol duties as well as for biological and other survey work, and had a well-lighted and equipped laboratory on the main deck and ample accommodation for the Department's technical staff as well as for the ship's officers, engineers and crew. Her two sets of triple expansion engines, supplied

by David Rowan & Co. of Glasgow, gave her a speed of 12½ knots under natural draught conditions, and 14½ knots when working under Howden's forced draught system.[17]

While this was his view of the vessel as a product of the yard at that time, the *Helga* was to have a much more important role in history than John Smellie could ever have foreseen.

To understand the importance of this ship in the perspective of Irish maritime history, we must go back almost 200 years to 1731, when the Dublin Society (later the Royal Dublin Society) was founded. This august body was most active from its inception in promoting the Irish Fisheries and many papers were produced on various issues. In 1887 the society set up a fisheries committee, with the main aim of collecting data on the condition of the fisheries in Irish waters. The committee discussed whether a commission should be established or a single person should be appointed to carry out the task. It says something for the common sense of the committee that they decided on a one-person approach and named the Rev. William Spotswood Green as the person for the job. The Rev. Green had previously led scientific expeditions on behalf of the Royal Irish Academy. In 1887 he toured fishing ports in west Cork and in 1888 he visited the east coast of the United States to study the industry there. In the last decade of the century research cruises were also made round the coast of Ireland by the Royal Dublin Society, which were part funded by the government.

In 1891 the Congested Districts Board was established by the British government to promote local industry in Ireland through subsidies and technical education. In the maritime sector, nets were provided for fishermen with education in their use, as well as the construction of landing slips and piers, many of which still exist. In addition, larger fishing craft were introduced to fishing communities. The two main types of ship were the Zulus from Scotland and the Nobbies from the Isle of Man.

At that time, research cruises were being carried out by two chartered steam yachts. In 1899 a floating laboratory was established in the west by the Royal Dublin Society aboard the *Saturn*, a 220-ton vessel bought with government assistance. Her hold was converted into a laboratory and openings were cut in the hull for windows. During the summer months, she was towed and moored off the island of Inisbofin.

At this time the British fishing fleet was rapidly developing, with the introduction of steam drifters and trawlers. These vessels directly affected the Irish fishing trade, as they had a catching capacity and range of operation that could not be matched by the local sailing boats. Trawlers from Milford Haven and Fleetwood, to mention only two ports, fished in Irish waters, taking large catches which were frozen on board. Their operations caused such alarm that the Steam Trawling Act of 1899 was enacted to protect fish stocks. This gave power to the Lord Lieutenant, on the advice of his fishery officers, to close certain marine areas to steam trawling. However, the inspectors of fisheries complained that the Coastguard and Royal Navy, who were charged with the task of enforcing this protection, were largely ineffective.

In 1899 the British government established the new Department of Agriculture and Technical Instruction for Ireland. This was to be the first government department in Ireland. It took over the Royal Dublin Society laboratory and the fishery functions of both the Board of Works and the Congested Districts Board except for the supply of boats to fishermen. In October of that year a steam yacht named *Helga*, built in 1891, was purchased from a Major General Gore. A vessel of 345 tons built at the Ayr yard of S. McKnight, she was commissioned as a fishery cruiser, the first in Ireland.

The importance of the coming of the first *Helga* as a fishery cruiser in Irish waters during the last year of the nineteenth century has been overlooked by most historians. The vessel and her more famous successor were the first vessels under the direct control of a government department in Ireland and empowered to enforce its laws at sea. The significance of taking this role from the Admiralty and giving it to the Irish administration was lost on Whitehall for twenty years until the formation of the Irish Free State.

For eight years the yacht *Helga* seems to have had a very successful career. However, she was not completely suitable for her task, in spite of alterations carried out when she was bought by the department in 1899. In 1907 an offer was made to buy her and the department decided to sell her and build a vessel exactly to their requirements. The first *Helga* was sold and her name changed to *Constance*.

In the face of stiff competition from many other British yards, the tender of the Dublin Dockyard Company was accepted for the new vessel, and its keel, designed by James Maxton, a Belfast naval architect, was laid on 20 December 1907. The new ship (ON 123147), also called *Helga*, was launched on 16 May 1908 and named by Mrs T.W. Russell, wife of the deputy head of the fisheries department. Exactly one month later she underwent speed trials on the Clyde and in July she was handed over and commenced her work, which lasted until the Great War in 1914. During this period scientific officers from the department embarked from time to time, undertaking research and sampling of fish stocks in the laboratory situated on the main deck below the bridge. In addition to a searchlight mounted on the bridge, the *Helga* was fitted with a gun on the forecastle. This fired a three-pound solid non-explosive shell, to put a shot across the bows of any trawler that did not obey her signal to heave to. The cruiser was capable of a higher speed than most trawlers, with another two knots in hand when using her forced draught system.

Following the outbreak of war, enemy German naval activity in Irish waters was limited, except for the mining of the battleship HMS *Audacious* off Lough Swilly in October 1914. However, all this changed in January 1915, with the increased submarine operations round the coast and the first sinking of merchant ships by U-boats. Following this, Kingstown (Dun Laoghaire) and Larne were established as bases for armed trawlers and drifters carrying out anti-submarine patrols. In March the *Helga* was requisitioned by the Royal Navy and commissioned as His Majesty's Armed Yacht, while retaining her peacetime name. Her small gun was removed and a larger 12-pound weapon was fitted in the bows of the ship far forward. Naval equipment was also installed, including a wireless cabin on the afterdeck. It is thought that this refitting was carried out by the Dublin Dockyard Company. In addition members of her crew, as merchant seamen who were enlisted into the Royal Naval Reserve, remained with the vessel, although a RNR lieutenant commander was appointed as captain. She was stationed at Kingstown and, together with armed trawlers, she carried out patrols northwards to the Mull of Galloway and south to Wicklow Head. In particular these patrols were to oversee the protection of the mail steamers running to Holyhead, which were now carrying troops in addition to civilian passengers.

Just one year later the *Helga* entered into the mainstream of Irish history when she became involved in the Easter Rising, after responding to a military request for help. The Rising began on Easter Monday, 24 April 1916, when the General Post Office in Sackville Street and other buildings in the city such as the Royal College of Surgeons, Boland's Bakery and Liberty Hall were seized. After the occupation of the GPO, telegraphic communications between Dublin and London were cut off. Apparently news of the Rising only reached Whitehall in mid-afternoon through naval messages. First to know were the Admiralty, as the information was contained in a naval signal transmitted from the Kingstown base and received by the post office wireless station at Seaforth near Liverpool, which was then passed by land line to London:

Armed Sinn Féin rising in Dublin today have seized Post Office stop Telephonic and telegraphic communications with remainder of Ireland cut off stop Troops called out stop Phoenix Park seized reinforcements from the Curragh now on their way stop .

Captain Henry Aplin, RN, commander of the Kingstown base, at once recalled the *Helga*, together with the accompanying trawlers which were on patrol. Later that day, in response to a request from the military in Dublin, the *Helga* and a trawler arrived in the Liffey. In the evening troops were brought from the Curragh camp by rail and taken through the tunnel which ran from Kingsbridge (Heuston) Station to Cabra and then on to the passenger terminus at the North Wall for the London North Western Railway vessels (beside Spencer Dock and the Royal Canal). They took control of the north bank of the Liffey below the Customs House. The *Helga* carried troops downriver to protect the Pigeon House generating station and remained in Dublin for the night, presumably moored at the North Wall Extension under a military guard. The following is extracted from the armed yacht's bridge log during the Rising:

25 April. At Dublin.

Steamed out and made fast in River berth. Guns, crew and rifle party standing by for all emergencies.

(5.20 a.m.) Proceeded up River. Two rounds from gun fired into mill (near Grand Canal Dock) held by rebels.

(2.15 p.m.) By request of military C.O. commandeered 34 short deals from quay for defence for gun platform and bridge.

Built up barricade and coaling irons on front part of gun platform and front of nav. bridge – sand bags placed round fo'cle (3 p.m.).

Proceeded (10.45 p.m.). Rebels attacking Power station at Pigeon Ho. Fort. Anchored off Pigeon Ho. Fort (11.45 p.m.).

26 April. Proceeded up River. Stopped near Customs House. Opened fire on 'Liberty Hall' in conjunction with the military.

Fired 24 rounds (8. a.m.). Backed down river.

Off Pigeon Ho. Fort, 26–27.

27 April. Proceeded up River (12.00 a.m.). Opened fire on building of Dublin Distillery. Fired 14 rounds into it (12.15 p.m.).

Ceased fire (12. 30 p.m.) and backed down River. Boarded steamer *Campbeltown* and searched her for fugitive enemy.

27–30 April. At Dublin.

1 May. Depart Dublin.[18]

Some accounts of Easter Week have claimed that the ship fired at the GPO. However, her gun, being a naval weapon, was not able to elevate high enough to fire over the Loop Line Bridge. In the bombardment of Liberty Hall the bridge also got in the way, so it appears that she fired under the bridge between the support pillars. From my observations from City Quay and on Matt Talbot bridge, the ship was probably moored in the river on the line of this present-day bridge.

Contemporary photographs show that Liberty Hall sustained some shell damage but remained standing, while the premises on the far side of the laneway between the Hall and Lower Abbey Street was partly demolished. Perhaps the gun crew were given the wrong target, which would not be surprising considering the bad communications that existed on all sides in the city at that time. The Dublin Distillery building mentioned is at the southern side of Pearse Street at the corner of Grand Canal Quay on the city side of the former opening bridge. The building was empty, although Mr de Valera's unit, who were occupying Boland's Bakery, hoisted a Republican flag on top of a tall chimney to draw fire.[19]

An interesting sidelight of the Liberty Hall shelling is contained in a letter from the secretary of the Department of Defence, dated 5 March 1966, on the occasion of Golden Jubilee of the Rising, to Frank Robbins, who had fought in 1916. The letter quotes a story told by Captain Tom McKenna, who served as a junior mate in the early 1930s aboard the *Muirchu*, as the *Helga* became in 1922. It records that Captain P. Duane and Chief Steward J.

Longmore told McKenna that they had both refused to take part in the shelling of Liberty Hall and had been put in irons for a time. However, the story could not have been true, as the gun crew would have been specialist ratings and furthermore, the refusal to carry out such an order in wartime would have been entered into the ship's log and would have been a court-martial offence. Such conduct would have been dealt with most severely by the naval commander in chief in Ireland, Admiral Sir Lewis Bayly. Perhaps the reason for Duane and Longmore's story is that by 1932 there was a new Irish republican government, and the captain and the steward as employees of the Department of Agriculture were afraid for their jobs. Their story could not be challenged because the ship's log was sealed in London. In fact, Captain Duane, as a Lieutenant RNR, was on watch during the shelling and initialled the log. Moreover, according to the Kew documents, Duane 'was mentioned in dispatches twice' – this was the next best thing to being awarded a medal.

Another example of the confusion existing during the 1916 rising, is the entry in the *Helga*'s log: 'Rebels attacking Power station at Pigeon Ho. Fort' on the night of 25 April. There is no record of any assault on the fort or the electricity station.

Following this diversion, the *Helga* returned to anti-submarine patrolling for the rest of the war. As the number of U-boat attacks increased, in 1917 the City of Dublin Steam Packet Company, which held the Royal Mail contract, requested naval escorts for the *Leinster* and *Ulster*, the two ships operating the Kingstown to Holyhead service. This plea was rejected by the Admiralty and naval vessels were only provided for important occasions or persons.

On 4 April 1918, when the *Helga* was on patrol off the Isle of Man, she sighted a slick of oil. The ship then worked up to full speed and followed the track to east, where she encountered the wake of a submarine. A periscope was spotted which then submerged. The *Helga* passed over the point where the periscope was last sighted and dropped two depth charges on the possible track of the submarine. After depth charging, air bubbles were seen and quantities of oil appeared, so more depth charges were dropped. The ship maintained an all night watch and next morning oil was still coming to the surface. An armed trawler then towed a deep sweep with explosives attached in the area.[20] When minesweeping trawlers arrived they located an object on the sea bed, and more depth charges were dropped. On day three of the operation further charges were dropped. Although the *Helga* was credited with sinking a U-boat, in post-war years this claim was considered to be doubtful. The supposed submarine attacked or sunk could not be accounted for in German records, but for the rest of her life the *Helga* carried a star on her funnel to mark this 'sinking'.

On the morning of 10 October 1918, the *Helga* was taking on coal alongside the Traders Wharf, at the Old Coal harbour near the coastguard station in Kingstown, when news arrived that the *Leinster* had been torpedoed. The mail vessel had sailed earlier for Holyhead and was two miles off the Kish lightship when she was hit. Coaling was stopped, steam was raised and the *Helga* cleared the harbour to render assistance. The mail steamer, which had almost 800 people aboard, including troops, had been struck by a torpedo at 9.50 a.m. fired from the submarine UB-123, commanded by Lieutenant Robert Ramm. This struck just forward of the bridge and the order to abandon ship was given by Captain Birch. A second torpedo struck the vessel as the lifeboats were being loaded. The *Leinster* sank about ten minutes after the second torpedo hit.

When the *Helga* reached the scene she commenced picking up survivors, together with the destroyers HMS *Lively* and HMS *Mallard*, the USS *Winslow DD-53* and the USS *Cushing DD-55*. Some 200 survivors were rescued and landed at Kingstown. However, over 500 lives were lost, including some 300 troops whose deaths were concealed at the time. The U-boat never reached home and it is thought that she was lost in the joint British/American mine barrage laid off the north-east coast of Scotland to prevent U-boats and surface craft breaking out into the North Atlantic Ocean. On 11 November, the 'War to End All Wars' ended with the Armistice on the Western Front. Following the end of the conflict the *Helga* was released by the navy and returned to the Department of Agriculture and Technical Instruction to resume her peacetime role.

First Export Order Completed

Returning to the story of the Dublin Dockyard, in 1909 the first vessel launched was the *Kairaki* of 462 tons gross (ON 76080), which must be termed the shipbuilder's first export order, as she was built for the Kaiapoi Shipping & Trading Company of Kaiapoi, a small port on the South Island of New Zealand near Christchurch. She had a deadweight of 400 tons on a draft of 8 feet 6 inches and was 160 feet in length, 28 feet 6 inches in beam and 10 feet 6 inches in depth. Registered in Lyttleton and described as being for her owner's general cargo and livestock trade, Kaiapoi had received tenders from forty yards to build the vessel, before the Dublin Dockyard was successful.

The *Kairaki* had a very short life, as she was lost off the west coast of New Zealand in 1914, with her entire crew of seventeen. However, she was to be the first of five ships built in the Dublin yard for New Zealand over the following eighteen years.

The second ship to come from the yard in 1909 was the *Rhona* (ON 128489), of 640 tons, completed in July, with a length of 188 feet 5 inches and a beam of 28 feet and propelled by a 87 HP engine. She was also the second order for the Dublin firm Michael Murphy Ltd.

On 6 September the third ship of the year, the *Balneil 11* (ON 127996), ran trials. She was a ship of 704 tons and built for the Wigan Coal & Iron Company Ltd of Lancashire. She was named for Lord Balneil, whose family owned coalmines in the area, and replaced a vessel of the same name built twenty-three years earlier. Her dimensions were: length 185 feet, beam 27 feet 8 inches, depth 17 feet 4 inches.

The last ship completed in 1909 was the *Lord Stalbridge* (ON 124625), which ran her trials on 25 November. She was an interesting passenger vessel ordered by the Shropshire Union Railway & Canal Company, Chester, and intended for service on the Manchester Ship Canal and the River Mersey. She was a twin-screw vessel, 105 feet in length, with a beam of 22 feet 6 inches and moulded depth of 11 feet. Propelled by two compound steam engines, she had a higher than normal speed of twelve and one quarter knots. While accommodating 200 passengers, she was also equipped for towing and could function as a tug when required. The *Lord Stalbridge*, conveyed passengers from the Woodside Railway station at Birkenhead on the Wirral, opposite Liverpool across the River Mersey to the Princess Landing Stage for embarkation on liners. By 1922 the ship had been purchased by the Manchester Ship Canal Company and re-registered in Manchester, while retaining her name.

The *Shipbuilder* magazine at the end of 1909 recorded the Dublin yard's output for that year as being five ships totalling 1,809 tons. Since only the above vessels have been recorded, it must be presumed that the fifth vessel was a barge.

The first ship for 1910 was described by Smellie as a twin-screw collier. The term collier was the normal term used in describing a coastal vessel which carried bulk cargoes, mainly coal, from England, Scotland and Wales to Irish ports. Since the new vessel was a coal carrier her task was dirty and unglamorous, but she played an important part in servicing other ships. She was in fact a self-propelled coaling barge working in Holyhead harbour, providing coal for the cross-channel steamers at the Welsh port. Named the *Herald* (ON 128853), she was ordered by the London

North Western Railway Company and had a gross tonnage of 347, with a length of 147 feet, a beam of 27 feet and a depth of 11 feet 6 inches. With a deadweight of 400 tons on a draft of 8 feet 6 inches, she was propelled by a small 19 HP engine. Built under Lloyd's Special Survey, she had a well extending almost her full length under the hoppers, which delivered coal by gravity into buckets. These were then raised by two Holland Johnson elevators and tipped into scoops leading into the ship's coalbunkers. The spent steam from the lifting gear engines was not wasted into the air, but fed into the coal to dampen down the dust. She had a loading rate of 200 tons per hour. The two Dublin-built coaling barges, the *Herald* and the *Nancy*, were in continuous use during the Second World War as all passenger and cargo ships were coal-burning up to 1948. According to G.V. Gwynn Jones the *Herald* had an early form of bridge control, with two levers controlling each engine. When one of these was pushed the vessel went ahead, when the other was pushed the vessel went astern. This propelled the barges round the harbour at a very slow speed and their reliability was exemplary.[21] Both these barges were scrapped in 1952.

In 1910 three further vessels left the yard, the first being a lightship for the Commissioners of Irish Lights in Dublin. Named *Penguin*, she was 102 feet (length) by 24 feet 3 inches (beam), by 13 feet 4 inches (depth) and was designed by the commissioners' naval architect George Idle, MINA (Member of the Institute of Naval Architects). According to John Smellie, the framework of the vessel was of mild steel, 'the whole of the bottom plating is of the best quality iron to better resist the corrosive action of sea water, marine growths etc.'[22] The next vessel, the yard's second overseas order and their first for the New World, specifically Canada, was a coastal passenger vessel named the *Cheslakee* (ON 130309). The last ship of 1910 was the *Slieve Foy* (ON 127474) built for the Carlingford Lough Improvement Commission, Newry. A small vessel, 102 feet 3 inches in length with a beam of 22 feet 6 inches and twin screws, she was designed both as a tug and a buoy tender for maintaining the navigation marks in Carlingford Lough. She had a derrick capable of lifting 5 tons fitted forward on deck. Her design specification required that she must not incline more than seven degrees from the vertical when a buoy was swung from side to side on board the ship. She was propelled by two steam compound engines developing 82 HP, which gave the ship a speed of 11.5 knots. While intended for service on the lough between Counties Down and Louth, she had an eventful interval in her career, when in 1915 she was taken over by the Admiralty for salvage work, a situation which lasted until 1919. Her first naval task was during the ill-fated landings in the Dardanelles where so may Irishmen were killed while serving with the British army. She was scrapped in the 1960s at Ringsend.

The year 1911 saw an output of only two vessels from the yard, both for shipowners who were already customers. The first of these was the *Cheloshin*, the second ship built for Canadian owners, and the other was the *Enda* (ON 132859) for Michael Murphy Ltd and the largest ship built by the dockyard for that company. She had a length of 202 feet and a beam of 30 feet 6 inches, with a gross of 842 tons, driven by a 53 HP engine.

Four ships were built during 1912. The first was a dredger named *Curraghour* (ON 86660), constructed for the Limerick Harbour Commissioners, which had similar dimensions to the very successful *Portlairge* delivered to the port of Waterford five years earlier. Her particulars were 140 feet (length) by 29 feet 6 inches (beam) by 12 feet 6 inches (depth) and she was built to Lloyd's highest class, with a deadweight capacity of 550 tons and a gross of 393 tons. Her dredging equipment included two Priestman cranes with grabs capable of lifting 80 tons of dredged material per hour. Divided into ten watertight compartments, she was able to safely lie aground when the tide was out. Her propelling machinery was supplied by Fisher & Co., Paisley, Glasgow, and consisted of surface condensing engines developing 45 HP. She was delivered in June.

On 1 May, a vessel was launched which was to become renowned over the next forty-six years as the main lifeline for the Aran islands. She was the *Dun Aengus* (ON 121008), owned by the Galway Bay Steamboat Company Ltd, 12 Eyre Square. Steamship services were introduced on the west coast in 1871, when the Galway Bay Steamboat Company obtained the paddle vessel *Cittie of the Tribes* to act as a tug to assist sailing ships using Galway harbour. In the summer of 1872, the company commenced a service across the bay to Ballyvaughan, County Clare, carrying passengers for the Lisdoonvarna Spa and for naturalists visiting the Burren. In 1891 the company started a year-round service to the Aran Islands, which was subsidised by the Congested Districts Board to provide transport for fish catches to Galway. This was part of the task of the development of the fishing industry and bringing fish as fresh as possible to the market.

In 1893 a new steamer specially built in South Shields was delivered to the Galway Bay Steamboat Company. Named *Duras* and only 96 feet in length, she was named after the residence of Major J. Wilson Lynch, the chairman of the Congested Districts Board. An indication of the vessel's priorities was given when the master of a sailing ship complained that the Galway vessel would not tow his ship. The master was quickly informed by the harbour master that the steamer's job was the carriage of fish and not towage.

After almost twenty years of service, it became clear that the Galway Bay Steamboat Company needed a larger ship for their Aran Islands' trade. The *Dun Aengus* was 120 feet in length, with a beam of 24 feet and moulded depth of 10 feet 6 inches. She was driven by a single compound steam engine supplied by Ross & Duncan of Glasgow, which developed 94 HP, giving a speed of 11.25 knots. Her deadweight capacity was 200 tons and her gross was 234 tons. While the vessel could get alongside Kilronan

Pier on the largest island, Inis Mór, depending on the tide, she had to lie off the smaller islands. There the passengers and cargo were carried by currachs to and from the shore. Cattle swam out to the ship, where they were lifted aboard by the ship's derrick, which was just aft of the forecastle, and lowered into the hold for carriage to Galway. Her low freeboard made these cargo and livestock operations relatively easy compared with her successor from the same yard in 1958. During the 1920s–1950s she was the only lifeline to one of the most exposed island communities in the world. On the completion of her successor, the *Dun Aengus* was sold to Haulbowline Industries Ltd, and broken up at Passage West, County Cork. At the end of her life, she made news when she sent out a distress message after getting into difficulties on her final voyage from Galway, and the corvette, LÉ *Macha-01*, was sent to her assistance from Haulbowline. She made Castletownbere in safety, before reaching her last resting place.

The next ship launched was the *Wheatlands* (ON 132827), which left the slipway on 18 July. She was owned by Spillers & Bakers Ltd, 240 Bute Street, Cardiff, where the ship was also registered. She had dimensions of 162 feet 4 inches (length) by 25 feet 7 inches (beam), with a gross of 499 tons. Propelled by a 97 HP engine, she was completed in September.

A LIMITED COMPANY IS FORMED

After eleven years of successful trading, Smellie and Scott wanted to extend their activities and decided to form a limited company. On 12 November 1912, the Dublin Dockyard Company Ltd was incorporated. The directors were the original partners, Walter Scott, MINA, and John Smellie, MINA, together with Robert Crawford, MINA, the chief draughtsman of the yard, and William Alexander the yard manager, both of whom according to John Smellie 'had rendered the company signal service'. Sir John Purser Griffith, M.

Inst. CE, the former chief engineer of the port, was also invited to join the board. John Smellie noted: 'The board of directors was thus composed of men who had considerable business and technical experience, and who were well qualified to inspire the confidence of clients and workmen alike and to ensure a further successful expansion of the Company's affairs.'[23]

The most interesting person to work for the company was Sir John Purser Griffith, described later as the 'Grand Old Man of Irish Engineering'.[24] John Purser Griffith had joined the Dublin Port & Docks Board in 1871 as a young engineer under Bindon Blood Stoney, rising to become first his deputy and then his successor in 1899. He had sought retirement early from his board post because of his total frustration over the board's financial policy. As early as 1901, Purser Griffith had written a memo to the board on the subject of its financial policy, backed up by figures that supported his view that the future of the port would be jeopardised if the board did not make adequate provision for a programme of continued improvements. He said in a report submitted to the Port Board in 1901 that 'Dublin from its geographical position and lines of communication, is the natural commercial gateway to the greater part of Ireland, and should be treated as a national and not merely a local asset'. Purser Griffith wanted to have the harbour dues increased so as to provide money for development, although the 1902 Port Act prevented the Port Board from using accumulated revenues for this purpose and also restricted the financing of new works using borrowed money. He saw the refusal to listen to his ideas as being due in part to the powerful shipowners lobby on the board, who preferred ocean-going ships to berth in Belfast, to discharge their cargoes there and have these transshipped to Dublin in their own coastal vessels. Following the passage of the 1902 Act, permission had been obtained to spend £200 and £9,000 to construct a second graving dock, just after the reopening of the shipyard. However, the Port & Docks Board's failure to increase their revenue prevented any progress and it would be another fifty-five years before that dock was built.

It must be remembered that Purser Griffith was an employee at the time and although he could attend board meetings, together with the harbour master and law agent, he was there to give professional advice only. The board members did not see finance as being part of Purser Griffith's official duties. He therefore decided in 1912 that the only course left open to him to continue his fight for financial reform, was to become a member of the board, so he retired and was succeeded in his old job by his son John William Griffith. The Dockyard Company was seeking representation on the Port & Docks Board and the time was now opportune for Purser Griffith's move. Purser Griffith was knighted at Buckingham Palace in 1911, in recognition of services representing Ireland on the Royal Commission set up in March 1906 'to enquire into and report on the canals and inland navigation in the United Kingdom'.

The first ship launched by the newly incorporated Dublin Dockyard Company Ltd, which took to the water on 12 November 1912, was the *Sligo* (ON 126964). She was ordered by the Sligo Steam Navigation Co. Ltd for their cargo and livestock service between Sligo and Liverpool. The *Sligo* followed the general design of cargo vessels built by the yard, which had their machinery aft with a long raised quarterdeck and a forward well deck. This design was much favoured by the shipowners of the time, as it gave good freeboard and excellent stability with good propeller immersion, both in loaded and light ship conditions. However, the *Sligo* had her well deck built up by high bulwarks to the quarterdeck level. These kept out smaller seas, but in rough weather conditions heavy seas could fill this well and endanger the stability of the ship. In the case of this Sligo-owned vessel, her owners must have specified the design for the protection of livestock carried in open pens in this well space. She was a vessel of 182 feet in length by 28 feet beam and 12 feet 10 inches in depth. Her gross was 515 tons, with a deadweight of 560 tons on 11 feet 6 inches draft. Her propelling machinery, supplied by Messrs McColl & Co. of Belfast, gave her a loaded speed of 11 knots when new.

The *Sligo* remained with her north-west owners for only a few years, when she was sold to the Limerick Steamship Company Ltd. She was one of no less than twelve ships bought by the Shannon-side company between the years 1915 and 1918. Almost all of these vessels only flew the Limerick house flag for one or two years before being sold on or becoming war losses. The exception was the *Mungret*, as the *Sligo* became when she was purchased in 1917. She remained trading for the Limerick Company until 1934, when she was sold to Scotland. Her purchasers were Messrs William Robertson Shipowners Ltd, Glasgow. They renamed her *Nugget* in accordance with their tradition of calling vessels after semiprecious stones. Her new owners had her high well deck bulwark plating removed, as they were carrying heavy bulk cargoes with a high weight to density ratio, such as stone and coal. She was a regular visitor to Ireland, carrying coal to ports on the east and south coasts, then sailing in ballast to north Wales to load stone as a return cargo. On many occasions, having missed a high tide, she could be seen berthed alongside Sir John Rogerson's Quay, Dublin. Then shortly before the next high water, she would proceed down the river with hatches uncovered and enter the small Pigeon House harbour to unload. The dockyard's output for 1912 was 1,641 tons gross.

The first ship built in 1913 was the *Summerfield* (ON 135446), launched on 5 February and registered as owned by the Zillah Shipping and Carrying Company Ltd of Warrington, Lancashire, with W.A. Savage of Liverpool as the manager. Her dimensions were 182 feet (length) by 28 feet 7 inches (beam) with a gross of 687 tons. The company, which was more commonly known as Savages in later years, operated a large fleet of bulk vessels in the Irish Sea right up to the 1960s.

The last ship of that year, completed in December, was named the *Patrica* (ON 132984), a vessel of 781 tons gross, built for Michael Murphy Ltd. Her dimensions were 192 feet 7 inches by 30 feet 6 inches.

The Great War

At this stage ominous war clouds were gathering in Europe and the world was about to torn apart by the greatest conflict in history. The first launching for the year 1914 was the *Streatham* (ON 136049), a cargo steamer of 1,207 tons gross of the raised quarterdeck type, for John Harrison Ltd of London. She was a self-trimming vessel of 1,700 tons deadweight, 226 feet by 35 feet 3 inches by 16 feet 7 inches, and propelled by a triple expansion engine supplied by Ross & Duncan of Glasgow.

The second ship that year and the largest constructed in the yard up to that point, the *J. Duncan* (ON 136938), was launched on 25 July. She was a vessel of 1,832 tons gross, ordered by the J. Duncan Steamship Company Ltd, Cardiff. While described at that time as a long raised quarterdeck steamer and a first class collier, she was different to previous Dublin-built cargo vessels because her machinery was amidships instead of aft. She was actually constructed to the plans of an older *J. Duncan* which had been lost. Her owner, J.T. Duncan, began business as a shipbroker in 1883 and later went into shipowning. He was one of a number of Welsh shipping companies who held British Admiralty contracts. These were for carrying Welsh coal to British naval bases such as Devonport and Portsmouth for warships, and also across the English Channel, where the French navy used Welsh coal because of its steam raising properties. The *J. Duncan* was specially designed to meet Admiralty requirements for going alongside warships and was fitted with eight long pole derricks with powerful winches, with two at each of the four large hatches. Her dimensions were

260 feet by 38 feet 4 inches by 18 feet 6 inches and she had a deadweight of 2,400 tons. She was described in the *Shipbuilder* magazine as having 'unusually comfortable' accommodation for officers, engineers and crew.[25]

J.T. Duncan and company had very close Irish connections with the Shamrock Shipping Company Ltd, established in 1897 in Larne by Thomas Jack. J.T. Duncan was his agent in south Wales and fixed coal cargoes for his ships. Their association was so close that, in return for holding onto the Antrim company's business, Mr Duncan agreed to operate only one vessel in the French and Bay of Biscay coal trades.

The *J. Duncan*, remained with this one owner for her entire career. The naval use of coal dropped from 2.5 million tons per year at the end of the 1914–18 war to just under 200,000 tons in 1928 as oil fuel took over. In later years the Dublin-built vessel found employment carrying coal across the Bay of Biscay and also to Irish Free State ports from the continent during the Economic War in the 1930s. After the Second World War she still was engaged in tramping round these islands, including calls at Dublin, until she was scrapped in 1956.

The outbreak of war in August 1914 brought changes at the yard both for the staff and in the work undertaken. According to John Smellie, a good number of its tradesmen were lost in the early weeks of the war, when they joined up. Some were sent back when the submarine menace was 'causing anxiety', when it was considered that these men would 'better serve their country by assisting to reproduce lost tonnage'. On the staff front he relates that on 4 September, a meeting of the employees was held to consider making weekly contributions to the National Relief Fund set up by the Prince of Wales (later King Edward VIII) and the men agreed unanimously to make a weekly levy on platers of one shilling per man; riveters six pence per pound per squad; caulkers, drillers and blacksmiths, three pence per pound per man;

with engineers, shipwrights, joiners, painters, plumbers, riggers, sawmillers, patternmakers and labourers six pence per man per week.[26]

On that same day, the first direct communication from the naval authorities in London since the outbreak of hostilities was received by the dockyard. According to Smellie, this was a telegram which read: 'It is of the greatest importance that the *J. Duncan* should be completed as quickly as possible as she is urgently required by the Admiralty.' This vessel was still fitting out but she was completed by the end of the month and ran her trials on 1 October, when a speed of 11.25 knots was reached.

Later in October agreements were made by the dockyard with the two government departments in London concerned with the prosecution of the war. These were the Admiralty for the navy and the War Office for the army, who had lost no time in drawing commercial firms into the war effort. On 23 September 1914, a contract was signed between the Admiralty and the Dublin Dockyard Company Ltd for the maintenance and repair of His Majesty's ships and other vessels that could be accommodated at the yard. Work was also carried out for the British Ministry of Shipping, which became responsible for all merchant shipping and for whom the yard continued working until two years after the conflict ended.

Before 1914 many battalions of the British army were stationed in Ireland, including the famous Irish regiments of the time such as the Dublin Fusiliers, Munster Fusiliers, Connaught Rangers and the South Irish Horse, who all had their headquarters on the island. After the outbreak of war all military units had to be carried to France, both men and equipment. This included horses in the case of cavalry regiments, or guns for the artillery batteries together with wagons and stores. The main movements took place through the Port of Dublin because of its proximity to the Curragh, the largest military establishment in Ireland, while the North Wall

Extension was taken over for military use. Civilian vessels were requisitioned as troop transports and these had to be fitted with horse stalls, extra ventilation and even cookhouses, according to Smellie.[27] One presumes that the extra cooking facilities were needed because the ships galleys were not large enough to feed the number of troops aboard. A number of these ships were adapted by the Dockyard Company and in addition the yard undertook other war work, such as converting trawlers and other craft taken over by the Royal Navy, which were armed and equipped for mine-sweeping and anti-submarine duties. The Admiralty had, by April 1915, requisitioned 975 out of the total of 1,400 trawlers under the British flag for naval operations.

The last vessel launched in Dublin in 1914 was the *Shoreham* (ON 136054), which took to the water on 21 October for John Harrison Ltd, 49–51 Eastcheap, London. Her dimensions were 200 feet by 30 feet 6 inches and she had a gross tonnage of 805 tons.

In January 1915, Sir John Purser Griffith was elected to a seat on the Dublin Port & Docks Board as a nominee of the Dockyard Company, although John Smellie makes no mention of this. The eminent engineer was now apparently in a position to champion his finance ideas on a level playing field, but he was not to remain in the position for long.

In February 1915, the dockyard company had issued war badges with an identity certificate to each permanent employee and later the dockyard was placed on the Protected Establishments List, so as to avoid manpower losses through recruiting. However, the threatened conscription in Ireland never materialised, so this protection ultimately proved unnecessary.

The first ship to leave the slipway in 1915, on 3 March, was another for John Harrison of London. The vessel was the *Eltham* (ON 136058), a raised quarterdeck type vessel with engines aft and two hatches in the forward well deck. The foremast was between hatchway numbers one and two with a single hatch behind her open bridge on the quarterdeck and she was rigged with a mizzen mast abaft the funnel. She was 188 feet by 28 feet 6 inches by 13 feet 7 inches, with a gross tonnage of 687.

The volume of war work soon began to put pressure on the yard in a number of ways, including the need to increase the number of building slipways, as well as problem of the shortage of quays to berth the number of ships being repaired. When the yard was established fourteen years previously, the Lord Mayor of Dublin, Tim Harrington, MP, who facilitated the reopening, had envisaged the creation of a large shipbuilding enterprise on the Alexandra Wharf to the east. However, Messrs Scott and Smellie had been more realistic in their outlook and had felt that in the shipbuilding industry of that time, it was questionable to have a bigger yard than existed to meet Dublin's needs, so Harrington's dream remained unfulfilled. Another concern in 1915 for the management was the condition of the two graving slipways, which had been constructed between 1830 and 1840 and to which the Port & Docks Board had made no improvements since they were built.

There was also the fundamental problem caused by the layout of the Alexandra Basin. On the eastwards side, the water area was completely open to the sea, which meant that there was no protection for the graving dock, fitting-out wharf and building berths during east or south-easterly gales. The sea had in fact eroded the foreshore in front of the yard with the result that by 1915 the launching ways had become so undermined that they had to be to be supported at the water's edge on six-foot-high timbers. In what later came to be known as the Spur Wharf Controversy, the *Shipbuilder* reported the dockyard drawing the board's attention to these matters.[28]

John Smellie goes into great detail about an application made by the dockyard in early January 1915 to the Port & Docks Board to provide more shelter and extra berths for ships being repaired.[29]

The board did not reply at once, but asked the harbour master and the engineer to prepare a joint report on the situation, which they submitted to the board on 22 January. The officials put forward two solutions, the first being their preferred choice. This was to construct a spur wharf in a south-easterly direction from the west end of Alexandra Wharf, for a distance of 400 feet, which would give the dockyard a deep water lying-up berth and give shelter to the graving dock entrance. Their report admitted that in easterly or south-easterly gales the sea became very rough in the basin and that several ships had been damaged, while also reporting that during such weather it was impossible to dock any vessel. Their second proposal was to extend Alexandra Wharf to the east, which would allow a lying-up berth at the west end and at the same time not reduce the amount of public berths. This report was not passed to the dockyard, but was given to the board's Berthage Committee for consideration, who ruled in favour of the extension of Alexandra Wharf. When the shipyard was informed of the decision, they protested very strongly that the wharf would not solve the problem of congestion nor provide the shelter or the extra berths needed near the yard.

As a result the matter was referred back to the two officials and on 15 May 1915 they reported again to the main Port & Docks Board that the spur wharf could be shortened to a length of not less than 300 feet, with a minimum width of 40 feet. This would ensure the stability and safety of the structure, which would stand against wind and sea in a 24-foot low water spring tide. The cost of building this would be £15,000 pounds. On 21 May the secretary of the board informed the dockyard that the following resolution had been passed: 'That the matter be deferred for twelve months and meanwhile the engineer would take any steps that are absolutely essential to protect the Dockyard Company's frontage, and restore the land that has been washed away.'[30] This work was promptly and efficiently carried out, but the spur wharf matter dragged on for two more years.

The *Shipbuilder* of August 1915 reported that: 'A proposal to co-opt Walter Scott of the Dublin Dockyard Company onto the Port & Docks Board was defeated by 13 votes to 8 and a trader's representative was selected'.[31]

The last vessel built in 1915, which took to the water on 16 June, was a second lightship for the Commissioners of Irish Lights. Constructed at a cost of £1,310 and named the *Petrel*, she was a sister ship of the *Penguin* completed in 1909, and was constructed with an iron hull and decks with steel frames with five watertight compartments. Her lantern was manufactured by Messrs Merrick of Cork and her design was based on the results of simulations carried out at the National Experimental Tank at Teddington near London, which tested the performance of the ship under sea conditions using a specially constructed model. *Shipbuilder*, which gave a description and news of her launch, also carried a notice from the Commissioners of Irish Lights, signed by H.G. Cook, the secretary, inviting tenders for the purchase of the lightship *Osprey*, built on the same site in 1868 by Walpole, Webb & Bewley. The forty-seven-year-old vessel was acquired by Mr Galsworthy of Appledore, Devon, for the sum of £5,125. The *Petrel*, which was the second ship of that name, served with the Commissioners until 1968, when she was sold to the Hammond Lane Metal Company Ltd, Dublin. They resold her to the Down Cruising Club for use as a clubhouse vessel at Strangford Lough. She was towed there by the Commissioners' Lighthouse Tender *Isolda*, which was fitting, as the towing vessel herself was a product of the same yard in the 1950s.

Although not directly shipbuilding, it is worth looking at the other war work performed by the Dockyard Company. As has been noted at the outbreak of war, agreements had been signed with the War Office and contracts were entered into to supply the Royal Engineers with bridging stores, mining cases, trunks, telegraph poles, ladders and pontoons. According to John Smellie:

'About one hundred of these [pontoons] were supplied to carefully detailed drawings and built of first-class yellow pine, covered with canvas, and treated for water tightness. They had to be capable of interlocking with others made in many parts of the country and specially accurate workmanship was essential.'[32]

In July 1915, when aircraft and shells were in short supply, the directors of the dockyard were anxious to assist the production of munitions. Mr Smellie was invited by the War Office to visit the Farnborough Royal Aircraft Factory to study the possibility of building aircraft in Dublin. He felt that while the work was exacting there would be no difficulty in doing the work in Dublin except for the cost of erecting the factory. The dockyard board considered the matter and informed the War Office that the company would build an aircraft factory, provided that the government would establish a flying centre in the Curragh camp or at some other location in Ireland, so that there would be continuity of work for the new factory, which would be expensive to construct. Although the company was willing bear the cost of building the factory, the War Office would not agree to the airfield project. The company then decided to go into shell production in any case and a shell factory was built within the shipyard estate without government help.

In December 1915, the Dublin Dockyard War Munitions Company Ltd was established by Messrs Walter Scott and John Smellie, with Sir John Purser Griffith as the chairman. The new factory received a contract from the Ministry of Munitions to supply 50,000 eighteen-pound shells. Machinery to produce 2,000 shells per week was ordered from a company in Manchester. In order to make sure 'that the factory was a model one for its size', several manufacturing facilities were visited in England. The most interesting aspect of the new facility was that the workforce would be 'girl labour', as the contract stipulated that only 5% of the total number of employees could be men or boys. Smellie recounts that it was initially felt that there would be difficulty in obtaining girls, as the munitions factories in Britain were located in industrial areas where female factory labour displaced males gone to the Front, a situation that was not a factor in Dublin. However, he went on to pay tribute to their female employees and said that any fears that the directors had about getting suitable labour had proved to be groundless: 'While the factory was being erected and the machinery installed a dozen chosen young ladies were sent over to Messrs Vickers of Barrow-in-Furness for a six weeks' course of instruction ... these girls came back highly capable of teaching others and no difficulty was experienced in obtaining a good output from the very start of production, with but few discards.' There seems to have been very good morale in the factory, perhaps due to a bonus paid for both overall and personal output. The 200 girls employed soon became highly efficient and were quick to adapt to the machinery. Smellie also paid tribute to the company chairman Sir John Purser Griffith, who took a great interest in the staff. This is not surprising, as when he was the engineer with the Port & Docks Board he had also shown a strong interest in the welfare of the men under his employ.[33]

There were two launches in the first month of 1916. The *Ferga* (ON 139593), which slid down the ways on 21 January, was built for the Dublin General Steamshipping Company (Michael Murphy Ltd). This was their fourth vessel from the yard and a sister ship of the *Patrica*. The other ship launched that month was the *Dulwich* (ON 139126). With dimensions of 240 feet 3 inches by 36 feet by 18 feet 3 inches and with a gross tonnage of 1,460 tons, she was a vessel of a new design created by the yard. Even before leaving the yard she attracted publicity, as while she was being fitting out in February, the harbour master, Captain Webb, asked the shipyard to move her to allow an oil tanker to discharge at the Alexandra Wharf. The company refused to move the vessel 'as they felt that their own berth was unsafe owing to failure of the Port & Docks Board to carry out their obligations.'[34] The Port Board took the shipbuilders to court, according to the summons: 'For failing to regulate the *Dulwich* in accordance the Harbour Master's directions.' The magistrate held that the dockyard had to obey the harbour master and he imposed a fine of £1 with £5 costs.

While the next launch did not take place for another nine months, other momentous events were taking place in Ireland. On Easter Monday 1916 the GPO and other buildings in Dublin were seized by nationalists led by James Connolly, Tom Clarke, Pádraig Pearse and Joseph Plunkett to name but a few. The 1916 Rising, however, seems to have had little impact on the Dublin shipbuilders. John Smellie fails to mention it in his book and the only reference to it is found in the *Shipbuilder*, under the heading of 'Shipbuilding in Ireland': 'Nothing to report from Londonderry and Dublin yards. In the first named the scarcity of labour is hindering progress and in the latter, the untoward events of the past few weeks in and around Dublin, have delayed work, although the Dublin Dockyard establishment escaped injury during the insurrection.'[35]

The last ship for 1916, launched on 28 October, was the *Western Coast* (ON 137530), a vessel of 1,394 tons gross tonnage similar to the *Dulwich*. She was ordered by Messrs Powell, Bacon & Hough Lines Ltd of Liverpool, for their general cargo trade. Later in the 1920s this company became Coast Lines Ltd, a conglomerate which was major force in British and Irish cross-channel trade for over forty years.

One other vessel was launched in Dublin during October that year. She was the *Zoe*, a small tug built in Ringsend Basin by the Ringsend Dockyard.

Before leaving 1916 it is worth recalling that two of the vessels launched had only brief careers. The *Ferga* did not even see a full year of trading, because on 16 February 1917 she was intercepted by a U-boat, captured and sunk fifteen miles south of Bardsey Island in the Bristol Channel, without loss of life. The *Dulwich* sank on 18

June 1917, when she struck a mine seven miles off the Shipwash Light Vessel while on passage from Seaham to London with a cargo of coal. Despite being sunk, she later became of importance to the prosperity of the Dublin Dockyard.

The Shipyard Extension

The Great War was now in its third year, and the shipyards and the Dublin Dockyard were busy working for both the Admiralty and the Ministry of Shipping, including repairing vessels damaged by enemy action, mounting defensive guns aboard merchant ships and the fitting of minesweeping gear on converted trawlers. In October 1916 no less than 312,000 tons of merchant shipping had been sunk and by April 1917 the figure had more than doubled, increasing to 852,000 tons. The Dockyard Company came under intense pressure from visiting Admiralty officials and the Controller of Shipping, to increase their output of tonnage.[36] Apart from personal verbal exhortations, letters and telegrams were sent from Whitehall, including one from Prime Minister Lloyd George in Downing Street.

Once again the *Shipbuilder* commented early in 1917 on the shortage of berths, by reporting in February that 'the Dublin Company had applied to the Belfast Harbour Commissioners for land as they needed space'. The March issue also reported on this issue: 'The question of the quay extension is very unsettling at the moment … the Dublin Dockyard may take advantage of the Belfast offer.'[37] The Dublin Dockyard may have been following in the footsteps of Lord Pirrie and playing Belfast off against Dublin, but Smellie makes no reference at all to a Belfast approach. The April issue of *Shipbuilder* leads its report from Ireland as follows:

> The most important happening in the Irish shipbuilding industry last month was the settlement of the long-standing dispute between the

Dublin Dockyard Company and the Dublin Port & Docks Board. The dispute has dragged on for two years, and the terms were only carried by the casting vote of the Chairman of the Board. It has been agreed that so much of the land on the east side of the Graving Dock as is not used in connection with the working of the dock will be let to the Dockyard Company at a rent of £250 per annum. The Board will also lease to the company a portion of their yard on the west side of the graving dock. The company will pay yearly £80 per acre for this land. The dockyard would give a sum of £3,000 towards works to be carried out, while the Board would spend not more than £8,500 of the port fund. The dockyard to take over all the employees not required in the Board's engineering department. The extension of the Alexandra Wharf was to be undertaken immediately and the spur wharf shall be started.

The report concluded that 'since the dispute had been settled the company have booked an order for a large steamer'.[38]

John Smellie stated that the new lease for the extra ground was signed by both parties on 17 September, but that the company had been given the right of entry to the site two months earlier in July. That same agreement promised that the Port Board 'would proceed with all reasonable dispatch' to construct the spur wharf originally discussed two years previously, with the dimensions 400 feet in length and 80 feet in width, and to give the Dockyard Company unobstructed right of access from their premises to the pier. However, despite this agreement the wharf was never constructed.

The extra land gave the yard a water frontage of 165 feet, permitting two new building berths, Nos 4 and 5, to be established and allowing vessels of up to 420 feet in length to be built. According to the *Dublin Commercial Year Book* there were between 750 and 800 employed in the dockyard at this time.[39] In June, the *Shipbuilder* reported that wages in all the Irish shipyards were raised by an extra 2s 6d per week per man and that 'Messrs Baily Gibson, who had applied to the Port & Docks Board for a site on the Liffey for shipbuilding and repairing work, waited on the board on December 23rd ... They could not recommend any expenditure of capital at the moment.'[40]

THE LONDON COAL SHIPS

At the outbreak of war the office of the Controller of Shipping was established by the government to co-ordinate all wartime ship construction. This included the allocation of contracts for new ships to yards that had spare building capacity and free slipways.

The British capital, London, had used gas since the nineteenth century and the amount of coal used in its production was immense. In the year 1913 a total of nine million tons of coal was imported by sea, mainly from the north-east coast, which was carried in a fleet of vessels chartered by the various London gas companies. However, as the war progressed shortages of supply occurred as result of a number of factors: the Admiralty's need for colliers to carry coal for the fleet caused more colliers to be requisitioned; war losses of ships sunk by mines or U-boats; and delays caused by naval re-routing orders. In 1915 the Coal Advisory Committee was set up to regulate this trade and was made up of representatives of the two main London gas producing firms, the Gas Light & Coke Company on the north side of the Thames and the South Metropolitan Gas Company on the southern bank, together with the main industrial coal suppliers and shipping companies. Its work was to ensure that sufficient ships were made available to carry the coal needed for essential purposes. At this stage the convoy system of escorting ships to protect them from U-boat attacks had not been established, owing to resistance at senior level in the Royal Navy, although it was later introduced in 1917 following the personal intervention, it is said, of the Prime Minister David Lloyd George.

This shortage of shipping caused increased freight rates and the gas companies were forced into buying their own ships to carry cargoes. The South Metropolitan Gas Company purchased four vessels in 1915, although by 1917 three of these were lost. The Gas Light & Coke Company likewise bought four ships in 1915 and a further four in 1916. In all, ten second-hand purchases were made, mainly of older ships because of their cheaper prices. The Gas Light & Coke Company also began ordering new vessels in England, but the South Metropolitan's first building contract was allocated to the Liffey yard by the shipping controller, presumably on account of its vacant slipway. The *Dulwich*, while a typical raised quarterdeck steamer with her machinery amidships, had accommodation for both officers and crew around the engine and boiler casing. This was instead of the more traditional location of sailors and firemen forward in the forecastle. The captain and steward's quarters and the saloon were at the front of the superstructure, while the mates and engineers had cabins on port and starboard, with the fireman and sailors on the deck below. This vessel had very large hatches to facilitate unloading by grabs and the floor of its No. 4 hold was raised to the top of the top of the shaft tunnel to form a tank top, so as to permit the grabs to fully empty the space. The cargo deadweight was 2,330 tons.

Although the *Dulwich* herself was lost at sea after only eighteen months of service, her design was selected as a standard ship type by the Controller of Shipping. Her design was called the C5 and to maximise shipbuilding efficiency, the dockyard was asked to supply the details of her construction to other shipyards. Fourteen vessels of the type were constructed in four British yards, while Dublin built a further nine for the London gas companies.

The next C5 constructed was the *Lambeth* (ON 140414), of 1,536 tons gross and completed for the South Metropolitan Gas Company in November 1917. She had a slightly increased deadweight tonnage and was the only ship to come from the yard that year. The first ship in 1918 was also a C5 type, the *Kennington* (ON 142435), launched on 3 March and completed in May, again for the South Metropolitan Gas Company. She became a war loss almost overnight, as on 12 June she was sunk in the North Sea by a German submarine UB-108, some fifteen miles east of Flamborough Head. She was on passage from London to the Tyne in ballast, probably returning north having discharged her first cargo.

The second completion for that year was another C5 vessel, which also launched in March. This was the *Amiens* (ON 142583) of 1,548 tons gross, which was delivered to the European Gas Company Ltd. She was sold in 1926 to Harries Brothers & Company of Swansea and was sunk by German aircraft on 14 April 1941, while on passage from Cardiff to Portsmouth with a cargo of coal, all aboard being saved.

The third launching for the last year of the First World War was handed over to the South Metropolitan Gas Company in November, the month of the Armistice. She was the *Brixton* (ON 142671), which had her quarterdeck extended by 3 feet with an increased depth and breadth. Her deadweight was 2,450 tons and her dimensions were 240 feet 3 inches by 36 feet 3 inches by 18 feet 4 inches. She was the last C5 built to the original design with a raised quarterdeck. This feature was eliminated in all following ships in order to simplify construction.

The *Shipbuilder* makes very interesting reading for the latter part of 1918 with news of Irish events: 'Another shipyard for Dublin; the Northern Ireland Shipbuilding Company of Derry seeking powers to obtain more land; That concrete shipbuilding was proceeding successfully at Warrenpoint and that the Committee of the Newry Urban Council is to advertise the town as a shipbuilding centre.' Another Derry item that made the news columns, was the court case in Dublin before Mr Justice Ross between the aforementioned Northern Ireland Shipbuilding Company and Messrs Ben Cromwell Ltd, contractors of Liverpool. The shipbuilders were asking Messrs Ben Cromwell Ltd to annul a contract to build 100 houses for their workers, under the Court's Emergency Provisions Act 1914-1917, because there was no material. After two days of the hearing, a settlement agreed by both parties was accepted by the judge.[41]

PEACETIME RETURNS

At the end of the Great War in 1918 the Dublin Dockyard Company Ltd, like all other shipyards in the United Kingdom had a full order book for the Controller of Shipping, including five 2,450-ton deadweight standard ships and two larger vessels. The first peacetime ship, which had been ordered as the *War Liffey*, was launched on 2 February 1919 as the *Bermondsey* (ON 143169), just under three months after the end of hostilities. She was the first of the improved C5 type, with dimensions of 240 feet by 36 feet 3 inches by 19 feet and had a gross tonnage of 1,561. She was delivered to the South Metropolitan Gas Company in April.

The yard's next launching, which took place that same month, was the *Catford* (ON 143334), which had been laid down as the *War Avoca*. She ran trials in July and was again handed over to the South Metropolitan Gas Company. The third ship of the year which took to the waters of Alexandra Basin on 16 July 1919 was both the largest built to date by the company and also the first vessel to come from the new shipyard extension, which had been leased from the Port Board just two years previously. Named the *Halo* (ON 143426), although laid down as the *War Brigade*, she was capable of carrying 3,350 tons deadweight on a draft of 19 feet 3 inches. Built to Lloyd's highest class, her dimensions were 285 feet by 41 feet 9 inches by 21 feet 3 inches. She was also the first of two new ships for the Gas Light & Coke Company Ltd. This company had, by the end of the war, lost eleven of the eighteen ships they had bought since 1914, most of which had been relatively old. So the company decided both to order new vessels and to purchase more suitable ships for their post-war fleet, and the *Halo* was their largest unit. She was towed to Glasgow to have her triple expansion machinery installed by Messrs David Rowan & Company and was completed in September.

The actual launching date of the fourth ship of the year from the dockyard is unclear, but was possibly August or September because of the extra fitting-out time required, as she was a twin-screw passenger ship for India. This was the *Jayanti* (ON 133361), built for the Bombay Steam Navigation Company Ltd and ordered for the company's Bombay to Goa service. A vessel of 318 tons gross, she was constructed to comply with Lloyd's Special Survey rules for their coasting class and had dimensions of 176 feet by 28 feet by 9 feet 6 inches to the main deck. Propelled by two sets of triple-expansion engines supplied by Ross & Duncan of Glasgow, she ran trials on the Skerlmorlie Measured Mile in the Firth of Clyde on 16 November 1919, when a speed of 14.75 knots was reached. An interesting fact about the ship is that the 1921 Mercantile & Navy List gives her as registered in Bombay in 1920, but her building date is given as Dublin 1913. The reason for this could be that her keel was laid that year, but owing to the war, construction was suspended. This would explain her allocated official number 133361, which dates from about 1913.

The last launch for 1919, which took place on 9 October, was that of the *Old Charlton* (ON 144292), which was the seventh ship for the South Metropolitan Gas Company, with dimensions of 240 feet by 36 feet by 21 feet 6 inches and a deadweight of 2,500 tons. Ordered originally as the *War Fal*, her machinery manufactured by Messrs Rowan & Company of Glasgow was installed in Dublin and she was completed in December.

The total output by the Dublin Dockyard for that year was 7,860 gross tons. However, as 1919 came to an end, the shipbuilding and the labour scenes in Ireland were entering very stormy waters. Shipwrights' wages had doubled since 1914, but in October the

Shipbuilder reported that 'members of the Amalgamated Society of Engineers in Dublin were seeking wage parity with Belfast'.[42] The item concluded by saying that 'the matter would be put to arbitration'. The political situation in Ireland and the War of Independence which was taking place added to the unrest.

By 1920 the shipbuilding industry throughout the United Kingdom was starting to adjust to the changed needs of peacetime. Most vessels ordered under the wartime building programmes were for the Controller of Shipping and these had been finished and handed over. The Admiralty had cancelled many naval contracts and some warships were even scrapped part way through their construction. There had been some hysterical reaction towards the end of the war about the perceived shortage of building berths, with some large British shipowners even attempting to tie up these berths for up to ten years. However, two unforeseen factors then distorted the British shipbuilding industry: the post-war slump and war reparations. Under the Treaty of Versailles, Germany had to cede all merchant ships over 1,600 tons gross and half of those between 1,000 and 1,600 tons to the victors, and also surrender a quarter of her fishing fleet. Great Britain, because of her huge war losses, had been allocated the biggest share of the German vessels. For example in the twelve months ending in September 1921, 2.5 million deadweight tons of enemy shipping was offered for sale, including 49 passenger ships, 328 cargo steamers, 29 trawlers and 28 sailing vessels! The war had also increased the total number of building berths in Britain; in one sector alone the number increased from 450 in 1914 to 650 in 1920, so things were very tough for shipyards in the immediate post-war years.

We saw earlier that the Controller of Shipping had chosen the Dublin Dockyard Company's plans of the *Dulwich*, as a standard type of ship design, but there were in all some fifteen different types covering various tonnage sizes. One of the other types, developed by the Tyne Iron Shipbuilding Company Ltd, Newcastle upon

Tyne, was for a 5,000 tons deadweight cargo steamer. The first launch from the Dublin yard in 1920, the *Glenstal* (ON 138912), which took to the water on 19 February, was one of these. The *Glenstal* was the largest ship ever built in Dublin and the second constructed in the shipyard extension. Ordered as the *War Cloud*, she was bought by the Limerick Steamship Company Ltd from the Controller of Shipping, but only remained with the Shannon-side owners for about a year.

With a poop deck, bridge and forecastle, she had five holds and five hatches served by ten derricks. Her dimensions were 331 feet by 46 feet 6 inches by 25 feet 6 inches. Built to Lloyd's highest class, under their Special Survey rules, she carried 5,150 tons deadweight on a draft of 21 feet 8 inches. In March she was towed to Glasgow to have her triple expansion machinery installed by McKie & Blair, which gave her a speed of 11.25 knots, while her three single-ended boilers were supplied by David Rowan. In 1921 the Adelaide Steamship Company Ltd, Newcastle, New South Wales, South Australia, purchased and renamed her the *Aldinga*, although she did not change her port of registry until 1925. She remained with them for some thirty years, then in the early 1950s she was bought by a South African company, the Neptune Shipping Company, and became the *Natal Coast*. In April 1955, while on passage between Durban and Matadi, she ran into a fog bank south of the Cunene River and was wrecked on the notorious Skeleton Coast near Swakopmund. The loss of the old vessel was apparently the last straw for her owners, as they went out of business soon afterwards.

In March 1920 the first of the labour disputes, which according to Smellie plagued the Dublin Dockyard for the remainder of its existence, commenced. This dispute was caused by a claim served by the Irish Transport & General Workers Union (ITGWU), who demanded that the Clyde Agreement be abolished and that new conditions be introduced for dinner-hour working. In addition, they called for one week's pay be given in lieu of notice of dismissal and for increases on the rates paid of three pence per hour for new work and four pence per hour for repair work. On 26 November 1919, a general increase in wages had been granted in England. Following this, strikes occurred in Belfast and Larne, where a pay rise was granted after two weeks, while in Derry increases were given to clerks for overtime and holiday working. All of these raises soon became known to Dublin workers.

The ITGWU's demands for Dublin workers were submitted on 26 March. John Smellie later claimed that the ITGWU had little or no reason for their demands, as member's rates of pay had risen three times since pre-war and the working week had been reduced from fifty-three hours to forty-seven hours per man, compared with the craft workers. He noted that efforts were made to have the strike called off, with initial meetings in the yard, then at Union headquarters followed by the Ministry of Labour and in the Mansion House.[43] An Irish office of the British labour ministry had been set up in July 1919.

The withdrawal of labour lasted for eleven weeks and only ended when pressure was brought to bear on the ITGWU by other unions and by the company's argument that 'a victory for a section of the workers now meant defeat for all in the not too distant future'. On 30 June 1920 all the employees returned under the existing terms and conditions. Smellie wrote that while the strike was without rancour, all work stopped and raw materials and equipment could not be obtained. He was very bitter about the part played by the ITGWU and felt that the union had deliberately targeted his company because it was the largest shipbuilding industry in the port, while they had ignored other shipbuilders. Although the others are not identified, he could only have been talking about the shipbuilding facility which had been established at the east end of Alexandra Wharf, Dublin Shipbuilders Ltd (see chapter 4).[44]

As a result of the strike, permanent damage was done to labour relations and also to the future stability of the yard. From the end of this dispute, there commenced a period of labour unrest, with constant inter-union disputes in the yard on a weekly and even a daily basis. These were led by the craft workers, with the joiners and riveters taking a leading role. According to Smellie, every attempt by the management to economise was examined and opposed, while 'the motives of one union were constantly challenged by others'. Time-keeping fell below normal especially among the ironworkers. Little attempt was made to take advantage of the current high rates of wages and company bonuses for good time-keeping. He claimed that the major part of the 44,000 man-days of production lost for the year 1920 was caused by the actions of the ITGWU, which body, apart from flexing its muscles in Dublin, had also caused disputes in Rushbrook, County Cork, with the Wharf and Riverside Workers Union.[45]

When John Smellie made these statements four years later, it is fair to say that it was still too near to the events for him to make objective comment. It must also be appreciated that he wrote as the employer and co-founder of the Dublin Dockyard, who had revived the shipbuilding industry in Dublin just twenty years earlier and so had a somewhat more proprietary interest in the enterprise than most. Although living in Dublin for two decades, he was also a Scotsman and probably did not fully understand and appreciate the changes taking place in Ireland and her politics. At this time there was turmoil in the labour movement; for example the ITGWU, which had 5,000 members in 1916, by 1920 had a membership of 120,000. Most of the craft unions up to this point had been British based and now attempts were being made to establish local unions for skilled workers. An illustration of how times were changing is shown by the fact that in 1916 nineteen out of the thirty-seven unions affiliated to the Dublin Congress were British, but in 1921, while union numbers had risen to forty-two, only thirteen were now British. In addition there was a growing tide of militant trade unionism and by 1920 many of the trades councils had rejected the normal titles of 'Trades' or 'Labour' for the name Workers' Councils.

The immediate result of the withdrawal of labour in March 1920 in the Dublin Dockyard was that the launch due to take place on 20 April of their next vessel had to be postponed. The *Shipbuilder* for June reported that dockyard had been closed since early May 'owing to strike of labourers and the management intimate that dockyard will remain closed until better councils prevail. The SS *Brockley,* awaiting launching for the South Metropolitan Gas Company is still on stocks owing to the strike.'

This closure caused the departure of a number of the firm's skilled workmen to England and diverted several repair jobs from the Liffey to other yards. The men who left Dublin would have had little difficulty in getting jobs in Britain, as there was a shortage of craftsmen there. That June issue of *Shipbuilder* carried another important item of labour news: 'During May a new trade union was formed in Dublin under the name The Irish Engineering, Shipbuilding and Foundry Workers Union. It is a purely Irish organisation and seeks to enrol all workers at present in the ASE, Iron Moulders, Boilermakers and other cross-channel unions. The Belfast workers will not join the new organisation, which is, however, meeting with support in Dublin and the south.'[46] The trade unions in Ireland were now becoming fragmented and split on a north/south divide.

After work resumed in June, the *Brockley* (ON 145012) was launched on 5 July, as the *Shipbuilder* in August reported: 'Cargo steamer 240 feet BP [between perpendiculars] by 36 feet by 21 feet 3 inches. A 2,500 tons deadweight vessel, and the eighth for the South Metropolitan Gas Company for their special trade. She is of the flush deck type and has two holds, forward and aft free from obstructions. A large cellular double bottom is fitted throughout and large fore and aft peak tanks and a deep tank are also provided, thus giving ample ballast to enable her to make light passages in heavy weather. The triple expansion engine and boilers made by J.G. Kincaid of Greenock will be installed in Dublin by the builders.'[47] After running trials in September the vessel was handed over.

The September 1920 *Shipbuilder* carried further news about the development of the labour movement: 'The newly formed Irish Union of Shipbuilding, Engineering and Foundry Trade Workers, has so far failed to get a footing in Belfast, but during August a branch was formed in Cork. The society claims a membership of close on 2,000 of which 1,200 are in Dublin. But its chances of supplanting the English unions in the north under present conditions and indeed under any conditions are hopeless.'[48] This was a reference to the action in July when 3,000 employees were forced out of the Belfast yards because of their religion. 'A number of these prominent socialist workmen included leaders of the 1919 strike for a 44 hour week'. This only accelerated the replacement of British unions in the south of the country, who were seen not to have supported their Catholic members.

The next ship to be completed was another C5 class for the London coal trade, launched on 28 August and named the *Jetblack* (ON 145083), which had been ordered as the *War Calder*. It is not known if her propelling machinery and boilers, which were supplied by J.G. Kincaid, were installed in Dublin or Scotland. She completed trials on 4 November, after which the 2,500 tons deadweight vessel was handed over to the Gas Light & Coke Company of London, who had taken delivery of the *Halo* the previous year. The 27 November also saw the launch of the *Finola* (ON 145533), the last long raised quarterdeck machinery aft vessel built by the yard, which was the sixth ship for local shipowner and long-time customer Michael Murphy Ltd. This 1,100 tons deadweight ship with dimensions 207 feet by 30 feet 6 inches by 15 feet 3 inches was intended for the company's Dublin-Swansea-

Cardiff and Liverpool-Birkenhead general cargo services and she ran trials on 6 February 1921.

The last cargo vessel launched in 1920, which took to the water on 14 December, was the *Orlock Head* (ON 145413), which had been ordered as the *War Trent*. Smellie noted that she was the yard's standard [C5] design modified to meet the requirements of her owners, The Ulster Steamship Company of Belfast.[49] This ownership is clarified by William Harvey, who records that the archives of G. Heyn & Co. Ltd show that the vessel was constructed with steel left over in the dockyard intended for vessels in the war programme, which had been cancelled. The government and the shipbuilders approached G. Heyn & Company and offered the steel at a discounted price to construct a vessel. This was accepted, as it was a good deal for all – the surplus steel was sold, the shipyard received an order at a difficult time and the owners got a cheap ship to their own design.[50]

This new 2,450 tons deadweight vessel had a poop deck, bridge and forecastle, and dimensions of 240 feet length by 30 feet 6 inches beam and 21 feet 3 inches depth. She was equipped with six double derricks and was designed for the Head Line's continental and Baltic trades, in which they had been engaged for many years. They carried timber and paper pulp from ports in Sweden and Finland, and general cargo from the Low Countries. She was towed to the Clyde on 12 January to have her triple expansion machinery installed at Greenock by the engine builders Messrs J.G. Kincaid & Company. However, after her sea trials she was taken over by the owners in an incomplete state and brought to Belfast where her fitting out was completed, as she could not return to Dublin because of a joiners strike. This was most ironic, as the tradesmen in Belfast who finished off the vessel had themselves been expelled the previous year by the Carpenters and Joiners Union in England because they had refused to come out on strike in support of a dispute in Britain. The *Orlock Head* sailed on her maiden voyage on 12 March 1921. Along with the *Jetblack*, she was the last ship constructed for owners in the UK by the dockyard. The total tonnage of ships launched in Dublin for 1920 was five steamers of 8,672 gross.

In the latter half of 1920, arising from their constant difficulties with the workforce, the directors of the dockyard were very apprehensive about the prospects for future ship-repair contracts. Apart from these headaches, they were also becoming concerned about the non-performance by the port authority of the legal contract entered into three years before to provide extra building capacity to meet wartime demand. That document included a clause committing the Dublin Port & Docks Board to have the Spur Wharf constructed 'on or before the first day of April 1919', yet nothing had happened in the interim. By November 1920, since eighteen months had elapsed since the stipulated date without any sign of building work commencing or indeed any word of explanation as to the delay being received, the dockyard wrote reminding the Dublin Port & Docks Board of 'their definite engagement' to build the wharf. They pointed out that damage was still being sustained both by ships fitting out and those under repair because of the lack of protection that this pier would provide. They also noted that there was an additional expense incurred and inconvenience caused when vessels had to be shifted 'second off', whereby one vessel was tied up to a quay and a second moored outside the first, or when they had to be anchored in Alexandra Basin, to allow work to proceed aboard. Attention was drawn to the port's facilities, which were no better than eighteen years previously when the yard opened and to the fact that the only dry dock was still without a crane. Smellie noted that no action was taken in response to their letter and another eighteen months would pass before the dockyard again felt compelled to write and ask about the lack of progress in this matter.[51] However, by the time a definite reply came it would only be of academic interest, as by then all building and repair work had come to a standstill in the Port of Dublin.

THE DOCKYARD COMPANY HEADS FOR CLOSURE

The last full year of shipbuilding for the Dublin Dockyard Co. Ltd, commenced with the launch of the steamer *Brynymor* (ON 143974) on 10 February 1921. This 4,100 tons deadweight steamer was ordered by the Tor Maritime Property Company of Jersey, Messrs Letricheux, and managed by Letricheux and David Ltd, Swansea. She was the first of three Frederikstad-type ships to come from the yard and had the following dimensions: length 300 feet; beam 44 feet and depth 23 feet 6 inches. She had clear holds with four large hatches and the well decks were clear of all obstructions so that they could be utilised for timber cargoes. The vessel only ran her trials on 10 October, after fitting out for eight months. This gap appears to have been caused by a delay in steel deliveries, a material which had been in short supply the previous year and this shortage continued into 1921. She was the last seagoing ship to fly the Red Ensign launched from the yard, as all those following were built for overseas.

The first foreign order to come off the stocks was launched the following month, on 28 March. This was the Norwegian vessel *Mascot* of 1,823 tons gross for A/S Nordsjoen of Christiania (now Oslo), with R. Pederson as manager. Described in the *Shipbuilder* as a 3,050 tons deadweight Frederikstad ship with dimensions of 278 feet by 42 feet by 20 feet, she had her winches on the poop deck, bridge and forecastle decks with timber cargoes stowed in the well decks. Smellie makes no mention of this vessel nor is there any date known for her sea trials. She seems only to appear in the Lloyd's Register for a year under this name.

The next overseas ship was the *Saint Marguerite II*, of 1,845 tons gross, built for the French owners Société de Navigation à Vapeur Daher of Marseilles. This was a sister ship of the Norwegian vessel, although it carried a slightly lower deadweight of 3,000 tons. Her machinery was supplied by Rankin & Blackmore of Greenock and she ran trials on 14 October 1922. All her working life was under the French ensign and she was sunk in 1943 by a British submarine in the Mediterranean Sea during the Second World War, while on passage from southern France to Italy.

During the first half of 1921 shipbuilding throughout Ireland entered a very troubled time. Mention has already been made of wage increases at the Larne Shipbuilding Company, but there was another company in that County Antrim port, the Olderfleet Shipbuilding & Engineering Company, whose yard had only been laid out in 1919. In the closing months of the previous year, the *Shipbuilder* had reported that both companies were busy, with the Olderfleet yard completing a new slipway to build 3,000-ton ships. In September, while five vessels were on order, only four had been laid down and these were delayed by a shortage of steel. The Larne Shipbuilding yard had five vessels on the stocks, with further orders on hand, and on 30 October launched the largest ship ever built in that port. She was steamer *Kerrymore*, built for John Kelly of Belfast, which was owned by Robert McCowan & Sons Ltd of Tralee. The *Kerrymore* was registered in that Kerry port until being scrapped.

However, by April 1921, the *Shipbuilder* was publishing a very different story: 'The Olderfleet yard has been placed in liquidation and the Larne Shipbuilding Company was in crisis, and in the latter firm a shareholders meeting had been called for the purpose of putting the company into voluntary liquidation.' By the May issue the report was worse: 'The Larne yard has been put up for sale by the liquidator and Olderfleet was closed.'[52] In just six months the town had been turned upside down with the virtual disappearance of its shipbuilding industry. At the time a large number of contracts had been cancelled and almost new second-hand ships could be bought at a price cheaper than it cost to build new vessels.

To return to Dublin, in August a resolution was tabled, voted for and passed at a meeting of the city council in response to a letter from Alderman Alfie Byrne, calling for a conference to be held to discuss the repair of Irish lightships. This conference brought together the trade unions, corporation members and the board of the Commissioners of Irish Lights. However, the September issue of *Shipbuilder* reported an adjournment of the event, so as to allow the shipbuilders in the city to attend. But there is no record of any subsequent meeting being held or of any decisions to improve matters.

SS *Bocamaule*

The next launch from the Dublin Dockyard took place on 3 September 1921, when the first of two vessels ordered by Messrs Duncan Fox & Co. of London on behalf of South American principals took to the waters. She was the *Puchoco*, of 2,515 tons gross, and her owners were the Compañía Carbonifera y de Fundición Schwager of Valparaíso in Chile. John Smellie wrote about these two ships, built at a time when it was practically impossible to obtain steel plate and bars at home, and he noted that the steel had to be imported from America. 'The vessels were built to Lloyd's highest class and to exacting specifications, as their trade routes, off the west coast of South America, were far distant from ready assistance in case of breakdown.'[53] Their dimensions were 300 feet by 44 feet by 20 feet with a deadweight of 3,500 tons and the triple expansion propelling machinery was supplied by David Rowan & Co. Ltd of Glasgow. The second ship, the *Bocamaule,* was launched on 29 October and named by Mrs Royale, wife of John Royale, head of the engineering department of Duncan Fox & Company and daughter of their senior partner, Mr Woodsend. The *Bocamaule* ran successful acceptance trials at Skelmorlie on the Firth of Clyde towards the end of February.

The start of 1922 saw the first issue of the *Shipbuilder* painting a very dark picture of the industry in Britain, with the cancellation of orders, which had started in 1919, still in progress and the collapse of the freight market in 1921. The cost of building ships at the end of the year was high and the sale price of a general cargo ship less than half of the building cost. The prospects for the new year, it reported, were not good, as there were practically no orders placed in 1921. In its April edition, the *Shipbuilder* noted: 'The shipbuilding industry in Dublin is hard hit by the prevailing conditions and at a meeting of the Dublin Port & Docks Board on 14 March it was intimated that the shipyards of the port were practically closed down.'[54]

The previous years' depression in Britain was now affecting Irish yards and that prospects for the year were not good was an understatement. During the 1914 to 1918 conflict, a war bonus had been paid in twelve instalments to shipyard workers, the last of which was given in June 1920. These did not form part of the basic wage and by the time the scheme ended the total bonus amounted to 26 shillings and 6 pence. Pre-war, a shipwright earned forty-two shillings a week, but when the last payment was made in June 1920, he was taking home eighty-two shillings a week – almost a third of his wages was made up of this bonus pay. On 19 January the shipbuilding employers in Britain told the unions that they proposed to withdraw the war bonus in two stages. After negotiations on the matter broke down, on 26 March most employers posted notices in the yards that ten shillings and six pence would come off on 29 March, with the remaining six shillings being deducted on 26 April. The Dublin Dockyard did not put up their yard notices until April, with the first deduction to take place on 19 April and the second on 17 May. A general strike took place, with all labour being withdrawn. John Smellie wrote that a conference was quickly called at the Ministry of Labour. This meeting resolved that the workers should return to their jobs while the employers would withdraw the notices. Smellie notes that following this, while work was resumed, the dockyard was out of the running to tender for large repair contracts because of the price differential between Dublin and other shipbuilding and repair centres elsewhere in Britain and the north of Ireland.[55]

Another long-term problem was also causing problems for the dockyard's directors. No action had been taken by the Port Board since the November 1920 letter outlining the difficulties of moving ships for repairs and the lack of the promised spur wharf. The company wrote again in May 1922 complaining about the unsatisfactory situation and that work on the wharf had not even commenced. As a result of these representations, the Berthage Committee of the Port & Docks Board passed the following resolutions: 'The Committee unanimously agree that the Harbour Master be instructed to give priority of use of 300 feet of berthage immediately east of the graving dock when required for ship repairs, until such time as the new spur wharf is completed.' Also, the committee recommended 'that the new spur jetty be commenced immediately, as until this jetty be completed, the cause of complaint will not be met. Meantime, Engineer to report fully as to advisability of extending the present fitting-out jetty.' While Smellie acknowledged that the members of the Port Board were alive to the fact that the Dockyard Company was not receiving the fair treatment to which they were entitled, still nothing happened following these resolutions. In June the company again pressed for a reply to their letters, but once more without success.[56]

In July 1922 representations were made to the Minister for Industry & Commerce, Ernest Blythe, by the Joint Shipbuilding Trades Committee and the employers that (a) a commission be set up by the government to enquire into the difficulties confronting the industry and (b) that the government subsidise or assist the industry. On 11 August a conference took place at the Ministry of Labour, at which the government side said (1) they did not see any use appointing a commission of inquiry and (2) they could not entertain the granting of a subsidy, especially in view of the great destruction of property taking place at that time.[57] The Civil War was then raging.

Despite the problems facing the dockyard, the unions said they could not accept any further cuts in view of the prevailing conditions and the fact that wages in other spheres were not being reduced. The employers for their part insisted further work was impossible to obtain because of the wide disparity between the wages paid in the Port of Dublin and the wages paid for the same classes of work in other ports. At this stage the Dublin Dockyard Company was still paying the full war bonus to the workers, so after this meeting the company posted notices on 23 August informing the workers about the details of the reductions as follows:

Shipbuilding and Engineering Trades – Withdrawal of 16s 6d of 26s 6d War Bonus.

As pointed out in detail at the various meetings held at the offices of the Ministry of Labour, between the Dublin Shipbuilding and Repairing Employers and the Dublin Shipbuilding Trades Joint Committee, it is no longer possible to secure work on the present wages scale, and notice is hereby given that it is absolutely necessary that wages be reduced to the same level as obtain in competing ports.

To make the break as easy as possible, the reduction intimated shall take effect as below:

> 5s 6d Reduction per week as from pay commencing Wednesday, 6 September 1922.
>
> 5s 6d Reduction per week as from pay commencing Wednesday 4 October 1922.
>
> 5s 6d Reduction per week as from pay commencing Wednesday 1 November 1922.[58]

The unions had insisted since April that they would not agree to any further reductions of the wages, so three days later, on 26 August, they withdrew all labour and never resumed their positions, forcing the eventual closure of the yard. All of this time the directors of the dockyard were still awaiting a reply from the Port Board regarding the construction of the new spur wharf and they wrote again in September demanding that the Port Board 'should forthwith carry out its obligations under the September 1917 agreement'. This matter was passed to the port's New Works Committee, and on 29 September their finding was sent by the secretary of the Dublin Port & Docks Board to the yard, which was: 'I am directed to state in reply to your letter of the 26th inst. that the board are prepared to reserve temporarily 300 feet of the Alexandra Wharf for ships being repaired, the question of the building of a spur wharf to remain over pending the preparation of a plan drawn up under expert advice for improving the Port of Dublin.'[59]

John Smellie wrote: 'As the result of years of supplication, and of twenty-one years of activity in the service of the Port of Dublin, the only concession as regards increased berthage for vessels under repair which the Port Board was willing to make was this temporary use of 300 feet of the Alexandra Wharf. With regard to obtaining expert advice, it is the writer's opinion that no better advice could possibly be obtained than tendered by the board's own officers, who were more in touch with the Port's detail requirements than any outside person could possibly be.' After two months of deliberation, the Dockyard Company's secretary replied on 8 December as follows:

> Under the agreement dated 19 September 1917, the Port and Docks Board definitely contracted under seal to erect the spur wharf. This contract was entered into only after the most mature and careful consideration by all parties. By the same agreement my company undertook obligations which it has faithfully performed, and it has paid the considerably enhanced rent which it, by that agreement, undertook to pay.
>
> I am therefore directed to state that my board cannot agree to your suggestion, i.e., 'The question of the building of the spur wharf to remain over pending preparation of a plan drawn up under expert advice for improving the Port of Dublin.' It is very difficult to see why such a suggestion should now be made, having regard to the very careful consideration given to the question in 1917, and to the fact that my company on its side has faithfully performed its obligations, and to the further fact that, as appears in the accounts of the Port and Docks Board, rather considerable sums have already been expended by the latter in the preparation of the work.[60]

The yard's letter went on to state that without jeopardising the Dockyard Company's rights in this matter, the board would consider favourably a suggestion from the Port Board 'to defer for a further period of not exceeding one year from this date the construction of the spur wharf' provided that the 300 feet of accommodation for repairs was given. The company were, however, not prepared to waive the 'benefits' of the 1917 agreement. However, nothing further transpired following this correspondence.

The action of the Port & Docks Board in not keeping to the terms of the 1917 lease appears to have been the last straw for the Dockyard Company and John Smellie in particular. He seemed to feel that while it was one thing for the unions to act unreasonably, it was a very different matter for a statutory body comprising 'gentlemen' to repudiate a solemn agreement. Smellie concluded his comments on this long running saga by saying: 'It appears that the Port Board, in breaking the bargain which it made, neither rendered a high service to the Port of Dublin, nor showed an example of good faith-keeping which could be followed by other contracting parties.' It is interesting that John Smellie was so fixated on the spur wharf at a time when the whole future of his yard was in jeopardy.

In the last month of 1922 further attempts were made to address the labour problems in the dockyards and meetings took place at the Ministry of Labour on 5 and 12 December to try to solve the wages question. The unions, according to Smellie, made it clear that their position was that the shipbuilding industry would be better scrapped than allow trade union workers and their standard of living to be degraded. Following the failure of these talks, the Minister for Industry & Commerce invited both sides to meet him at his office on 22 December. At this meeting, the Minister said he did not accept that the cost of living in Dublin was higher than other ports and that wages must come down from war levels. Also in view of the destruction being caused by the Civil War and possible claims by other industries, he could not see his way to recommend that a subsidy be paid. A suggestion made that dole money currently being paid could be dealt with in 'a manner helpful to the industry', was not found practical.[61]

However, before we leave 1922, note should be taken of a headline in *The Irish Times* on Friday 8 September, which read 'New Shipyard For Dublin – Suggested Large Outlay'. This was a report on a meeting of the Dublin Port & Docks Board the previous day, and it recorded that the chairman, David Barry, who presided, had interviewed A.V. Poskitt, who had sent a letter to the board about a proposed shipbuilding, ship repairing and marine engineering works at the North Wall Extension, and had discussed the project with him. Mr Poskitt said that 'he had great concerns behind him', but he had nothing definite to show for the proposal except his word. The chairman told Poskitt that while the board and its members would welcome any project he might bring forward and give every assistance to him, the board should have guarantees of his ability to carry out the scheme laid before them, before they could commit themselves to the huge expenditure of money required. When Poskitt asked about the nature of the guarantee required, the chairman told him that a huge capital sum would be required to reclaim the land needed and moreover, that it would require an act of parliament to gain permission to do this. The minimum security that the board would need was £2,000 per acre reclaimed.

Further discussion on the matter prompted Alderman Alfie Byrne to ask if there was any hope that anything would come of the scheme. Despite the chairman's pessimism, Byrne thought that the board should do everything it could to encourage the shipbuilding and engineering industry in Dublin. If the guarantee of £2,000 per reclaimed acre was going to stop the scheme, he believed they should be able to come to an arrangement with Mr Poskitt. In reply to a question about seeking a government grant for carrying out the work, the chairman concluded the discussion, noting Mr Poskitt had said that 'he would give the Irish people the privilege of subscribing two-thirds of the capital', and adding that the proposer's idea of the cost of building four graving docks was rather hazy.

The following day's *Irish Times* stated that a letter had been received from Mr Poskitt regarding the above news item, in which he took issue with the reported remarks of Mr Barry that the cost of the four docks was rather hazy. Poskitt claimed that 'the matter is receiving the serious attention of one of the oldest and most distinguished firms of shipbuilders in Europe, by whom cheap scepticism on the part of Mr Barry is not likely to be regarded as evidence of the goodwill of the Port & Docks Board. The cost of the proposed graving docks being exclusively the concern of those who are considering installing them, was not a question for discussion between the writer and Mr Barry, who, however, if he is interested may rest assured that the matter is in capable hands.' Poskitt is quoted further: 'He made no objection to the board requiring guarantees, but in view of the vital importance of having additional land available within a reasonable time, that if the proposed enterprise should be decided on, we would much prefer to carry out the reclaiming ourselves. Mr Barry was to find out the longest lease the board would be prepared to grant and the minimum rent to be charged.'

The Dublin correspondent of the *Shipbuilder* mentions the project and the letter in the press in the October 1922 issue. He felt that Poskitt was trying to convey the impression that the Port Board had tried to throw cold water on the plan and agreed that if there was any substance in the move it was unlikely that any obstacles would be placed in the way, because there were so few industries in Dublin Harbour. However, nothing further happened with this project. It is not clear who A.V. Poskitt was and who he represented, but in view of the difficulties being experienced locally in shipbuilding and the excess capacity in Britain, it seems an extraordinary proposal for the time to contemplate the setting up of a new yard and the construction of four dry docks.

THE END

The year 1923 opened with the *Shipbuilder* reporting in February that the shipbuilding and repairing industry in Dublin had fallen on evil days and that the matter was discussed at the January meeting of the Port & Docks Board. A strike had been in progress since September at the Dublin Dockyard, leaving the company unable to compete with the Clyde, as their wages were 55% higher. That month the Port Board intervened without success.[62] By this time the directors of the shipyard had decided that the situation at the dockyard was unsustainable and in February 1923, a letter was sent to the shareholders together with a statutory notice of meeting.

It is worth reproducing this letter, a copy of which resides in the archives of Cambridge University Library:

STRICTLY PRIVATE AND CONFIDENTIAL – Not for Publication.
The Dublin Dockyard Company Limited.
Alexandra Basin,
North Wall,
Dublin,
5 February 1923.

Dear Sir or Madam,

The directors of the Dublin Dockyard Co. Ltd have with great regret come to the conclusion that the interests of the shareholders can best be served by the company no longer continuing in business, but being voluntarily liquidated. The present position of the company is such that it is solvent both as regards its creditors and its original capital, and accordingly if the company is wound up at the present time no loss should be sustained by the shareholders.

On the other hand, the directors realise that should the company endeavour to continue in business on the present scale, a very heavy loss must be anticipated. Unfortunately, owing to the unsettled political condition of the country and owing to the labour position, the company cannot hope to be entrusted with sufficient new construction work to prevent such loss. The directors therefore feel it to be their duty, although with the greatest reluctance, to advise their shareholders the company can continue in business only at heavy loss and that accordingly the only wise course to be adopted is that the company should wind up voluntarily while it is in a solvent position.

The directors have come to this decision with the greatest regret, as they realise that your company represents an essential industry in the development of the Port of Dublin. They hope however, that it may prove possible to form a smaller company which would take over such of the assets of the present company as might be serviceable and necessary and which could continue in business on a smaller scale, until better conditions obtain.

This letter is intended by way of explanation of the enclosed notice, and the matters referred to will be explained more fully by the directors at the meeting to which the notice refers.

By order of the board,
James Carmichael,
Secretary.

That meeting of shareholders and creditors took place on 20 March 1923, when it was agreed to wind up the company and place it in voluntarily liquidation. John Smellie writing about that March creditors' meeting said it was 'with the greatest reluctance and regret' that the directors adopted the only wise course, that of placing the company in voluntary liquidation while it was still solvent.[63] This was done because the yard was deprived of its ability to compete for new and repair work and to execute any work obtained, there was no alternative but to seek new ownership.' The *Shipbuilder* commented in March: 'The [financial] position of the yard is exceptional, but it is impossible to successfully construct ships under the conditions, which obtain in Dublin at present.'

The *Shipbuilder* continued the tale of woe, reporting that the situation had gone from bad to worse and shipbuilding and repair on the Liffey had come to a complete standstill. In fact that statement was only partly correct, as one vessel under construction had just been launched from the Dublin Dockyard in February. This was a small grab dredger for the Sligo Harbour Commissioners, which was being built by dockyard apprentices who were excluded from the withdrawal of labour. The magazine also reported that 'the Dublin Dockyard has dismantled a steamer under construction, with a view to sending the material to [their yard at] Irvine for re-erection'.[64]

The dredger was the *Elsinore* (ON 146031), which had dimensions of 93 feet 6 inches, by 24 feet 6 inches, by 9 feet 6 inches, with a capacity of 200 tons of spoil on a draft of 8 feet 3 inches. It was built to Lloyd's highest class, had additional strengthening on the bottom and the hopper doors were of an improved design. A towing arrangement had been fitted to allow the vessel to act as a tug. Her triple expansion propelling machinery was supplied by Messrs William Beardmore & Co. Ltd of Coatbridge, Lanarkshire, and it was installed by the yard in Dublin. The *Elsinore* had a gross of 156 tons, cost £9,000 to build and could dredge to a depth of 31 feet. She ran sea trials on 4 and 5 April in Dublin Bay over a course of 1.33 miles and a mean speed of 7.3 knots was obtained. It is interesting that this was the first recorded instance of a vessel running trials in Dublin Bay, as previously all locally built ships had gone to the Clyde for this. She appears to have had a working life of about twenty years and was laid up during the 1940s and 1950s. She was sold by the Harbour Commissioners for scrap in 1957 for £2,000 to the Hammond Lane Metal Company Ltd, Dublin, and broken up at Sligo.

There is no clear information as to whether the steamer mentioned by the *Shipbuilder* was dismantled on the stocks and the steel sent to Irvine. Research shows that Messrs Mackie & Thompson, who operated a shipyard at Irvine in 1924, delivered Yard No. 493 to Messrs Michael Murphy Ltd of Dublin.[65] This vessel, named *Grania*, had the same dimensions as the *Finola*, built by the Dublin yard in 1921 and similar propelling machinery was supplied by Ross & Duncan. However, if there was a strike and a picket on the Dublin yard, how was the hull taken down? Perhaps Walter Scott, one of the founding partners who had been managing director of a shipyard in Ayrshire before coming to Dublin in 1901, used the contacts he presumably still had with the industry in that area, even twenty years later.

Although John Smellie records the fact that the Dublin Dockyard was taken over by Messrs Vickers Limited as one of its many subsidiaries, the sale of the yard did not become public knowledge for many months and the shipping press continued to recount the ongoing impasse in Dublin. In May 1923 *Shipbuilder* stated 'business stagnant at Alexandra Basin', while in June it reported 'Industry dead on the Liffey and little prospect for resurrection'. As late as September the *Shipbuilder* was still reporting that the dockyard was for sale, and in its October issue it simply said: 'Dublin dead'.[66] Only in the November 1923 issue did news of the takeover of the shipyard appear, when the purchasers were revealed as Vickers Ltd. This company became better known in later years as Vickers Armstrong Ltd, when Vickers Ltd joined together with W.G. Armstrong Whitworth & Company Ltd, and had yards in Cumbria, on the west coast and on the north-east coast of England, as well as Dublin.

Winding up letter to shareholders of the Dublin Dockyard Company on the decision to close the company down owing to continuing losses in 1923.

So came the end of what must be considered the golden age and the two most productive decades of shipbuilding and repair on the River Liffey, when some sixty vessels, constructed for owners in Britain, France, Norway, Canada and New Zealand were launched, as well as the canal barges and pontoons for the British War Department during 1914–1918. In the end the directors and shareholders of the Dublin Dockyard Company got more than £3 for each share when the company was bought out, five times more than they were asking. The new holding company established to own and operate the Dublin facility was styled Vickers (Ireland) Ltd, and while the news only became public in November, the records in the Companies Office in Dublin reveal that company had in fact been incorporated some five months earlier, on 26 June 1923, with the registration No. 7177.

CHAPTER 3

THE CANADIAN SHIPS

Before we leave the story of the Dublin Dockyard completely, we must recall the vessels built by the yard for Canada. Between 1910 and 1913, the Dublin Dockyard completed four vessels for Canada, which, because of the contribution they made to the maritime history of the Pacific coast of that country, are worthy of particular mention. The first two vessels were passenger ships ordered by the Union Steamship Company of Victoria, British Columbia. Strangely only one of these is given a short description by John Smellie in his book. Perhaps this omission could be accounted for by the fact that they were towed to Belfast to have their engines installed and both were fitted out there because of a lack of carpenters in Dublin to complete the passenger accommodation.

The *Cheslakee* slid down the slipway in May 1910. With a length of 125 feet, a beam of 28 feet and a moulded depth of 17 feet 9 inches, she was built to the highest class of the then existing British Corporation Register of Shipping, a classification society similar to Lloyd's Register of Shipping. However she was launched with only the main deck and crew's quarters completed. The propelling machinery, a triple expansion steam engine built by Messrs MacColl & Company, gave a speed of 11.5 knots, although on trials on 2 June, over six runs on the measured mile, a mean speed of 12.15 knots was obtained. Her nine-hour trials were concluded to the 'complete satisfaction' of Gordon T. Legg, the managing director of the owners.[1]

The *Cheslakee* departed Belfast on 29 June 1910 under the command of Captain J.W. Starkey and arrived in Vancouver eighty-nine days later on the morning of 16 September. The voyage was made via Cape Horn, with stops for coal at St Vincent, Montevideo, Cornel and San Francisco. After her arrival in British Columbia, a contract was placed in October with the Wallace Shipyard of North Vancouver to complete the superstructure and passenger accommodation. Twenty-three cabins with fifty-six berths were fitted and the vessel was given a British Columbia coast licence for 148 passengers and 120 tons of cargo when she entered service in December 1910.

While the new ship had steamed through the Atlantic Ocean, round Cape Horn and up the Pacific Ocean without mishap, the new Canadian-made superstructure affected her stability. On her maiden voyage northwards, she rolled and at one point in her passage through the Surge Narrows, she listed to such an extent that she threatened to capsize. She quickly earned a bad reputation among the loggers and other passengers, and was known as a 'cranky ship'. However, she continued sailing for another month before disaster struck. She departed Vancouver at 8.20 p.m. on 6 January 1911 bound for her first port of call at the settlement of Van Anda, where she arrived at 3.20 a.m. and disembarked seven passengers and freight. At that point there was a moderate sea with a south-easterly wind. Just ten minutes after leaving the jetty a strong gust of wind caught the vessel, causing her to list dangerously. When she failed to come back to an even keel, Captain John Cockle took the advice of the pilot Robert Wilson and turned back to the pier, put a gangplank ashore and commenced disembarking the passengers.

However, the ship started to take on water through an open ash chute on the port side, which was now under water, so the pumps were started. She soon listed further, causing the gangplank to slip and fall into the water, throwing the people on it into the sea. Seven people were drowned including one logger, a child, three women and the ship's cook. While conflicting stories were told of the event, it was clear that some lives were lost because some of the passengers waited to dress before abandoning ship, and were still on board when it sank.

A marine court of inquiry was established on 20 January 1911, and having heard all the evidence from both crew and passengers, it found that the ship was most likely top heavy because of the new superstructure fitted in Vancouver. The sinking of the *Cheslakee* was the only accident involving loss of life in the history of the Union Steamship Company of Victoria aboard all their vessels and in the thousands of voyages they made along the hazardous coasts of British Columbia and Alaska. The *Cheslakee* was raised by the B.C. Salvage Company and towed to Esquimalt, Victoria, where the owner's manager, E.H. Beazley, had the ship cut in two and a new mid section inserted, lengthening the vessel by 20 feet. The ship's name was changed by special sanction from the federal capital Ottawa and she resumed service as the *Cheakmus* in June 1912. Her new dimensions were length 145 feet, beam 28 feet and moulded depth 17 feet 6 inches. For the remaining twenty-nine years of her life with the company she traded successfully up and down the coast of British Columbia, calling at the little piers that served isolated settlements and logging camps.

In 1937 the *Cheakmus* underwent a major and extensive refit when the passenger accommodation was modernised. Two years after the outbreak of war in 1941, she was cut down and converted into a tugboat and sold to the United States' government for $70,000. She retained her name and was used by the US Army Transport Service for towage and carrying cargo on the Pacific coast. At the end of the conflict she was bought by a private company named Foss, who kept her for a short time, after which, in spite of efforts to preserve the vessel, she was sold and broken up.

The next ship built for Canada and the Union Steamship Company by the Dublin yard was the *Cheloshin* (ON 130805), which was ordered at the not inconsiderable cost for those days of $140,550 by Gordon Legg at the end of 1910. She was a much larger ship than the *Cheslakee*, with a length of 175 feet 5 inches, a beam of 35 feet, a moulded depth of 14 feet and a gross tonnage of 1,134 tons. She had a passenger certificate for 191 persons, 66 in cabin berths and 95 others on deck settees, and a cargo capacity of 150 tons. After launching, she was towed to Belfast to have her two triple expansion engines, developing 1,420 IHP (indicated horsepower), installed by Messrs MacColl & Company.

During her trials on 25 September 1911, she achieved a speed of 14 knots on the measured mile. Three weeks later she sailed from the Lagan again with Captain Starkey as master and after a passage of seventy-two days arrived in British Columbia on 28 December 1911. She made her maiden voyage from Vancouver to Skenna River, Prince Rupert and Port Simpson on 24 February 1912. Contemporary newspapers described her as one of the smartest vessels on Canada's west coast, with her staterooms finished in oak with sliding windows and some cabins even having hot and cold running water. Only six months later she underwent repairs at the Wallace yard costing $30,000, during which time she was converted to burn oil fuel. After twenty-five years of uneventful service, the *Cheloshin* had a major refit in 1937 lasting three months, again at the Wallace yard at a cost of $81,000, when all the cabins were modernised with hot and cold taps. The lounge, smoking and dinning-rooms were rebuilt, and the sliding windows were replaced with portholes. During the war she continued to maintain sailings, but by 1945 the company was in difficulty and had only three ships.

On 12 November 1947, at 6.45 a.m., the *Cheloshin* ran aground in the dangerous Chatham Channel on the approaches to Vancouver. Captain Harry Roach ordered the pumps to be started, which controlled the flooding, and the vessel managed to steam ten miles to Mistal Island, where all forty passengers and cargo were safely discharged. The damage was not as serious as first thought and only one boiler was out of commission, so her crew of thirty-five were able to remain aboard. She was repaired and returned to service. Just two years later, on 6 November 1949, the *Cheloshin* went ashore for the last time in thick fog while inward bound to Vancouver. She grounded at Stanley Park near the local Siwash Rock and her twenty passengers were landed by lifeboat and continued their journey into the city by bus. When the fog lifted thousands of onlookers thronged the shore to the see the stranded vessel and hundreds of pleasure craft circled watching the efforts to refloat the vessel. All attempts to salvage the ship failed and the Union Steamship Company abandoned her; she was put up for sale 'as is' on 18 November 1947. Six days later she was bought for $1,600 by a Victor David, an amateur salvage man. In spite of predictions that he could not salvage the ship, he proved everyone wrong and the *Cheloshin* was patched up and pulled off by two tugs in January 1950 and taken to North Vancouver. It was the intention of Mr David to convert the vessel into a floating fish processing plant, but his plans were dashed by government regulations prohibiting this. After fifteen months she was sold to a San Francisco scrap company and in May 1951 she was towed, together with another former Union Steamship vessel called the *Cassiar*, to California and broken up.

The exact circumstances of the vessel's grounding are not clear, but one former ship's officer alleged that the company was at fault for not having the vessel's radar set, which had broken down, repaired at Powell River before she resumed her voyage to Vancouver. The lack of this radar was thought to be a contributory factor to her loss.

THE FISHERY CRUISERS

Five years after the completion of the Irish fishery cruiser *Helga*, the first of two similar vessels for the Canadian government was launched. She was the *Malaspina* (ON 136044), which took to the water on 5 July 1913. The second vessel, the *Galiano* (ON 136047), was launched on 14 October the same year.

The two vessels were described by John Smellie as: '[fishery] patrol vessels … the orders [for these] were doubtless placed as the result of the excellent reputation that the *Helga* had made for herself'. Their dimensions were somewhat greater than the Irish vessel, with a length of 162 feet, a beam of 27 feet, and a depth of 14 feet, and they were constructed to Lloyd's 100 A1 Class, the highest rating from Lloyd's. '[With] very full specifications, they were … well suited for patrol and surveying work and for the training of cadets. The accommodation was tasteful and somewhat extensive with refrigeration and other provision for long voyage service,' claimed Smellie.[2] The *Malaspina* was named for an area on Vancouver Island and during trials on 28 and 29 August 1913, including a six-hour continuous steaming test, reached a speed of 14.8 knots under mild forced draught conditions. The ships' propelling machinery consisted of two sets of triple expansion engines developing 161 HP, which were supplied by Messrs David Rowan & Company of Glasgow.

Both ships were registered in Ottawa, the Canadian capital, and for 1914 are recorded as owned by the Dublin Dockyard Company – it can be assumed that the contract called for both ships to be delivered by the builders to the west coast of Canada. The following year the Minister for the Naval Service of Canada is given as their owner. Although the ships were intended for operation by the Department of Marine & Fisheries for fishery duties, they also acted as tenders carrying supplies and staff to the many isolated lighthouses along the north-west Pacific coast.

Following Britain's declaration of war on 4 August 1914, the ships were assigned to patrol off Cape Flattery at the entrance to the channel leading to Vancouver and the *Malaspina* was armed with a 6-pounder Hotchkiss gun. The two vessels were taken over by the Royal Canadian Navy and commissioned in 1917, retaining their original names. HMCS *Malaspina* hoisted the White ensign (i.e. became a British warship) on 1 December, under the command of Lieut H. Newcombs, RCNVR, and HMCS *Galiano* followed suit on 15 December with Lieut Robert Pope, RCNVR, a former merchant officer, as her first and only commander. She was the only Royal Canadian Navy ship lost during that war. On 29 October 1918, the *Galiano* was at anchor off Triangle Island, a tiny treeless rock in Queen Charlotte Sound, landing supplies for the lighthouse. Later that day when Lieut Pope sailed for Ikea Island further north during a gale warning, he had aboard a lady passenger named Brunton, the wife of the lighthouse keeper, who was taking passage to a dentist ashore. At 3.30 a.m. the following morning, the radio operator at Triangle Island, Jack Neary, picked up an SOS from the ship saying 'Holds full of water … sinking …' That was the last ever heard from HMCS *Galiano*. Tragically the SOS was transmitted by Michael Neary, Jack's brother. There were no survivors and only the engine room skylight and three bodies were recovered. Among the twenty-seven lost were two seamen aged only fifteen and sixteen.[3]

The other vessel, HMCS *Malaspina*, was engaged in contraband control in the Strait of Juan de Fuca, until she was decommissioned on 31 March 1920 and handed over to the Department of Transport to resume peacetime duties. In 1923 the fishery cruiser was at the centre of an international incident when she encountered a fishing vessel poaching in Barkley Sound. The American fishing vessel *Siloman* refused to stop when ordered and attempted to escape. The *Malaspina* opened fire with her 12-pounder gun and one shell hit the fishing craft, causing the death of a fisherman. Again in 1929 the ship came to prominence, when she arrested five American fishing boats and took them into Prince Rupert, where the skippers were charged with violating Canadian fishery regulations. During the prohibition period, the *Malaspina* had many engagements with rum-runners attempting to illegally import alcohol into the United States. She was retired about 1938, but following the outbreak of the Second World War, she was recommissioned into the navy on 6 September 1939, again as HMCS *Malaspina*, under the command of Lieut Comdr W. Redford, RCNR, for patrol and examination duties. In 1943 she became part of HMCS Royal Roads, a shore training establishment.

At the end of the war she was decommissioned and in December 1946, she was sold by the Canadian War Assets Commission to Capital Metals Ltd of Victoria for scrapping. However, this did not happen as she was gutted and the hull was sold to the Powell River Company, a lumber firm further up the British Columbian coast, where she was scuttled to form part of an artificial breakwater to protect their log-holding pond. Perhaps something still remains to this day of the *Malaspina* among this scuttled fleet, which includes a number of US Maritime Commission Ferro-concrete ships built during 1944, which were also sold to Capital Metals at the end of the war.

CHAPTER 4

THE RINGSEND DOCKYARD & DUBLIN SHIPBUILDERS LTD

Mention was made earlier of the comment by John Smellie about other yards not being targeted by the ITGWU in 1922 and his comment could only refer to Dublin Shipbuilders Ltd. It is now time to tell the story of that company, which lasted only five years. This yard is forgotten and unknown to most people outside Ringsend and the East Wall Road areas of the port. The story starts back in 1776, when the Grand Canal Basin at the entrance of the River Dodder was excavated and opened. As part of this development, three small graving docks were built just inside the entrance lock gates, which were unique, as they did not need a pumping system to be either filled or emptied. When a ship required repairs, the sluices in the dock gates were opened, which allowed water from the basin to flow in and when the levels outside and inside were equal, the gates were opened and the vessel entered. To dry out the graving dock, sluices at the other end were opened and the water drained into the River Dodder at a lower level and when repairs were completed, the cycle was repeated allowing the craft to leave.

By about 1840 some 100 boats a year were being dry docked, but the operations were not particularly profitable for the Grand Canal Company. In 1851 the company received an offer 'from parties of unquestionable respectability connected with the shipping interests of the port of Dublin', to take over the lease of the Ringsend Basin including the dry docks.[1] The Canal Company directors decided to lease both of these for the sum of £300 a year. A thirty-year agreement was entered into with the group headed by Messrs Wright, Pike and Barrington. Frederick Barrington also took over the operation of the Camden and Buckingham locks, giving access to the Liffey from the Grand Canal. Barrington developed the dry dock business and built his first iron craft for the Canal Company almost straightaway, as has been noted in an earlier chapter. However, his dockyard company does not seem to have been a success, as by 1870 the group were attempting to get out of their lease, but without success. In 1881 when the Canal Company regained possession, they hired out the dry docks to boat owners, who then made their own repair arrangements. This continued for the remainder of the century, although by the first decade of the 1900s, the dry docks and the Canal Company yard seem to have been under-utilised.

We do not know if the Grand Canal Company actively sought outside operators, or if they were once again approached from outside. However, on 28 February 1913, an agreement was entered into between William McMullan of 11 Leahy's Cottages, Sandymount, and the Canal Company to lease the three docks with an adjoining cottage on the quayside. Contemporary books and newspapers refer to the Ringsend Dockyard Company, the name under which McMullan carried out his business. Although Ruth Delaney describes the chief draughtsman William Alexander as being involved in the establishment of the firm, the only person legally mentioned is McMullan. Incidentally Mr Alexander had resigned from the Dublin Dockyard Company to join this new firm.

The new enterprise engaged in general ship repairs and dry docked small vessels up to 140 feet, which were able to enter the canal basin. They also carried out repairs to larger ships afloat at the quays. In October 1916, the new firm built their first vessel, a sub-contract from Messrs McKie & Blair of Glasgow. This was a small tug, the *Zoe*, ordered by the British India Steam Navigation Company of London for service in the East African port of Mombasa. According to the November issue of the *Shipbuilder*: 'She had five water-tight compartments, with a length of 62 feet and was in every way up to date.'[2] By 1917 the company was also constructing barges for the British War Office.

The December 1917 issue of the *Shipbuilder* reported that 'Messrs Bailey and Gibson have applied to the Dublin Port & Docks Board for a site for shipbuilding and repair work. They waited on the Board on 23 November 1917, who resolved to give them details of the terms offered to Messrs Workman Clark of Belfast. The board could not recommend any expenditure of capital at the moment.' The next issue of the *Shipbuilder* reported that 'the Dublin Port & Docks Board in December 1917 considered the application from Messrs Bailey and Gibson could be carried out for £20,000. Agreed by a majority that £20,000 be deposited and the board would carry out the work. A 25% refund to be made when the yard was established, and the offer would remain open until early January 1918'.[3] The amount of this refund was later increased to one third. The work to be carried out by the board was the preparation of the site so that the shipbuilders could lay out their yard. When Dublin Shipbuilders was formed in 1918, the Ringsend dockyard became part of the company.

In May 1918 it was reported that: 'The proposed yard for Bailey and Gibson will have a capital of £150,000, £50,000 of this to be called up immediately, however matters are not definitely arranged with the board'.[4] On 30 May a deed of agreement was drawn up with the Dublin Port & Docks Board for the designated site. In June a start was made to lay out the new shipyard at the east end of Alexandra Quay west (just where present-day Ocean Pier begins). A new company styled Dublin Shipbuilders Ltd was incorporated on 8 July 1918 with the registered number 4586. The first directors were given as William George Bailey, Adam Henry Gibson, Edwin W. Booth and William McMullan. The new company's letterhead had in brackets under its title: 'With which is incorporated The Ringsend Dockyard Co.' and the address is given as Grand Canal and Alexandra Basins. William McMullan is described as the managing director and the registered office was given as 39 Nassau Street.

Looking back ninety years, it must be said that the yard was established at a very uncertain time. The Great War was ending and the directors could not have been certain that there would be a demand for new ships in the future. Furthermore the new yard did not commence any construction until two years later – although the keels of two ships had been laid, any further progress was delayed until 1920 owing to the shortage of steel. In January 1921 *Shipbuilder* reported that the company hoped to launch the first of four coasters in mid-April of that year. However, even before the first launch took place, one ship, an 850 tons deadweight coaster for the Abram Steamship Company of Glasgow, was offered for sale on the stocks.[5] Their first hull only took to the water on 12 May 1921, she was Yard No. 14, the *Craigavon* (ON 145421) ordered by Messrs Hugh Craig & Co., coal importers of Royal Avenue, Belfast. The new vessel, a raised quarterdeck coaster, had a gross of 682 tons and dimensions of 186 feet by 28 feet 9 inches by 13 feet 3 inches with an 850 tons deadweight. Her triple expansion machinery was supplied by Messrs Ross & Duncan of Glasgow.

The *Shipbuilder* described the launching in its June issue as 'being carried out by Miss Phyllis Maxton, daughter of the owners' consulting engineer and that the owner's representative present was James Maxton, Naval Architect Belfast.' The report continued: 'The Alexandra Road yard is now fitted with the most modern appliances for speedy and economic construction of sea-going vessels. After the ceremony guests were entertained in the canteen.

Three hundred men are employed there. Shortly after the launch the ship was towed to the Clyde to have her propelling machinery installed by Messrs Ross & Duncan of Govan.'[6] The new vessel ran trials on the Skelmorlie measured mile in the Clyde on 2 September 1921. However, she had only a very short trading career of six years, as she was posted as missing on 23 November 1927, while on a voyage from Glasgow to Britton Ferry in the Bristol Channel with a cargo of coal. The last sighting of the Belfast ship was on 28 October by the coaster *Stanwell* off Milford Haven. It should be remembered that at that time small vessels did not carry radio equipment and the only practical way of sending a distress signal was by rockets, which had to be seen by a passing vessel or from the shore for a rescue bid to be launched.

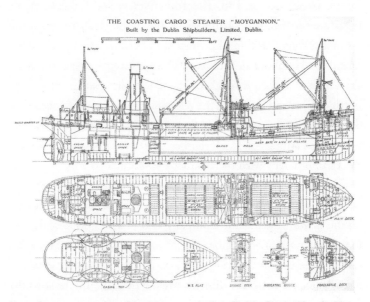

General arrangement plan of the *Moygannon*, built in Dublin Shipbuilders for Newry owners in 1921.

The second vessel built was Yard No. 16, the *Moygannon* (ON 127478), with a gross of 681 tons, for the Newry & Provincial Coal

Company Ltd. She was launched on 26 July and was 171 feet by 25 feet 6 inches by 12 feet, with a deadweight of 545 tons. A very detailed report appeared in the December 1921 *Shipbuilder*, where the ship was described as being 'of the usual coasting type, with machinery aft and a long raised quarterdeck extending well forward of mid-ships. The captain and mate's cabins are arranged in the lower bridge house at the break of the front end of the quarterdeck with their saloon. The rooms for two engineers and a steward were arranged in a deckhouse abaft the engine casing. The engineers' mess room and galley are placed between the engine and boiler casings. The crews quarters for four sailors and two firemen are in the forecastle, with their galley on the starboard side.'[7] The County Down owner went bankrupt in 1924 and the ship was bought by Joseph Fisher & Co. Ltd, also from Newry, for £10,000. Apart from use on the cross-channel coal trade, she was also employed on long voyages carrying herrings from Lerwick in the Shetland Islands to Hamburg in Germany. On her return voyage in ballast, she called at Runcorn in Cheshire, where she loaded salt for the north of Scotland. In 1938, the *Moygannon* was renamed the *Agba*, conforming to the nomenclature of vessels in the Fisher fleet, which were called after trees. In December 1940 she sank in a collision in the Firth of Clyde with the steamer *Mano*.

The third ship from the new yard was the *Kylebeg* (ON 146275), which was launched on 23 September 1921. She had been ordered by the Abram Steamship Company Ltd of Glasgow, exactly two years earlier on 24 September 1919, at a cost of £40,000, and was a sister of the *Craigavon*, with a gross of 681 tons and a deadweight of 870 tons on the same dimensions. By the time she took to the water, the vessel was at the centre of litigation. She had been sold on the stocks in February of the previous year by the Abram Company to The Westville Shipping Co. Ltd, Cardiff, for £58,700, on the understanding that the keel had been laid, the tank tops were being put in and the frames bent and that erection had commenced. She was then resold by Westville the following month, for £65,000 to the British Hispano Line Ltd, making the former a profit of £6,300. However, these owners were much more diligent in their purchase, with the result that, following a survey in June 1920, they found only the keel had been laid owing to the shortage of steel. The Hispano Company repudiated the contract, perhaps with some relief, as freight rates by that time had fallen through the floor.

The dispute over this contract went to law and was appealed through the courts system right up to the House of Lords, where the Abram Company lost the case. After launching, the *Kylebeg* was towed to Glasgow to have her propelling machinery installed by William Beardmore & Co. of Coatbridge, and there she was offered for sale. By 7 December 1921, the vessel had been inspected and bought by a Captain Sydney Holm from New Zealand on behalf of the Dunedin Whangarei Shipping Co. Ltd, Murray Place, Dunedin. Captain Holm had come to Britain looking for a vessel for this newly established company. After her arrival in New Zealand, the ship was renamed *Holmdale*, and re-registered in Dunedin as No. 3 of 1922. For the next sixteen years she sailed between the mainland of South Island and the Chatham Islands. In 1937 she was re-engined as a motor ship with a 725 BHP (brake horsepower) Polar Atlas diesel. She remained with these owners for another nineteen years until 1956 when she was sold to Victor International of New York, who registered her in either Liberia or Panama. As the *Pacific Pearl*, she sailed for Japan with a cargo of scrap, but was seized in Yokohama as a result of a writ for money owed of over two million Yen. She was abandoned by her American owners and put up for auction. Bought by the Kinbara Kisen KK at the end of 1957, she was placed in the Japanese coastal trade, and re-named *Pacific Maru*, registered in Tokyo. She was lost after running aground off the Japanese coast on 12 December 1965 while carrying a cargo of coal.

The last ship launched by Dublin Shipbuilders as Yard No.

19, was the *Lady Anstruther* (ON 146285), ordered by Noble Explosives Ltd of London, which took to the water on 31 December 1921. She had a gross of 498 tons, with a deadweight of 650 tons and dimensions of 173 feet by 26 feet 6 inches by 12 feet 9 inches and was to be used for the transport of explosives from the company's factory at Irvine, Ayrshire, Scotland, to ports round the UK and Ireland. Her triple expansion engine was supplied by William Beardmore & Co. of Coatbridge, and the ship ran trials on the Clyde on 18 February 1922. At same time the *Shipbuilder* for March 1922 reported the yard's output for 1921 as four ships, totalling 2,371 tons gross, with two further ships on the stocks, one plated and one with keel laid. It noted, however, that the prospects of the yard were not bright.[8]

Despite what Smellie had claimed, the labour situation in this new yard was similar to that at Dublin Dockyard and a complete withdrawal of the workers took place from September 1922. By July 1923 the yard was for sale.[9] Finally, almost three years later, on 28 June 1926, the directors agreed to the voluntary winding up of the company and a liquidator was appointed. The two ships mentioned as incomplete on the ways were never finished or launched by Dublin Shipbuilders, although the more advanced of the two did eventually sail. She was a raised long quarterdeck steamer.

The other ship, *No. 16*, appears to have been ordered from Belfast, as the November 1922 issue of the *Shipbuilder* reported: 'Dublin Shipbuilders are engaged in litigation with Messrs Cullen, Allen & Co. Ltd of Belfast, over a contract to build a steamer entered into with John Kelly Ltd, of Belfast.' It is not clear what the outcome of this litigation was or if the case ever went to court.

The framed vessel, Yard No. 15, remained abandoned on the stocks for a number of years until she was eventually purchased by Henry Robb Ltd, shipbuilders on the Firth of Forth, and was dismantled and brought to Scotland, where the new owners had an established yard at Leith, the port for Edinburgh. The

Scottish company commenced the reconstruction of the vessel as a speculation as their Yard No. 113 and at first thought was given to increasing her length. This was to be done by cutting the ship in two by hatch No. 2 on the quarterdeck, but it was decided instead to install a diesel motor and not a steam engine. This was a Fairbanks Morse 560 BHP engine, chosen because it took up much less space and thus allowed the cargo hold to be lengthened by 16 feet. The space saved in the hold was used for two mates' cabins and a wheelhouse was fitted in place of the original open bridge design. The ship was launched unnamed in November 1929, with a gross tonnage of 678 and 368 net, and offered for sale.

Once again another New Zealander came to the UK looking for a ship for the Antipodes. Lieutenant-Commander Alexander Frederick Watchlin of Auckland had seen service in the British navy as an RN salvage officer at Scapa Flow during the First World War, for which he was decorated with the Order of the British Empire. During the 1920s he owned and operated vessels in the timber trade in New Zealand and purchased the new Robb-built ship. He named her the *Port Waikato* (ON 160675) and sailed her to Auckland. In 1941 the *Port Waikato* was chartered to Holm & Company to replace a ship sunk by the German armed merchant cruiser *Komet*, the only raider to enter the Pacific via the Barents Sea. The Dublin-built ship spent the remainder of her life running alongside her sister ship the *Holmdale*, formerly the *Kylebeg*. In 1947 Watchlin & Company was taken over by the famous Union Steamship Company. In 1959 she was sold to the Lanena Shipping Company of Hong Kong and was scrapped in 1961.

While Dublin Shipbuilders Ltd was placed in liquidation in 1926, the company only ceased to exist on 16 March 1929. The delay in winding up the firm appears to have been due to the desire to establish a new company to take over certain assets of Dublin Shipbuilders. A new company, the Ringsend Dockyard

Company (Dublin) Ltd, was incorporated on 24 November 1928, with the objectives, as laid down in the articles of association, to take over from the liquidator of Dublin Shipbuilders Ltd the lease of the three dry docks in the Ringsend Basin granted to William McMullan in 1913, along with the buildings on the quayside. In addition, they would take on all the debts of that company, together with certain plant, machinery, tools and stock in trade owned by Mr McMullan in premises at Hanover Quay. This was on the far side of the basin where ships under repair were berthed. The creditors of the company were listed in great detail down to the sum of two shillings and sixpence due from W.A. Savage & Co., the Liverpool shipowners.

The only director listed from this new shipbuilding company was William McMullan, who was appointed managing director for five years at a salary of £500 per annum. The other shareholders were a cross-section of the Dublin business scene: Gabriel Brock, Dame Street, chartered accountant; William Weir, silversmith of Grafton Street; George Jacob, merchant; Hugh Kennedy of Parnell Street, from the well-known bakery family which owned the Ringsend Bakery. There were also two non-Irish residents, Henry Robb of Edinburgh, the shipbuilder who purchased and dismantled the incomplete hull, and John Mackie, chartered accountant, Victoria Street, London. The total paid-up share capital was £2,050. While the new company only came into existence in 1928, Mr McMullan had commenced building canal barges three or four years previously by himself.

There is some confusion as to the new company's first craft. One account records a ship called the *Enterprise* constructed by the Ringsend Dockyard Company Ltd (which was not a formal company at this point, but a trading name) in 1924 for the Grand Canal Company, which was transferred to Mrs C. Farrell in May 1930 and was operated as a 'hack boat', or traders vessel until January 1954 when she was sold to Coras Iompair Éireann, who had taken over the canal system at that time. She was then used as a traffic vessel until 1959, when she became an engineers' boat and renumbered *96E*. Eventually sold in 1993 to Messrs Conal Kerney and Derek Waters, she is still sailing as a floating theatre with the same name. The next was *No. 31M*, constructed at a cost of £1,100. In 1927, he had completed four vessels, *Nos 33M, 34M, 36M* and *39M*. *No. 36M* had a shallower draft for use on the Barrow navigation section of the waterway. All of these had the same dimensions of 60 feet in length with a 13 feet beam and are still afloat at the time of writing and being used for pleasure. These vessels were fitted with Bollinder hot bulb diesel engines – the make had been adopted in 1911 by the Canal Company to power their fleet.

In 1928 three Canal Company vessels were completed: *Nos 35M, 37M* and *38M*. *No. 35M* is still afloat. The following year the new Dockyard Company built their first vessels for the Canal Company: *Nos 58M* and *No. 61M*. The latter was a larger vessel than the other craft, designed to carry extra firkins of Guinness. It is now named the *Murrough* and is still afloat. In 1930 the yard delivered one vessel, *No. 65M*, the last constructed for seven years. During this time the Dockyard Company also carried out ship repairs for The Alliance & Dublin Consumers Gas Company Ltd, overhauls of lightships for the Commissioners of Irish Lights and of Arklow schooners, all of which could enter the Ringsend basin. Larger ships would have been attended to afloat at their berths in the port.

In 1937 two barges were built for the Canal Company, *Nos 76M* and *77M*. The first of these is still afloat. A third craft floated out on 27 September cost £1,175. She was *No. 113B*, a 'bye boat', the designation given to craft operated by private owners on the waterway. On 4 April 1938, four days after the close-down of the Vickers Dublin yard, the *Irish Press* newspaper carried a story under the headline 'Busy Dockyard' which stated: 'The Ringsend Dockyard has been busily employed during the last six months. Among the vessels overhauled by the Ringsend Dockyard (Dublin) in the Alexandra graving dock during the period have been the Port & Docks dredger *Sandpiper*, SS *Shamrock* belonging to Dublin Corporation and government fishery cruiser *Muirchu*. In all 22 ships have been slipped, while 29 vessels including tankers, coasting vessels and steamers of Irish Lights have been repaired afloat. Close on £5,000 was paid in wages between October and March, as much as £370 odd being paid in one week divided among 130 employees.'

At the end of 1938 the yard launched their largest vessel for the Canal Company, as the *Irish Press* reported on 9 December 1938: 'New Vessel for Service on Shannon'. She was the *St. James* (ON 159825), 73 feet long, with a 14.8 feet beam and a draft of 4 feet 8 inches. She had a Bolinder B type two cylinder motor, developing 80 HP, which gave a speed of 7 knots with 70 tons of cargo and she was also capable of towing one or more barges. There was space forward for a crew of three. Because she was too long to fit in the lock basins, she was not able to navigate the canal, and sailed to Limerick round the coast.

On 12 January 1939, the *Irish Press* carried the news that William McMullan, the founder and managing director of the company had died and that William Alexander, the technical manager, had been appointed managing director. McMullan's shareholding was transferred to his widow Jeannie Campbell McMullan. That year the company built their last two barges for the Canal Company, *Nos 78M* and *79M*. These had slightly different dimensions from the previous craft and were 61 feet 9 inches in length and had a 13 feet 3 inches beam. Also on 29 November 1939, *No. 118B*, the last steel barge built by the company, made her first trip. She was delivered to Messrs W.P. & R. Odlum, the flour and grain merchants. Her Bollinder engine was loaned from Grand Canal Company stock, as no new engines were available owing to the outbreak of the Second World War.

At the start of the Second World War, or the 'Emergency' as those years of conflict were officially described by the Irish government, the Ringsend firm was the only steel shipyard operating in the state. The first 'Emergency' work that the firm received, in late 1939, was the conversion of the Fishery Protection cruisers, the *Fort Rannock* and *Muirchu*, which had been taken over by the Department of Defence for use as patrol vessels for the newly formed Coast & Marine Watching Service. The *Muirchu* was undergoing her second conversion for war, while the *Fort Rannock* was a new vessel completed by the John Lewis yard in Aberdeen, Scotland, in 1937 and chartered to the Department of Agriculture for fishery protection. The work on the vessels included strengthening decks for a single 12-pounder gun, fitting machine-gun mountings on the bridge wings of the former trawler and providing extra accommodation for their larger crews.

The government also realised the need to transport turf supplies to the capital from the Midlands and through the Department of Industry & Commerce commissioned a series of non-propelled wooden barges for this task. The orders for the twenty vessels were allocated to different builders. Six came to Ringsend, six went to Thomas Thompson & Company of Carlow, three to the Liffey Dockyard, and five to the James Tyrrell yard in Arklow, famous for their construction of fishing boats and yachts. All these barges were 61 feet long, with a 12-foot 6-inch beam and a depth of 5 feet. They had a deadweight tonnage of 50 tons on a 3-foot 9-inch draft. It is thought that James Tyrrell at Arklow failed to build all five commissioned from him, as he felt it was more profitable to build fishing vessels for the north of Ireland than barges for the government at a set price of £1,000 each. Also for every three northern vessels completed a new engine would be released to Éire.

In 1944 William Alexander and his wife Edith became shareholders in the new Ringsend yard, as did Arthur Andrews a bank official. For the war years, the firm carried out repairs to wooden schooners from Arklow. At the end of hostilities normal business resumed, but times were changing and the larger modern ships were not able to enter the basin, which led to a severe decrease in work for the Ringsend Dockyard. On 20 August 1963, an Emergency General Meeting of the company took place in the offices of Craig Gardiner at 39–41 Dame Street, Dublin, at which it was resolved that the Ringsend Dockyard (Dublin) Ltd be voluntarily wound up under the Company Acts 1908/1959 and that Gerard O'Brien, Chartered Accountant of 39–41 Dame Street, would be appointed liquidator for the purpose of winding up the firm. By 5 January 1965, the process was complete.

CHAPTER 5

VICKERS RUN THE DUBLIN DOCKYARD

As we have seen, the shareholders of the Dublin Dockyard agreed to liquidate the company at their meeting on 20 March 1923 and John Smellie makes reference to the purchase of the yard by Vickers Ltd. However, the sale of the Dublin yard only seems to have come to public notice eight months later, when the *Shipbuilder* reported in November 1923: 'One of the most interesting announcements of the month is that Messrs Vickers Limited have embarked on an Irish venture, having purchased the shipbuilding yard of the Dublin Dockyard Co. Ltd in liquidation. Intimation to this effect was conveyed to the Port & Docks Board by the solicitor for the liquidator, who wrote that the premises, plant, machinery, fixtures, stock in trade, etc., of the Dockyard Company had been conditionally sold as a going concern to Messrs Vickers (Ireland) Ltd. Messrs Vickers would continue the shipbuilding and ship-repair business carried on by the Dublin Dockyard Co. Ltd, together with the various auxiliary businesses. The various leases under which the premises are held by the Dockyard Company from the board contained clauses restricting their assignment without the consent of the board, and application was made to the board for their consent to the assignment to the purchasers. The Port & Docks Board referred the matter to the Finance Committee, whose approval was a matter of form.'[1]

The report continued: 'Four of the directors of Vickers (Ireland)

Ltd, are on the board of Vickers Limited, viz., Mr Douglas Vickers, Sir Arthur Trevor Dawson, Bt, Sir Vincent H.P. Caillard and Mr J. Barr. Mr George Ridgeway (an official of Vickers Limited) will be managing director of the new company, with Mr D. Vickers as chairman and Mr Barr as vice-chairman. The Irish directors are Sir Henry Ford, a director of R. & H. Hall Ltd, grain merchants of Belfast, Dublin, Waterford and Liverpool, Senator Moran, an ex-chairman of the Port & Docks Board and Mr J. MacVeagh, an ex-MP and director of various Dublin companies. The company will not begin work till strikes in the port are over and of that there is no sign, although negotiations are proceeding with the Free State government and the trade unions on the subject. The Dublin Dockyard Co. Ltd, who had to go out of business as a result of prolonged labour troubles, built in all about 120 vessels, mostly coasters. They had five building berths, with a private jetty for fitting out. The dry docks and patent slips of the Port & Docks Board adjoin.'

The following paragraph in the same issue carried news from Cork: 'Haulbowline Island was visited on October 16 by representatives of the government, accompanied by the representatives of a very big concern who are said to be contemplating the purchase of the island and equipment. The company concerned is Sir W.G. Armstrong Whitworth.' While not of direct connection to Dublin at the time, Whitworth's was famous for shipbuilding and naval armaments on the east coast of England. Later in the decade the company got into financial difficulties and was bailed out by the Bank of England, following which it merged with Vickers Ltd, in 1927, to form Vickers Armstrong Ltd. It then became directly involved in Dublin.

The intriguing question of this takeover is why did Vickers Limited, a major British industrial group, come to Ireland? It must be recalled that in 1923 the Irish Free State was only two years in existence and the very bitter Civil War had just ended. Businesses had not regained pre-war production levels and the infant state was trying to cope with the damage caused to the railway system, communications and the destruction of buildings throughout the whole country. All economic indicators of the time were against any investment and while there could have been various reasons, which ranged from the Barrow yard slipways being occupied by ships or not wishing to build small ships on big berths, it still did not make any shipbuilding sense to come to Ireland, particularly since the collapse of the British shipping industry had left so many yards closed. Surely there must have been more than one small derelict shipyard in England or Scotland that would have met their requirements?

In the Vickers Ltd Archives, the first mention of the Dublin yard only appears in minutes of a London board meeting on 23 September 1923.[2] This records the decision to purchase the Dublin Dockyard Company being approved. However, the name of Vickers (Ireland) Ltd had appeared in the board's minutes three months earlier, at the meeting of 29 June 1923. These stated that 'a new company had been formed under the title Vickers (Ireland) Limited, with registered offices in Dublin to trade in the Irish Free State to act as agents for Vickers Limited. The capital is £50,000 in 50,000 ordinary shares of £1. These would be taken up by the company, except for 100 by each Director.' The company's office files in Dublin confirm the minutes, as the company was incorporated as No. 7171 on 23 July 1923. The difference between these two dates is important – while Vickers (Ireland) Limited was the vehicle which took over the shipyard, it was clearly not established for that purpose.

The story of just how the Dublin yard came to be acquired is found in these Vickers papers, where it has been possible to obtain an overview of the activities and scope of the group. While the minutes of board meetings between 1923 and 1938, when the yard closed, record matters discussed and decisions taken, one has to look beyond these for the background to events in 1923. First we must go to the 'official' starting point and the minutes for meeting of the main Vickers Limited board held on 23 September 1923: 'Sir Vincent Caillard reported on behalf of the Finance Committee, that Mr J.F. Barr, vice-chairman of Vickers Ireland Ltd had obtained an option on a dockyard in Dublin, the purchase price of which would be £63,000. Mr Ford, Deputy Shipyard Manager at Barrow, had visited the dockyard and made a complete detailed report and estimated the scrap value of the yard at £63,000, which does not include a 4,000-ton ship in an advanced stage of construction, which is included in the purchase price of the yard. Mr J.F. Barr is very sanguine. Hopeful that there will be plenty of good work, shipbuilding and repairs available for the dockyard. In view of the low price of the dockyard, Sir Vincent Caillard and Sir Trevor Dawson – in the absence of the chairman and General Lawrence – in view of the urgency to secure the option, decided that a deposit of £15,750 be paid forthwith, and a cheque had accordingly been forwarded to Vickers Ireland Ltd. The dock will be exploited by Vickers Ireland Limited and the above payment and any future payments will be regarded as a loan to them on the security of the Dock, marked APPROVED.'[3]

The following month's board meeting held on 29 October records: 'Dublin Dockyard. Sir V. Caillard reported on behalf of the Finance Committee, that a report on the Dublin Dockyard had been submitted by Mr John Barr, and the Finance Committee had agreed subject to the approval of the board, to complete the purchase of the Dockyard in due course, but that in the meantime, endeavours are to be made to obtain terms under the lease from the Dublin Port and Docks board. Approved.'[4]

The minutes of the board meeting held on 21 December 1923 recorded further progress on the Dublin Dockyard issue: 'Sir V. Caillard reported the purchase of the Dublin Dockyard had now been completed for a price of £63,000, as previously reported to

The *Simon and Jude*, a replica of William Petty's catamaran, which was constructed in 1991 at the Grand Canal Dockyard, Ringsend, Dublin, in co-operation with the Ringsend Community Workshop and the Irish Nautical Trust for Mr Hal Sisk.

Knight Commander: The first vessel built at the Bewley, Walpole and Webb yard in 1864. *Courtesy of the Quaker Library, Dublin.*

John Smellie, one of the two Scots, who re-established shipbuilding at Dublin in 1901. *Photograph by kind permission of the family.*

The first vessel built by the new Dublin Dockyard Company, the *Gertie*, taking shape on the slipway.

The steam tug *Anna Liffey* was the first vessel built for the Dublin Port & Docks Board in 1904.

Port Lairge: A very early photograph of the ship, which appears to have been taken shortly after she came into service. *Photographer unknown, courtesy of Brian Cleere.*

The *Dun Aengus*, built in 1912 for the Galway Bay Steamship Company for their passenger and cargo coastal service, including the Aran Islands.

The twin-screw fishery cruiser *Helga*, built in 1908 to the order of the Department of Agriculture and Technical Instruction for Ireland.

The patrol vessel *Galiano*, built for the Canadian government for patrol and survey work and the training of cadets. Commissioned into the Royal Canadian Navy in 1917, the *Galiano* sank in a severe storm, the only RCN vessel to be lost during the First World War.

The TSS *Lord Stalinbridge*, a twin-screw tender built to the order of the London & North Western Railway Company for the service of the Shropshire Union Railways, to carry passengers from the Woodside station on the Wirral side across the Mersey to the passenger landing stage at Liverpool.

The dredger *Curraghour*, built for the Limerick Harbour Commissioners with two heavy Priestman grab dredges.

The twin-screw sludge steamer *Shamrock*, constructed in 1905 for the Dublin Corporation main drainage scheme.

Two coasting vessels on No. 2 Patent Slip simultaneously undergoing repairs.
The near vessel is owned by Joseph Fisher and Sons of Newry, who favoured the
Dublin yard with much work over many years. The vessels are each sitting on a
carriage which was pulled out of the water on tracks by a powerful winch.

The *Eltham* was one of five vessels built by the Dublin Dockyard for John
Harrison Ltd of London and was typical of the long raised quarterdeck type of
ship, with machinery aft, greatly favoured by owners engaged in the coasting and
continental trades of the early twentieth century.

The *Halo*, one of the ships ordered by the Shipping Controller during the First World War. She was assigned to Stephenson, Clarke & Co., London, to assist in maintaining coal supplies to the main London gas works. She was the first vessel launched from the shipyard extension on land taken over from the Dublin Port & Docks Board in response to the government's appeal for extra tonnage to offset the immense shipping losses caused by German U-Boat sinkings.

The SS *Glenstal* was the largest vessel ever built in Dublin.

Vessels in the 1860 dry dock. Looking seawards, the nearest ship appears to be the Commissioners of Irish Lights' small tender *Ierne*, constructed to assist the building of the Fastnet Lighthouse.

The *J. Duncan*, built for Messrs J.T. Duncan of Cardiff in 1914 as a collier for bunkering British warships, photographed at the end of her days going astern out of Alexandra Basin in Dublin in the 1950s.

The *Holmdale*, launched by Dublin Shipbuilders from their short-lived yard at the east end of Alexandra Quay, Dublin. *Courtesy of the New Zealand Maritime Museum.*

The official party leaving the launching platform after the *Irish Fern* took to the water on 28 August 1954. The President of Ireland, Mr Seán T. O'Kelly, is escorted by Mr Hugh Lennox, managing director of the yard. At the top of the ramp is Mrs Phyllis O'Kelly, who christened the new vessel, escorted by Raymond A. Burke, one of the founding directors of the Liffey Dockyard.

The *SS Puchoco*, one of two ships built in 1921 for the Chilean Compañía Carbonifera y de Fundición Schwager of Valparaíso, on trials in the Clyde.

The *TSS Jayanti*, a coastal passenger vessel completed in 1918 for the Bombay Steam Navigation Company for their Bombay to Goa route.

The *Cheloshin*, a twin-screw passenger ship, the second of two vessels built for the Union Steam Ship Company of Vancouver for service on the west coast of Canada and delivered in 1911. She is seen fitting out in Dublin before her 14,400 sea mile voyage to Vancouver via the Straits of Magellan.

The *Orlock Head*, built after the First World War for Messrs G. Heyn & Sons of Belfast. She was a modified C3 type for the owners' special requirements.

The *Kilkenny*, a motor ship built for the British & Irish Steam Packet Company Ltd in 1937 for their cross channel trade, mainly between Dublin and Liverpool.

The *City of Amsterdam* in Alexandra Basin, Dublin, outward bound to the continent. The vessel, formerly the *Irish Fir*, was one of the wartime fleet of Irish Shipping Ltd, before being bought and renamed by Palgrave Murphy Ltd.

The *Isolda* (*Yard No. 171*), the first vessel built under Liffey management, ordered by the Commissioners of Irish Lights, Dublin.

The *Glencree* in the River Dodder, outward bound on passage to the Mersey to load coal for the Dublin Gas Works in Pearse Street.

Coill an Eo (*Yard No. 183*) was the last ship ever built in the Liffey yard.

The first ship from the Liffey Dockyard, the *Isolda*, in her final guise as the training and store ship LÉ *Setanta* of the Naval Service between 1976 and 1981.

The *Meath*, the largest vessel built by the Liffey Dockyard.

The motor tender *Blarna*. The first of two sister ships built for the Cork Harbour Commissioners in 1961, seen proceeding on trials in September of that year.

the board. The balance due is £47,250 for which amount a cheque had accordingly been sent to Vickers Ireland Ltd, to effect the completion. In recognition of the services rendered by J.F. Barr in connection with the purchase of the above yard, he has been paid the sum of £3,000 and the company had undertaken by letter dated 20 December 1923, to procure for him the allotment, free of cost, of 7,000 fully paid up shares in Vickers Ireland Ltd, when the dockyard is opened, subject to an undertaking on his part that the shares must be held by him for at least three years, and are not to be sold without first being offered to Vickers Ltd either at par or at 12½ years purchase of the average rate per cent of dividends paid in the three preceding years, whichever is the greater. Approved.'[5]

However, just one year later matters had changed dramatically as the minutes of the board meeting held on 19 December 1924 show: 'Sir V. Caillard reported on behalf of the Finance Committee with ref. to the board minutes 21/12/23 that the company had agreed to give 7,000 fully paid up shares in Vickers Ireland Ltd, on certain conditions to J.F. Barr free of charge. It had been (now) agreed to ten shillings per share i.e. £3,500 in full satisfaction of the above undertaking on condition that he resigns his seat on the board of Vickers Ireland Ltd. Agreed.'[6] Obviously this action was the result of a decision taken prior to that meeting to remove Mr Barr as a director of the Irish subsidiary.

This decision was not resolved on the board's terms, and after a meeting with Barr, Sir V. Caillard agreed to purchase the shares at face value, at which time Barr resigned.[7] What had caused the happy and intimate relationship between the board and Mr Barr to change from just one year earlier, when he was rewarded with a cash bonus of 5% of the purchase price, together with a further 11% of the price in free shares, is not recorded in the company minutes.

In November 1959, Vickers Armstrong produced a booklet, *A Short Account of the Vickers Group of Companies*, which devoted a couple of paragraphs to Vickers (Ireland) Ltd. In compiling material for the publication the editor, V.F.G. Pritchett, had sought information about their Irish subsidiary company, which had then been closed for twenty years. The person he approached for help was Frank Strickland, who had worked in the Irish yard and was then the commercial director of the Vickers Armstrong Ltd Naval Yard at Walker, Newcastle upon Tyne. On 21 October 1958, Pritchett wrote to Strickland, who replied on 24 October, saying: 'Just how Vickers came to acquire the Dublin Dockyard is a story in itself, and would not make favourable reading for the company.'

Strickland commenced his account of the 1923 affair, by going back to the end of the First World War, when Vickers, in common with other companies, embarked on the manufacture of 'peace products'. Vickers (Ireland) Ltd was formed to represent the group for the sale of their products in Ireland. Towards the end of 1923 they purchased the dockyard, which was, at that time, closed due to a strike. Its owners sold out while the going was good and they eventually paid their shareholders back £3 per £1 share. Strickland went on to record that the trades which were on strike at the time and whose members still refused to work in the yard until it was liquidated in 1938, were plumbers, engineers, blacksmiths, painters and joiners: 'In consequence, only blacklegs or non-union men could be employed, but there was agreement with the black squads, namely, platers, caulkers, riveters etc. ... Under these adverse conditions, we struggled along from 1925 to 1938, only to prove the old company correct – that there was no future – but in that time, in addition to doing an extensive amount of repair work, we built 55 vessels including several barges.' He lists the seagoing ships produced by the company: 'In association with P. & W. MacLellan of Glasgow we fabricated 3,000 to 4,000 tons of structural steelwork per annum. During the whole time we carried on the representation of the Vickers Group of Companies, and Mr Ridgeway continued to do this after 1938 when the company was wound up and I left.'

Strickland went on to say: 'The man who was responsible for Vickers buying the Dublin Dockyard was a John Fillians Barr; he was also primarily responsible for forming a separate company to represent the Vickers Group in Ireland, persuading them [the board] there were massive hydro-electric schemes for harnessing a river in the north of Ireland and another in the south. Neither of these schemes developed – the only one which did was the Shannon hydro-electric scheme, which was given to a German firm.' He concluded his letter by stating: 'There was no question at any time as to the quality of the output of the Dublin Dockyard, but it was only just that it could not be built economically and in competition with this side [England], due to labour difficulties and the extra cost of transport, materials etc. Although Ireland was primarily an agricultural country, we did obtain a fair share of the orders going for the Vickers Group of companies.'[8]

Along with that letter there are also three typewritten pages of an interview just a year later in Newcastle on 8 September 1959, in which Strickland gave a more in-depth account of the period between the wars, when he was in effect the Vickers representative in Ireland: 'In 1923 Vickers formed an agency in Dublin, and a man named John F. Barr became interested and went to Vickers House, where he met Sir Trevor Dawson [vice-chairman and managing director], and persuaded Dawson to form an Irish company. The Dublin Dockyard was for sale at the time. Barr with all the persuasiveness of a company promoter, got Vickers very interested in this, and at the time the owners were willing to sell for £12,000. Two representatives were then sent by head office to value the yard and they produced figures of £63,000 as scrap, or £194,000 as a going concern ... They did not take the elementary step of finding out that the directors were proposing to wind it up! A John Barr was also sent from the Barrow shipyard to get inside information. However while he was still engaged in his task, Vickers House cut him short and paid the Dublin Dockyard £63,000. He had no doubt that this was a case of the people in Vickers House being fooled by an astute and unscrupulous company promoter.'

It was only when Frank Strickland was sent to Dublin and installed as company secretary of the subsidiary that 'he found the document that told him the real truth. It was perfectly true that the attitude of the unions, and the impossibility of obtaining agreement with all of them, would prevent the yard from ever being worked efficiently if agreement with all of them was in fact sought. What they did therefore, was to obtain agreement with as many unions as possible and then go ahead. They got orders for repair work, structural steel and new construction, but so far as he [Strickland], could remember they made a loss every year except one. Nevertheless the business in Dublin brought some advantage to Vickers as it made their name known in Ireland and brought them some business there. Even so it was extremely hard to sell the company's peace products. Almost the only real success which they had was box-making machinery.'

The Vickers-Built Ships

According to Frank Strickland the Dublin yard reopened in October 1924 and from then onwards the London minutes only make occasional references to the group's investment in Ireland. In February 1926 a security bond was executed for the Dublin Port & Docks Board for a contract for tools. Later Commander C.W. Craven, RN, was appointed a director of the Irish subsidiary and in July, George W. Barr of the Barrow Works was also appointed to a seat on the Irish board.

The first vessel to come from the Dublin yard under Vickers ownership was launched on 24 August 1926. That afternoon's *Evening Herald* carried news of the event under the headline 'Tug Launched – interesting ceremony at the Port', which is worth reproducing:

Today the Dublin Dockyard Co., Vickers (Ireland) Ltd, launched the TSS *Kahanui*, a tugboat which has been built for service in New Zealand. This boat is the first boat launched under the Free State flag and the first built in the Saorstat. She is a new twin-screw tug built for the Wanganui Harbour Board of New Zealand.

She is 110 feet long by 24 feet beam, and 12 feet moulded depth, constructed of mild steel of the highest class at Lloyd's being built under their special survey. In addition to her capacity as a tug, she carries a very elaborate system of salvage and fire extinguishing plant. The accommodation is exceptional, the whole of the officers quarters being panelled in mahogany. The salvage gear consists of one 15-inch steam-driven centrifugal salvage pump with a capacity of 3,500 gallons per minute against a total head of 40 feet. The vessel has also a submersible electrical salvage pump capable of delivering 1,100 gallons per minute against a head of 35 feet. The fire pump is capable of delivering 1,000 gallons per minute against a total head of 30 feet.

The boat was launched at 12.30 p.m. today, in the presence of a large crowd of workmen and visitors. When the last prop had been knocked away, a bottle of champagne was smashed on her bows by Senator Moran, vice-chairman of the company, and the boat glided down into the water, where she swung round beautifully but with a slight list to the starboard due to the fact that the engines had not yet been installed, and the presence of some stores on her deck and her heavy superstructure, including the tall bridge and officers' quarters. From the Dublin Dockyard Co.'s premises, North Wall, she will be towed to Glasgow, where her propelling machinery will be fitted. This will consist of two sets of triple expansion surface condensing engines. Big cylinders 12 inches, 19.5 inches, and 3 inches by 23 inches stroke, supplied with steam from one large patent water tube boiler by a working pressure of 180 lbs per square inch. Thence she will proceed under her own steam to New Zealand. She is expected to average 200 knots per day on the voyage. She will be taken out by Captain Goodwin and a crew …

Since that date [Oct. 1924] the company have had 78 vessels dry docked and repaired in their yards, representing a gross tonnage of 70,000 tons. Work is progressing rapidly in the industry, and they employ on average 300 hands. On the slip behind the vessel launched today is another boat for the same destination, which is slightly larger, and will be finished in 8 or 9 weeks. She will be fitted with the largest semi-diesel crude oil engines carried by any ship afloat.

The tug was registered as *No. 4* of 1927 at the Port of Wellington. Further information on this vessel, the *Kahanui* (ON 151512), which had a gross tonnage of 207 tons, is contained in a thesis written in 1965, which is held at the archives of the Wanganui District Council: 'The contract for this vessel was let to Vickers in November 1925 at a cost of £30,470. She was built to carry a crew of fourteen, with the officers' accommodation forward of the machinery space which consisted of single cabins for the captain, mate, chief engineer and a spare. These were framed and panelled in polished mahogany with furniture to match. Next to these was a small pantry and storeroom. Access to the officers' quarters was obtained through the saloon on the main deck. The saloon was also framed and panelled in polished mahogany with upholstered settees and a large mahogany table. The ceilings of the cabins were cork-dusted and painted white, while the saloon had its beams boxed in and polished. The accommodation aft for the crew of ten men, who had to put up with only cork dusted and painted quarters. The officers' and crews' wash rooms, galley, lamp room and pump room were arranged under the bridge. The bridge deck contained a teak chart room and wheelhouse, and immediately aft of this was the wireless cabin with its 1.5 kilowatt transmitter and receiver and a berth for the wireless operator. The tug contained about sixty general lights apart from its navigational, towing and cluster lights and Morse flashing light.'[9]

The thesis also provides us with a history of the *Kahanui*'s service life. She was used about six times a year and took part in three salvage operations. One of these was the refloating of the steamer *Gale* seven miles south of Wanganui on 18 April 1928, when she managed to rescue the defenceless ship after the Wellington tug *Terawhiti* had failed. The second was a fruitless attempt to refloat the *Port Bowen* off a beach north of Wanganui in 1929 and the third was her assistance in the successful salvage of the *Wanganella* at Wellington in January 1947. During the war the tug was hired out to the government to earn money. From 1948 to 1959, the *Kahanui* was laid up and, although repairs and maintenance were periodically carried out, the ship's condition deteriorated. Improvements in engine designs and the cost of upkeep on a tug the size of the *Kahanui* made it almost impossible to sell, until in 1959 it was finally sold to a Wanganui contractor for £1,052.10. The buyers of the vessel, Messrs B. Bullock & Co., later had her scrapped. The upkeep and running of the vessel in all its years was £29,000, which was nearly balanced by its hire and salvage claims amounting to £24,500.

The estimate of the time it would take to finish the next ship in the *Evening Herald* turned out to be fairly accurate. Ten weeks later, on 26 October 1926, the new owners launched their second ship. She was the motor vessel *Southland* (ON 128592), ordered by the Bluff Harbour Board, on the South Island of New Zealand. This vessel was the subject of a very complementary article in one of the leading London shipping magazines of the time, *Syren & Shipping*. The article claimed: 'She was the highest powered craft in her class. This was on account of her particular multi-purpose role of motor tug, passenger ship and salvage vessel. During six summer months she would operate as an excursion vessel from Bluff to an island some 24 miles off the coast carrying 285 persons.' When the season closed the ship would act as a tug and pilot vessel for the harbour board. Her third role was that of a salvage ship and for this she was equipped with 'suitable gear', including a pump with a capacity of 70,000 gallons per hour.[10]

The *Southland* had a small forward hold to carry 65 tons of cargo served by a derrick, while the cabins for the five officers were also situated forward. The remaining ten members of the crew bunked and messed aft. She had four 18-foot lifeboats carried under Welin davits.[11] The ship's dimensions were an overall length of 145 feet, and 135 feet between perpendiculars. Her beam was 30 feet, and the depth to the upper deck 20 feet. She was propelled by two 6-cylinder Vickers-Petter diesel engines, each developing 600 BHP, which gave a speed of 12.4 knots on her trials over the measured mile off Kingstown. It is interesting that in the context of her role as a excursion ship she spent sixteen months fitting out, which is a very long time. She was taken out of service with engine trouble in the 1930s and laid up for a considerable time before being sold.

The passenger carrying tug *Southland* delivered to the Bluff Harbour Board in the South Island of New Zealand in 1927.

In November 1934 H.L. Tapley of Dunedin bought the tug and in December 1937, she was resold to Mollers Towage Ltd of Hong Kong. Three months later in March 1938, she was re-named the *Frosty Moller* and registered in Shanghai. On 5 May 1938 she towed the *J.A. Boyd* from Melbourne and on 21 May, picked up the *Moruya*. On 14 June, she put into Brisbane with engine trouble and arrived back in Shanghai on 22 July 1938. There her engines were removed and she was re-engined as a steamer with machinery from a former Royal Navy gunboat. On 20 November 1941, before the attack on

Pearl Harbour, she was taken over by the British naval authorities in Hong Kong and commissioned as an auxiliary patrol vessel. She was sunk in December. On the fall of that colony to the Japanese, the *Frosty Moller*, was salvaged and used by the Japanese Imperial Navy as a minesweeper under the name *Gennchi Maru*. There are conflicting reports as to when this Dublin-built tug met her end. The first states she was attacked and sunk by US aircraft somewhere south-west of Macau. The second account gives her lost in the same position on 24 January 1944, but named the *Harachi Maru*.[12]

In 1927 only two items appear about the Dublin yard in the London minutes of the Vickers Company. The first occurs in November when the board decided it was too expensive at £1,200 per annum to continue the registration of Vickers patents from the Barrow yards in the Irish Free State. The second appeared in the following month, where it was agreed to give a letter of guarantee to the Royal Bank of Ireland in respect of an overdraft of £12,000 to Vickers (Ireland) Ltd. That year also the yard commenced building for local owners. They received an order from Arthur Guinness Son & Company (Dublin) Ltd, for a steam river barge to carry the 'black stuff' from the brewery to the port. She was the *Farmleigh* (ON 146427), which was built to Lloyd's Class A1 for river traffic and the requirements of the Board of Trade. She had a length of 80 feet and a beam of 17 feet, with a net tonnage of 47 and a gross of 80. The propelling machinery, supplied by Messrs McKie & Baxter of Glasgow, was a direct acting vertical reciprocating engine developing 135 BHP at 165 RPM, giving a service speed of 7.5 knots with a full load of 100 tons. The vessel had an open hold, which had a capacity of 4,450 cubic feet, served by a Clarke Chapman steam crane lifting about half a ton.

Also the first two canal barges were completed for the Grand Canal Company of Ireland for the inland waterway system. These were the motor driven *No. 40M* still afloat as the *Sequoia* and the *No. 41M*.

Grand Canal Company barges laid up in St James' Harbour behind the Guinness Brewery. All of these were built either by Vickers (Ireland) Ltd, or the Ringsend Dockyard Company between the 1920s and late 1930s.

British Shipbuilding Giants Merge

At this time big changes were taking place in the British shipbuilding industry and in 1927 one of the major companies, W.G. Armstrong Whitworth & Co., got into financial difficulties having invested in papermills in Canada. This over-stretched the firm and the British government refused to intervene to help in spite of the company's major naval gun factory at Elswick. The company was rescued through a merger in 1928 with Vickers Ltd, to form Vickers Armstrong Ltd, a company which lasted into the 1990s. The Vickers shareholding in Vickers (Ireland) Ltd, was transferred to the new company. Two years later the share capital of the Irish subsidiary was increased, with £43,500 worth of shares allocated to Vickers Armstrong in reduction of loans to the Dublin yard. Also the 500 shares held by the Irish directors were acquired back from them at various times.

Maui Pomare, built in 1928 for the New Zealand government (Pacific Islands Administration) to carry fruit to the mainland. *Photo courtesy of the New Zealand Maritime Museum, Auckland.*

The next vessel from the yard was an interesting and specialised ship for the Cook Islands department of the New Zealand government, which was named *Maui Pomare* after the first Maori to be knighted. Her official number was 151514 and she was allocated the signal letters ZMFS and inscribed as *No. 65* of 1928 at Wellington. Her dimensions were 210 feet and 8 inches in length, with a 35-foot beam. The tonnages were 754 net and 1,203 gross. She was designed to provide a passenger and cargo service from both the north and south islands of New Zealand to Western Samoa, calling at the capital Apia, as well as Niue and Norfolk Island, all at the time administered by the Commonwealth government. The ship was fitted to carry bananas from these islands to New Zealand. The vessel had long forecastle deck with a small well just aft of the bridge house, which served as No. 2 hold, and a long poop deck continuing to the stern. The *Maui Pomare* ran trials in Dublin Bay on 28 January 1928, according to the *Irish Independent*, which reproduced a photograph of the official party aboard. *The Irish Times* of 2 March also published a photograph of the ship, with the caption noting 'that she left Dublin on Wednesday'.

From Dublin the ship went to Southampton, where she loaded cargo for Samoa and, with Captain F.K. Allen, a New Zealander, as master, left on her delivery voyage via the Panama Canal. It is interesting that a contemporary New Zealand newspaper in a lengthy account of the vessel, recorded that 'the ship's engineers overhauled the two 600 BHP Vickers-Petter engines after the Atlantic passage'. She crossed the Pacific without incident and reached Apia, where she discharged her Southampton cargo. She then loaded her first bananas, topping up at Niue, before reaching Wellington at the end of May 1928. She left Wellington on 4 June on her maiden voyage from New Zealand and at Niue and Apia she loaded fruit for Dunedin, where she was due on 27 June.

The *Maui Pomare*, was equipped to load 12,000 boxes of bananas in cool storage, 15,000 cubic feet in the fore hold and 21,750 cubic feet, in the after hold, with a further 4,230 cubic feet in the forward between deck, so that the fruit would arrive in the best condition at the terminal ports of Dunedin, Lyttleton or Wellington. Her passenger accommodation was in seven two-berth cabins on the main deck with two special cabins on the upper deck at an extra charge. The cost for a thirty-day round trip was £40. There were also sixteen 'drop' berths in the number one between deck, to cater for extra passengers between Auckland and Norfolk Island. On completion the ship carried five or six lifeboats under Welin davits, two on the forecastle deck, the remainder aft on the poop deck, although photographs taken some ten years later show one lifeboat less on the poop deck and plating extended on the fore deck to cover the cargo well at No. 2 hold. This vessel, like the *Southland*, seems to have been plagued by engine trouble during her lifetime and it would appear that the Vickers-Petter engine design was not a success. The vessel was re-powered in 1947 with a Fairbanks-Morse diesel motor manufactured in 1941. In 1961 the government sold the *Maui Pomare* to the Australian Pacific Steam Navigation Company, who resold the vessel to the Kimberly Shipping Company of Port Kimberly in western Australia and registered her in Panama. Early in 1968 she was sold to the Ming Hing Company of Hong Kong for demolition and by March breaking up had commenced.

As we have seen, Vickers (Ireland) Ltd commenced laying down the first vessels for Irish owners in 1927 and the first seagoing vessel, launched on 28 January 1928, was the *Isolda* (ON 142426), for the Commissioners of Irish Lights. The Lighthouse Tender was named by Mrs Andrew Jameson, wife of the commissioners' chairman. Designed by George Idle, MINA, the naval architect to Irish Lights, she had dimensions of length 198 feet, beam 32 feet 4 inches and depth 15 feet 9 inches. She had a gross of 734 tons. Her propelling machinery consisted of two sets of triple expansion engines supplied by William Beardmore & Company Ltd, Glasgow, developing 230 IHP, which gave a speed of over 12 knots. It is worth noting that the *Isolda* was the first new tender built for the lighthouse authority in twenty-four years. Their previous vessel, *Alexandra*, had been built by the Vickers Company at the Barrow-in-Furness yard, although at that time the company was called Messrs Vickers Sons & Maxim.

The following day's *Irish Independent* newspaper gave over two columns to the event and carried a cross section of the speeches given at the luncheon which followed the launching, although it did not indicate the venue. These are worth reproducing as they give an idea of the thinking of the time. The first speaker was Jeremiah McVeagh, a director of the builders, whose speech is paraphrased by the *Independent*: 'The company attached special interest to the launch, because the *Isolda* was the first ship, which they had built for Irish owners, and they appreciated the public spirit and patriotism of the Irish Lights board in placing the work in Dublin. That the Grand Canal Company had placed with them an order for the building of twelve barges and Messrs Guinness had entrusted them with their first order but he felt sure not their last commission.' He went on to mention all the Irish shipowners in Dublin, Drogheda, Waterford, Wexford and Belfast who had given much of their repair work to the Dublin yard. Not surprisingly he expected that, having built three ships for New Zealand, the company believed that they could also build ships for Ireland. He expressed the hope that the good example set by the Irish Lights board would see others follow. He continued: 'The shipbuilding industry everywhere is still much depressed, but the position with regard to this dockyard is, I am happy to tell you, more hopeful than it has been since it was reopened, and that fact is a source of relief and satisfaction to those of us who urged Vickers Ltd to throw themselves into the work of reviving this important Irish industry.'

The managing director George Ridgeway (the Vickers appointee from England) proposed the toast of the new ship coupled with that of her sponsor. The chairman of the Commissioners, Senator Jameson, in his reply said that they had given the contract to the company on its merits, as the Commissioners had to account to the Board of Trade for every penny they spent. He also noted that, whenever possible, his board would work with the Dublin shipyard, which they wished to see make a success of itself. The Dublin yard turned out first-class work at a price which would win an order. He hoped that capital (i.e. the money men) and labour would be able to settle their differences so that the company could keep to their estimates and fulfil their contracts. He concluded that if labour would back them up, he hoped to see the yard getting many contracts.

J.N. Dolan, parliamentary secretary to the Minister for Industry and Commerce, congratulated the company on obtaining the contract for the ship against keen competition and hoped it would be the first of many orders from Irish owners. He noted that since the yard had reopened they had been able to supply first-class facilities for the building and repair of fair-sized ships of all kinds and that Dublin costs were not unsatisfactory as shown by the success of the company in securing the building of vessel like the *Isolda*. He also stated that experts assured him that no better workmanship existed in ship-making anywhere else.

The final speaker reported at the ceremony was David Barry, the tone of whose speech suggests he was a shipowner: 'There is no reason whatever why vessels should not be built as successfully in Free State shipyards as Northern Ireland or Great Britain. Unfortunately there have been many difficulties in past years in regard to shipbuilding in Dublin and it is more gratifying now to hear that those difficulties had been overcome ... We are a body of poor men, we have to face all kinds of competition; the wages we pay are at least 50% above the lowest paid to crews employed by Continental shipowners generally. That is a serious disadvantage to us, and I hope that Senator Jameson and his colleagues on the Irish Lights Commissioners will give us a welcome respite by cutting down the cost of running the Irish service.'

Mr McVeagh concluded the proceedings by announcing that the yard had received an order for twelve barges from the Grand Canal Company. In fact the shipyard constructed no less than fifteen craft for that company in 1928. These were *Nos 42M, 43M, 44M, 45M, 46M, 47M, 48M, 49M* (still afloat as *Iron Lung*), *50M* (still afloat as *Venus*), *51M, 52M, 54M, 55M, 56M* and *57M*. The following year, two more barges were completed for the Canal Company, *No. 59M* and *No. 60M*. The former is still afloat as the pleasure craft *Countess Corinne*. As well as these, Messrs Guinness took delivery of two more steam barges, the *Fairyhouse* (ON 152265) and the *Knockmaroon* (ON 146430), both of which had the same dimensions as the 1927 vessel, the *Farmleigh*.

THE 1930s

The second decade of the Vickers ownership in Dublin yard opened with the completion of the *Clonsilla* (ON 152267), delivered on 26 February 1930, the *Castleknock* (ON 152268), delivered on 27 May and the *Killiney* (ON 156201), completed on 7 November, all for the Guinness Company. Also built were three further craft for the Grand Canal Company, *Nos 62M, 63M,* and *64M*, although following this there would be a gap of six years before any further vessels would be delivered to the inland waterway company. That year the shipyard also bought the iron steam barge *Moy* from Daniel Hayden, 9 The Quay, Waterford. She was a former Guinness vessel, built in 1897 by Ross & Walpole at the North Wall, but the reason for her purchase is not known.

Castleknock: A steam barge built for Guinness in May 1930 loaded with empty casks seen passing upriver under the Halfpenny Bridge loaded with empty barrels.

However, the major event of 1930 was the launch of the second merchant vessel for Irish owners, the *Sligo* (ON 152269), which took place on 30 July 1930. Ordered by the Sligo Steam Navigation Company Ltd, she was the second ship of the name to come from the slipways at Alexandra Basin, where her predecessor was constructed in 1912. Miss Jackson, the daughter of the chairman and managing director of the owners, carried out the naming ceremony. Interestingly in the full two columns report printed in the following day's *Irish Times*, they give only the initials or the Christian names of the gentlemen attending while the wives and daughters, including the vessel's sponsor, had to settle for Miss or Mrs as warranted! At the 'informal lunch' held in the workers canteen, the *Irish Times'* reporter took down in great detail the speeches, some of which are worth recording.

Senator Joseph Moran, then vice-chairman of Vickers (Ireland) Ltd, who presided, said in his remarks that 'the order for the *Sligo* was placed at a time when we were sorely in need of new work and was therefore most welcome'. He went on to note that he wished to congratulate the owners for keeping their business within the Irish Free State: 'Everyone present is aware that the shipbuilding industry has been for some years and is unhappily still suffering from a very deep trade depression and regret that even yet we cannot look into the future with any great optimism.' However, on a more positive note he mentioned that the yard had completed or was in the course of completing thirty-one vessels and barges, of which twenty-seven were for Irish owners. Another director, Jeremiah McVeagh, in proposing the toast to the Minister for Industry & Commerce noted that 'apart from the heavy capital investment, the proprietors have been paying wages at the rate of £50,000 per year. Vickers had with great indulgence and generosity, enabled their Irish company to keep the flag flying even in times of anxiety and gloom.'

The twin-screw *Sligo* had been designed by Messrs James Maxton & Co., naval architects in Belfast, and was of the shelter deck type. She was constructed under special survey of the Lloyd's Register to conform to their highest class, 100 A1, for the carriage of general cargo and livestock between Sligo and Liverpool. Her dimensions were an overall length of 231 feet, a breadth of 35 feet and a depth moulded to the main deck of 16 feet 3 inches. She was propelled by two sets of triple expansion machinery supplied by Messrs McKie & Baxter of Glasgow. In addition she complied with the regulations of the Board of Trade and the livestock requirements of the Departments of Agriculture in both the Free State and Great Britain. She had up-to-date pens for 275 head of cattle, as well as space to carry 500 sheep on the upper deck. In addition to the cargo space in the holds, she had refrigerated chambers for the carriage of dairy produce. Prior to her construction, model trials were carried out at the Vickers experimental testing tanks at St Albans.

Following successful trials, the *Sligo Champion* newspaper of 27 December 1930 reported that the *Sligo*, under the command of Captain Michael McLoughlin, had arrived in her home port on the evening of Sunday 22 December. The Sligo Steam Navigation Company Ltd was then one of the last three independent Irish cross-channel shipping companies operating between Britain and Ireland apart from the Railway Companies and the Coast Lines group. The others were the Limerick Steamship Company and the Wexford Steamship Company. In 1936 Coast Lines Ltd bought the Sligo Steam Navigation Company and the *Sligo* was allocated to the Burns and Laird Lines' Glasgow fleet and became the *Lairdsdale*. After the Second World War she was transferred to the Belfast Steamship Company and renamed the *Ulster Drover*. Almost thirty years later, in 1960, the *Ulster Drover* left from the North Wall, Dublin, on her last commercial voyage before being scrapped on the same day that the *Meath*, constructed for the British & Irish Steam Packet Company Ltd, was launched from the slipways of what was now the Liffey Dockyard.

The year 1931 was only nine days old when the yard completed another steam river barge, the *Sandyford* (ON 156213) and later that year two further craft were completed for the Guinness brewery, the *Seapoint* (ON 156205) and the *Howth* (ON 1562040), which brought the yard's total output for the St James' Gate firm over four years to ten vessels.

On Monday 12 October, the *Irish Press* recorded that 'a new barge for the Dublin Port & Docks Board, the largest and best steam hopper barge *Number Eight* (ON 156207) was successfully launched on Saturday [10 October] from the dockyard. She had a capacity of 1,000 tons of spoil, length between perpendiculars 165 feet, moulded breadth 33 feet and depth moulded of 15 feet.' Her gross tonnage was 635 tons and her triple expansion machinery supplied by D.W. Henderson Ltd of Glasgow, developed 74 HP which gave a speed of 7 knots. She was the second vessel for the board from these slipways, where the *Anna Liffey* had taken to the water in 1904. She would appear to have been the first hopper built for the board in fifty-eight years. The design of this vessel was the subject of a paper read at the meeting of the Institution of Civil Engineers of Ireland on 11 January 1932 by W.J. Mares, MINA, the general manager of the yard. His paper considered the various interesting problems encountered and went into great detail on the technical aspects and the hopper doors. The Proceedings of the Institution carried a full report and the resulting discussions.

On 21 October 1931, the *Irish Press* carried the headline: 'Reopening of Dublin Dock' and the report said: 'After three months the graving dock was put back into commission this week. In the interval the sea gates have been renewed by the Dublin Dockyard at a cost of £4,000. They replaced the original gates constructed in 1857, which were 40 feet in width by 25 feet high with ten separate water-tight compartments. Immediately after the removal of the cofferdam, the Irish Free State fishery boat was put into the dock. The vessel is going to be cleaned up and preparations are to be made for the fitting of the new gun to be used in activities against poaching trawlers.' Yet only two months later, on Saturday 12 December the same paper reproduced a photograph of empty building slipways under the heading: 'Dublin Deserted Dockyard'. It reported that 'when asked by Mr Lemass, TD, if he could induce the shipping companies using the port to get even 50% of their repair work done in Dublin, Mr Blythe [Minister for Finance] replied this was a business over which he had no control.'

The year 1932 opened with news of lost contracts for shipbuilding in Dublin. On Saturday 13 February 1932, the *Irish Press* carried a paragraph reporting: 'Tenders for Barges – The Dublin dockyards and their competition – in reference to Thursday's meeting of the Dublin Port & Docks Board at which the tender of the Ardrossan Dockyard Co. of £3,750 for three steel barges was accepted. This was against that of the Dublin Dockyard for £4,295 for two barges and of the Ringsend Dockyard Co. of £2,216 for one barge or £6,465 for three. W. McMullan, managing director of Ringsend wrote that wages did not account for more that 21.2% over wages paid on the Clyde and steel material by 71.2%, it would correct to say [*sic*] that shipbuilding costs in Dublin were 9 to 10% higher than the Clyde.'

However, there was good news two months later, as the *Irish Press* recorded on Friday 22 April: 'The Dublin Dockyard Company has secured the contract for the steam launch for the Dublin Port & Docks Board in competition with a cross-channel firm. A tender for £951, the lowest of three, was submitted by this firm at a meeting of the board yesterday. The work will be returned to the Free State, for the successful tenders were £300 less than the Ardrossan Shipbuilding Co. The *Irish Press* learns that no time will be lost on the order, for the launch will be required in seven weeks time for the Eucharist Congress.' The vessel was the small survey steamer *Erin* (ON 159813) and was 47.4 feet in length, 10.2 feet in beam, had a gross tonnage of 47 tons and was fitted with a 5 HP engine. She was renamed *Depthfinder* in 1938 and *Rosbeg* in 1947, to allow her name to be used that year for a new motor survey launch built in Malahide. She was fitted with a diesel engine in the 1960s and was sold by the board to Brian Crummy, a fisherman from Howth, County Dublin.

The following day, 23 April 1932, the paper carried a photograph of a pontoon being launched in Grand Canal Basin by the Ringsend Dockyard for the Electricity Supply board.

About this time the political landscape in the Free State was turned upside down when Éamon de Valera and his Fianna Fáil party came to power with the help of the Labour party. The *Irish Press*, as the unofficial party organ, highlighted all the activities of the new government. On 10 May it reported that 'Mr Lemass summoned representatives of various shipping companies to a conference at Government Buildings yesterday and discussed with them the question of having repairs executed in Irish ports, so that a share of the profits might be left in the Free State. The Minister also invited them to consider the employment of more Irishmen on their boats and suggested that 50% of the crews should be Irish. The companies replied that many boats were built in Dublin and repairs carried out here to as great an extent as possible and undertook to consider the minister's suggestions in other directions. These companies were the railways (Great Western of England and the London Midland & Scottish), B & I, Michael Murphy & Co., Palgrave Murphy & Co., Burns Laird, City of Cork Steam Packet Co., Sligo Steam Navigation Co. and Thomas Heiton & Co.'

Nine days later the same newspaper reported that 'deputations from various interests were received by Mr Seán Lemass, Minister for Industry & Commerce yesterday. One from the Boilermakers & Iron & Steel Shipbuilders Society, who pointed out that engineering works could be helped under the tax [tariff] by getting 50% of repairs to vessels trading and making profits at Free State ports done here. The Minister had already received representatives from several shipping companies. Headed by Mr Albert, Irish District Secretary of the Society, William McNally, Secretary of Dublin No. 1 Branch and Christopher Leahy, a Dublin boilermaker, who began an agitation for a tariff in the *Irish Press* before the present government took over.' It is recorded in the minutes of their

London board meeting of 15 May 1933 that: 'Vickers Ltd and Vickers Armstrong Ltd provided security for Vickers (Ireland) Ltd to carry out an order for £25,855 for steel erection work for the Great Southern Railway board.'[13] This work was carried under sub-contract by a specialist firm from Glasgow. The minutes for 15 September noted that the job had been completed.[14]

In 1934 the yard had a stoppage, as the *Irish Press* reported on 27 April: 'Over fifty workers who had been on strike for the past week at the Dublin Dockyard had returned to work the day before. The stoppage was due to an inter-union dispute and the paper understood that the Irish Brotherhood of Boilermakers had agreed to work with the firm's staff to whom objection had been made.'

In September, another merchant vessel, the steam collier *Glencree* (ON 159301), ordered by the Alliance & Dublin Consumers Gas Company, was launched. She was 142 feet in length, with a beam of 25 feet and 11.5 feet in depth. Her gross tonnage was 481 tons, with a triple expansion engine supplied by Aitchison Blair Ltd, Clydebank, Glasgow. She was slightly smaller than the other two ships in the Gas Company fleet which had been completed fourteen years earlier by the Lytham St Annes Shipbuilding yard in Lancashire. The Gas Company had wished to place an order for the first ships in 1920 with the Dublin yard, but it was unable to accept as at the time there was no berth available because of wartime construction waiting to be finished. The Gas Company vessels were constrained in length by the size of the Camden lock, the largest giving access to the Grand Canal Basin, where the gasworks was situated.

The *Glencree*, which was engaged in carrying coal for the gasworks across the Irish Sea, had a crew of eleven, consisting of the master, mate, chief and second engineers, as well as three seamen, three firemen and a cook. The normal passage time in good weather across to the Mersey was some fourteen hours, which allowed three round trips per week. She continued this trade under Irish neutral markings after the outbreak of Second World War hostilities and sailed without incident until the third year of the war. On 21 March 1941, while on passage from Barry in South Wales to Dublin in the company of the *Glencullen*, she was attacked at 5.20 p.m. by a German aircraft, which dropped a bomb 40 feet off the starboard side, causing slight damage. The ship was attacked again in spite of her neutral markings that evening, at 7 p.m., by another German plane, but there were no casualties and both ships docked in Dublin next morning.

Later that year, on 5 November, the *Glencree* was again subject to attack, this time with Captain C.H Bodels as master. She was once more in company with the *Glencullen* on passage from Barry showing her neutral lights, when at 6.30 p.m. a German aircraft made two passes over the vessel raking her with cannon or machine-gun fire. However the Belfast collier *Portavogie*, which was also in company with these ships, opened fire and drove the plane away. The *Glencree* was forced to divert to Fishguard and land her chief engineer, W.B. Brown, and second engineer, M. Moore, both of whom were wounded. There were no further attacks on Gas Company ships for the remainder of the war and the *Glencree* returned to peacetime trading until 1963 when, because of rising costs, the steamers were sold and replaced by motor vessels. The *Glencree* was sold to the Netherlands and was scrapped by N.V. de Koophandel at Nieuw Lekkerland during November 1963, after a career of thirty years.

FINANCIAL MATTERS

The year 1935 was one of mixed fortunes for the Dublin Dockyard. On 28 January 1935, the *Irish Press* reported under the heading 'Contracts for Dublin?' that the Dublin Trades Council had decided to take up the question of securing for Dublin the contracts for the building of two new cargo boats for the B & I Steam Packet

Company. A deputation was to be sent to the management in connection with the matter at an early date, but the Dublin yard failed to win the contracts. Two months later, correspondence between Dublin and London sheds an interesting light on how the Vickers operation was doing in the Free State. The chief Vickers accountant sent a letter dated 5 March to Dublin, seeking the turnover for 1934 where he quotes £60,668 for 1932 and £40,911 for 1933. The following day, the secretary at the yard, Mr F. Strickland, replied that the turnover for 1934 had been £76,370.

In 1935 the 'Royal Commission on the Private Manufacture and Trading in Arms' commenced sittings in London, which continued until 1937. Because of this, Vickers Armstrong, the parent company of Vickers (Ireland) Ltd, was required to appear and provide evidence to that commission about all of their companies including subsidiary firms. Therefore the Dublin yard had to account for its operations, which has left some interesting information on the company. In a letter dated 20 June 1935, marked 'Private & Confidential', George Ridgeway, the general manager of Vickers (Ireland) Ltd, stated: 'Dublin had not engaged in the manufacture of arms of any description, nor did they have any agreements with any firm engaged in the production of arms. Furthermore our present plant is not suitable for arms and munitions of war.' Under the heading 'Vessels of War of all Kinds', he went on to state: 'This yard has not hitherto been used for the building of naval vessels but could be adapted for the production of fleet auxiliaries of moderate tonnage.' In a further letter sent from Dublin two days later, Mr Ridgeway gave figures for the average number of employees for the five years from 1930 to 1934 as follows: 1930: 284; 1931: 218; 1932: 195; 1933: 207 and 1934: 262. He went on: 'Since we took over the premises in 1924, the yard has never operated to full capacity, manpower in Dublin in shipbuilding is definitely limited, and probably does not exceed 400 hands. Any increase would require to be secured by importing skilled labour or by intensive training.'[15]

On the front page of the *Irish Press* for 30 August 1935 a photograph appeared of the Finnish sailing vessel *Pamir* in dry dock, presumably in the care of the Dublin Dockyard for repairs. One of the last remaining windjammers of that era, she had arrived with grain from Australia on 13 August. She sailed from Dublin on 28 October under the command of Captain J.M. Mattsson bound back to Australia, a ninety-day voyage. Another interesting job carried out by the Vickers firm is mentioned in the *Irish Press* of Saturday 9 November that year. This is a photograph with the copy: 'Dead Pigs Shipped to Belgium. Last night 150 were loaded onto the *City of Ghent*. During the week the ship was fitted out for the Saorstat & Continental Steamship Company by the Dublin Dockyard with a new form of insulation in one of the holds. This new way of preserving the meat has been tried, a chemical evaporates into gas heavier than air and prevents bacterial growth and the vessel *City of Dublin* is to follow.' It concluded that a trial shipment had been made which was a success.

The Irish Times for Tuesday 28 January 1936, announced under the heading 'Shipbuilding in Dublin' that the B & I Steam Packet company had just placed an important order with the Dublin Dockyard Company for a cargo and cattle motor vessel with another to follow. Mr Ridgeway, the managing director, was quoted as paying tribute to the shipowners for placing the order for the ship with the yard.

On Thursday 12 March the yard launched a second steam hopper for the Dublin Port & Docks Board. This was the *Number Nine* (ON 159318), which had a length of 165 feet and a beam of 34 feet. Her triple expansion engine, manufactured by D.W. Henderson Ltd, Glasgow, developed 62 HP, while her gross tonnage was 682 tons. *The Irish Times* reporting the following day stated: 'Less than five minutes after the launch of a steam hopper barge from a slip at the dockyard, the keel plate was laid for the new steamship on the empty berth.' The paper also reported that eight barges for the

Grand Canal Company were under construction. These were *Nos 66M, 67M, 68M, 69M, 70M, 71M, 72M* and *73M.*

The London shipping journals also took note of the event, *The Shipbuilding & Shipping Record* reporting: 'Mr George Ridgeway the managing director of the Dublin Dockyard Company speaking at a luncheon following the launch of the Dublin Port & Docks Board's steam hopper *Number Nine* and the laying of a keel of a cattle steamer for the British & Irish Steam Packet Company the other day, said protective tariffs had assisted the structural steel side of the company's activities. Plant to handle larger units had been installed and last year the output had been increased to over 2,600 tons of fabricated steel. More than 300 men were employed in the yard, which had a wages bill of over £1,000 per week. W. Mares, the general manager of the Dublin Dockyard Company, referred to the shortage of skilled labour in the shipbuilding and other heavy industries. During the past few years very few young men had been trained in the industry. This was because parents were loath to allow their children to enter an industry which had not been prospering and because of trade union activities in restricting apprenticeship. Mr Mares thought the time was not far distant when some dilution of the skilled labour now employed would be necessary to cope with the increased work. Another difficulty of the industry was the inability of the rolling mills to cope with the demand for steel.'[16]

The *Irish Press* for Wednesday 27 January 1937, carried what was described as an exclusive story under the heading 'Dublin Dockyard Problem', with the sub-heading 'Hundreds of skilled men wanted yet none available.' It reported: '"If any skilled men in any branch of the shipbuilding trade is looking for a job, he will find one waiting for him at the Dublin Dockyard Company's yard," said the managing director Mr Ridgeway to an *Irish Press* reporter yesterday. In his office he showed me plans that are held up because of the shortage of men. "The trouble is that shipbuilding suffered most during the past years. The old hands drifted to other jobs. There were few apprentices because of union rules. The young generation brought few shipwrights, shell gangers, riveters, platelayers, roofers or other shipbuilding tradesmen. Belfast, the Clyde, the Tyne, other British shipbuilding ports, suffer most, first from the slump and second from the lack of men to tackle the revival." On the beams is the B & I cross-channel cargo vessel stretching 270 feet from stem to stern with 40 feet beam and 20 feet depth. Beside it are two big Canal Company barges under construction. [These were *No. 74M* and *75M*, the last built.] The *City of Dublin*, rescued from her grounding at Arklow, is in the next dock and around the ship are vast steel stanchions for new Irish cinemas in Waterford and Cork.'

The reporter continued: 'The company's agents went to Cork, Limerick, Belfast and Glasgow seeking shipwrights as the Free State could only supply fifty men. The Belfast and Glasgow men come and go, as their branch of the work in Dublin is held up for the lack of other tradesmen to complete intervening tasks. Ships to transport goods for new Irish trading concerns, for Dublin's new oil refinery, for Irish trawlers to compete with foreign fishermen must be built. "There is one way to increase Irish shipbuilding," said Mr Ridgeway, "and save it for Irish craftsmen. That is the institution of technical training for boys of early teens and the recognition of the craft as one of the important branches in future Free State technical instruction. Ships must be built," he added, "and men must be trained to build them."' The two canal barges mentioned in this report brought the number of such craft built for the inland waterways company in the decade to thirty-three.

The next public reference to the dockyard was somewhat tragic, as on 5 March 1937 the *Irish Press* reported on a murder trial in the Criminal Court, where a 23-year-old electric welder was charged with the murder of his 18-year-old sweetheart. It was stated in evidence that a steel plate had fallen on the man's head in 1930, while working in the dockyard and that he had suffered intermittent violent headaches since. He was found guilty by the jury, but with a strong recommendation to mercy, but was nevertheless sentenced to death. However, the same newspaper reported on 13 March that an appeal had been lodged the previous day on the grounds of insanity.

April saw the delivery of the largest ship from the Vickers period of ownership of the yard and the newspapers of the day following the launch were full of headlines such as: 'Dublin's Biggest Ship for 13 Years' and 'Striking Facts about Capital's Shipping and Shipbuilding Industries'. The *Irish Press* of 15 April 1937 opened its rather flowery account of the event as follows: 'To the cheers of hundreds of people gathered at Alexandra Basin, Dublin, the British & Irish Steam Packet Company's 1,500 ton cargo vessel, the *No. 169*, the biggest ship built in the state since 1924, was launched by Lady Glenavy yesterday. Lady Glenavy christened the ship *Kilkenny*, breaking a bottle of champagne, after which the vessel beautifully decorated and flying the tricolour and the B & I company house flag of white with a green cross was released and slid gracefully down the slip into the bay to the hiss of foam and the rattle of drag chains … The vessel designed for a speed of 14 knots was built by Vickers (Ireland) Ltd. The ceremony was broadcast from Athlone with a commentary by Mr Ted Halpin.'

The newspaper reported that before the christening of the vessel David Barry, Director of B & I, said that she would be the latest and most up-to-date ship of her kind on the high seas when she entered service in the early summer and that the Dublin Dockyard should be congratulated on the construction of such an important addition to the fleet of the British & Irish Steam Packet Co. Ltd. He noted that the vessel was designed and constructed to the latest requirements of the Departments of Agriculture both in the Free State and in Great Britain. The ship was to be in service on the Dublin, Drogheda and Liverpool trades and was fitted with all the latest improvements for carrying 720 cattle and 600 sheep, as well as having the most modern equipment for the rapid loading and unloading of cargo.

The overall length of the *Kilkenny* (ON 159788) was 276 feet, with a breadth of 40 feet and a moulded depth of 17 feet 11 inches. She was fitted with a cruiser stern, raking stem and was of the poop, bridge and forecastle type with topgallant forecastle and upper bridge. Possessing the most modern type of crew's accommodation in the poop, the officers and engineers were berthed amidships. The main propelling machinery was fitted by Harland & Wolff and consisted of one 2-stroke, single acting, direct reversing diesel airless injection engine from the Burmeister & Wain company with the enclosed forced lubricated trunk type working on the 2-stroke cycle and coupled direct to the propeller. The *Irish Press* continued: 'Afterwards about 100 guests were entertained to luncheon at the Shelbourne Hotel by B & I and Vickers (Ireland) Ltd. Mr G. Ridgeway, managing director Dublin Dockyard, presented a brooch to Lady Glenavy as a souvenir of the occasion. Sir Alfred Read, chairman of the B & I SP Co., proposed a toast to Vickers (Ireland) Ltd that this ship had been brought into the world in Dublin and he felt sure she would be a great success. He hoped the *Kilkenny* would carry a message of peace and goodwill to peoples on both sides of the channel. Vickers had produced a very suitable finely constructed, seagoing economical ship.'

A full account of the remarks by the next speaker, the managing director of the yard, George Ridgeway, was carried in *The Irish Times* of 15 April and is a good reflection of the difficulties facing the shipbuilders of the time. He said that the Dublin Dockyard 'appreciated that the B & I placed the order for the *Kilkenny* with them, which had been of great benefit in giving employment to a large number of men for over twelve months'. Ridgeway did not think any vessel had been constructed where more friendly relations existed between the staff of both companies. After all, he remarked, the shipowners, the shipbuilders and ship repairers had suffered the most during the downturn which all industries had experienced over the past seven or eight years. He suggested that if they had support from other companies regularly trading into Free State ports and particularly Dublin similar to that extended to them by B & I, the yard's position would be vastly improved. He noted that in 1930 the total merchant tonnage launched in Great Britain and Ireland was slightly over one and a half million, while in 1933 it had fallen to 137,000 tons. The depression in ship repairing was even worse and the number of their skilled men in Dublin was declining. He argued that it was essential to have work to keep the plant and their men going, so as to take advantage of any improvement in trade. Throughout the lean period the yard had not closed for one day, but this was solely due to the generosity of their parent company. The help and encouragement from their chairman and the work placed with them by the B & I Company, had assisted considerably in keeping the workers in employment. Without this support, it would have been difficult to keep the yard going.

Ridgeway went on to note how shipbuilding and the ship-repair industry in Ireland were not protected: 'The government has expressed sympathy with our industry and they must realise the importance to a port like Dublin. I understand that avenues are being explored, with a view to assist the industry in some way. There are 550 employees including 52 young people. The wage bill is £1,500 (pounds) and profits are reinvested, all are paid trade union rates and not one penny has been paid in dividends to Vickers Ltd.' He went on to state that if support was not given to the company that they would have to consider the advisability of continuing the industry in the port. His next remarks raise an interesting insight into the nationalist feeling in the country at the time: 'We have to meet statements to the effect that our company is not nationally owned. I think it should be known to those interested in such statements that Vickers Ltd purchased and reopened this yard in 1923 after protracted negotiations and on the advice and at the request of prominent Irish citizens, whose only interests were those of Dublin and the Irish Free State. Since then we have never ceased in our efforts to increase our turnover, our repair work has increased gradually and the *Kilkenny* launched by us today is the fiftieth craft launched by our yard.' Ridgeway ended with these telling words: 'I, therefore extend to anyone who may desire that our company should be nationally owned, and who will realise the possibilities of the company, if nationally supported, an invitation to get in touch with me, and they will find us helpful and reasonable.'

This speech should have been seen as a wake-up call and warning by the Vickers main London board as to their thinking and participation in the Dublin facility. However, it did not bring about any action or response, even though it was made in the presence of the responsible minister, Mr Seán Lemass. Just over ten weeks later *The Irish Times* headlines on Monday 28 June 1937 read: 'Blow to Dublin Industry – Shipbuilding Yard to Close'. The report said: 'The Dublin shipbuilding and engineering firm of Vickers (Ireland) Ltd, better known as Dublin Dockyard, have announced their intention of closing down as and from 31 December this year. The first intimation of the decision, which came as a surprise to the Dublin business circles, was conveyed to the employees on Saturday morning, when notices were posted on the premises … An *Irish Times* reporter learned yesterday that before the company decided to close down, the position was fully explained to the Minister for Industry & Commerce. In a communication addressed to Mr Lemass about a week ago, Messrs Vickers Armstrong Ltd of London pointed out that the company was the proprietor of virtually all the capital of Vickers (Ireland) Ltd, having purchased in 1923 the silent premises and plant of the Dublin Dockyard, with the intention of providing shipbuilding and ship-repair facilities in the Port of Dublin. During the period of operation of the company since 1923, the results to the shareholders have been disastrous, so that, in addition to the capital invested in purchasing the concern, and to some extent in re-equipping the works, a considerable sum has been lost in trading. The directors were convinced that the unfortunate results of this undertaking were in no way attributable to management and staff, but had been due to circumstances outside their control. They understood that on several occasions the difficulties under which the company was being operated had been brought to the notice of the Free State government. In 1935 Mr Lemass was informed that the views of the shareholders then were that, failing an immediate improvement in the trading results and prospects of the company, they would find it necessary to take steps to close down the works and shipyard. The results of the company for 1936 and trading prospects for 1937 were such that no justification could be seen for the company continuing to operate any longer than it was necessary to complete the contracts, which it had on hand, and the board of Vickers (Ireland) Ltd had been informed that steps must be taken to ensure the final closing down of the company by December 31 next.'

The letter to Lemass said: 'My directors regret that it has been necessary to take such a step, and appreciating, as they do, that continuation of the yard may be regarded as a necessity by the Free State government, they are anxious that everything possible should be done to ensure the continuity of affairs should the government or any other party wish to purchase the yard with a view to carrying on the business of the company. I am, therefore instructed to inform you that every possible help and information will be given by the board and officials of Vickers (Ireland) Ltd to the government or any other interested party who may be desirous of negotiating for the acquisition of our business.'

The Irish Times' report concluded with: 'the Lord Mayor of Dublin (Alderman Byrne) intends to call a meeting of all the Dáil deputies for Dublin with a view to urging on the Minister the desirability of taking over the yard as a national concern.'

That same month, on 17 June, the London board meeting minutes noted that 'Vickers Armstrong Ltd had agreed to extend the advances [loans] totalling £36,000 for a further period.'[17] The following month on 15 July 1937, the minutes recorded: 'A copy of a letter sent by Vickers Armstrong Ltd to the Minister for Industry & Commerce was laid on the table, of the decision to close the works of Vickers Ireland Ltd by 31 December 1937 and it is resolved that action be taken and is hereby confirmed.' No discussion took place at this Vickers main board meeting. All further references to the Dublin operation in September and October of the year, deal only with financial matters such as the loan of money by Vickers Armstrong Ltd to their Irish subsidiary and the repayment time of loans made.

The yard did not cease operation at the end of the year as proposed. The minutes of the first London board meeting for 1938 held on 20 January reported that 'an advance of £5,000 made by Vickers Armstrong to Vickers Ireland due for repayment on 9 December 1937 has been renewed with the same interest. The only one outstanding item noted.'[18] That same meeting under the heading: 'Sale of assets; with reference to minutes Ref. 1530 15/6/37, closing down of Vickers Ireland – It was resolved that acceptance of an offer by the Dublin Port & Docks Board to acquire for £15,000, the premises, plant, machinery, stock etc. of the Dublin Dockyard be and is hereby ratified. A copy of a letter 31/12/37 from Vickers (Ireland) Ltd, to the Dublin Port & Docks Board, confirming various conditions of sale, was laid on the table.'[19] While the Port Board owned and leased the land, the machinery was the property of Vickers.

Governmental Concern

Papers in the National Archives, Dublin, show that despite a lack of public action, the shipyard was very much on the official

193

mind at the beginning of 1938. There are letters from two state departments each enclosing a memorandum about the Dublin Dockyard.[20] These were to be placed on the cabinet table for the meeting that week. The first, dated 10 January, set out the position as seen by the Department of Industry and Commerce, while the second, dated 14 January, was from the Department of Finance and specifically addressed the Industry and Commerce document in disparaging terms. As a result Industry and Commerce withdrew their document the morning of the meeting.

The Department of Industry memorandum set out the history of the yard and its purchase by Vickers, with the comment that by the end of 1935 the company had lost £40,000. It also revealed that the Queenstown Dry Dock Shipbuilding & Engineering Company at Rushbrook, County Cork, which was taken over by the Furness Withy group in 1917, had requested a 10% subsidy toward wages in 1924, which was granted and ran from October of that year to March 1926, at a total cost of £3,500 to the state. It outlined the need for a ship-repair yard in the state and of the negotiations between the Dublin Port & Docks Board and the Vickers Company to buy the machinery for £15,000. It laid out a possible structure of a new company with 50% of the shares to be held by the board and the remainder controlled by the Industrial Credit Company, an Irish government bank. Finally it said efforts were being made to induce the trade unions to accept the same rates as Belfast and the Clyde paid, but so far without success, and noted that any new company would have labour difficulties.

The Finance document took a wide look at the shipbuilding industry both in Ireland and abroad, and pointed out that Dublin was on a level playing field with all shipbuilding material and equipment duty free. A Liffey yard would never be profitable, as repair work would only be 'patching up', to allow a vessel to proceed to Belfast or Birkenhead for permanent repairs. In view of the importance of wages, Industry & Commerce had put the cart before the horse in reaching an advanced stage of talks with the Dublin Port & Docks Board before reaching agreement with the trade unions on the matter of wage rates. The ICC was not in a position to take on any more financial commitments as it did not have money.'

That same Friday, 14 January 1938, the *Irish Independent*, reported the previous day's Port & Docks meeting under the headline 'Port Board to take over dockyard' and continued: 'The committee formed to deal with the problem raised by Messrs Vickers' decision to cease operations, has agreed to acquire the Dublin Dockyard on behalf of the Dublin Port & Docks Board pending the formation of a new company to take over and work the yard. This development was disclosed at a meeting of the Port Board yesterday, when it was stated by the chairman (C.M. Kelly) that the committee had had numerous meetings with the government, the outcome of which had been very helpful.'

On 3 March the *Irish Press* ran the headline 'May Not Cease says Port Chairman.' It went on to report 'indignation that the Dublin Port & Docks Board intended to suspend all negotiations for the reorganisation of Vickers Ltd until the shipyard was closed down. "It is a complete misrepresentation of the position," C.M. Kelly, chairman of the board said. "The board's anxiety from the start has been that the shipyard, the only one of importance in this part of Ireland, should not close down even for a day. While it was not the board's function, we went to the government and arrangements were got under way to have a new company formed to continue the shipyard." He said the new company might be ready to take over the day that Vickers Ltd ended their connection with the yard at the end of the month.' Meanwhile, Vickers in London noted at their meeting on 7 March: 'With reference board minutes, Ref. 1530 (15/7/37) and 1656 (20/1/38), relative to the closing down of Vickers Ireland, it was resolved that the board of Vickers Ireland be hereby instructed to take necessary action to liquidate the company voluntary at the appropriate time having regard to the various matters that they may decide should be disposed of prior to liquidation.'[21]

The next development in Dublin was an article in the *Irish Press* of 31 March 1938, which read: 'Position of Dublin Dockyard. Important reference is to be made at today's meeting of the Dublin Port & Docks Board on the future of the Dublin Dockyard, which closed down today. Having purchased the site from Messrs Vickers, who have decided to cease operations, the board may at an early time make decisions as to what company or interest will take over. All construction jobs and ship repair have been finished this week. For several weeks only a skeleton staff of 70 or 80 men carried on. The Dublin Trades Council recently proposed that the Government, Corporation and Port & Docks Board should co-operate towards a solution of the problem.' The article also noted that Major Hollwey, principal of the shipbroking firm of George Bell & Company, agents for Lloyd's of London in Dublin, had told the *Irish Press* that he believed a scheme was being arranged by which the close down would prevail only for a very short time.

In the following day's *Irish Press* the headline on the front page was 'Dockyard Contract Approved'. The article reported: 'The contract between Vickers (Ireland) Ltd and the Dublin Port & Docks Board for the continuance of the activities of the Dublin Dockyard Company were submitted to the Port & Docks Board yesterday and approved. No information as to the terms of the contract is forthcoming, but an *Irish Press* reporter understands that the formation of a company is being arranged and the interested parties being the Department of Industry & Commerce, Messrs Vickers (Ireland) Ltd and the Dublin Port & Docks Board. It is the concern of everyone connected with the venture that the temporary period of unemployment at the dockyard will be of short duration.'

The following Monday, 4 April, the *Irish Press* reported: 'Satisfaction at the action of Mr Seán Lemass, Minister for Industry & Commerce, in promoting a scheme for the continuance of the

Dublin Dockyard was expressed at a meeting of the Associated Smith Workers Association, held at 32 Lower Gardiner Street, Dublin yesterday.'

In London the board meeting held on 19 April noted: 'It was resolved that the action taken by the Directors of Vickers Armstrong in the following matters is hereby ratified. No. 1. In making on 7/5/38 a temporary loan of £1,000 free of interest to Vickers Ireland and No. 2. In purchasing from the former Directors of Vickers (Ireland) Ltd, 200 shares of £1 each in that company at par. Following these purchases the whole of the issued shares of Vickers Ireland is now beneficially held by Vickers Armstrong.'[22] However, the Dublin yard still needed more money, as the minutes of the London meeting on 16 June reported: 'That a further temporary loan was made by Vickers Armstrong to Vickers Ireland on 26/5/38, free of interest making a total advance of £1,250 was noted.'[23]

The next reference in the newspapers of the time was on 30 June, when the *Irish Press* reported that 'negotiations with a view to form a company to acquire the Dublin Dockyard and its operations are still in progress and it was hoped that a satisfactory outcome would be reached soon.' Again on 26 August, under the heading 'Conference to be held Today', *The Irish Times* posed the question: 'Will the Dublin Dockyard be taken over by the government and operated as a national concern?' prompted by the arrangements made by the Department of Industry & Commerce to hold a conference with department officials, and representatives of the Dublin Dockyard and the men's trade union. The following day the same paper reported that this conference had been held on the previous day and that the meeting had been adjourned to a later date.

The final reference to the Dublin yard at London board meetings occurred on 15 December where it was noted that the final meeting of Vickers (Ireland) Ltd in voluntary liquidation, was held on 15 November 1938.[24] Thus ended the involvement of the major English industrial group in Ireland. All the Vickers staff returned to Britain with the exception of George Ridgeway, who remained on in Dublin to act as the agent in Ireland for the Vickers Armstrong group. Any further steps taken in 1939 to reopen the yard were unsuccessful and the Port of Dublin was once again left without a large shipbuilding or repair capacity. The small Ringsend Dockyard Company was left to provide limited ship repairs to vessels using the harbour.

CHAPTER 6

HOW DUBLIN KEPT IRISH SHIPS SAILING IN THE 'EMERGENCY' YEARS

In writing about ship repair in Dublin during the Second World War, one again has to encompass a much wider view of those years, when outside events both at home and in Britain and beyond impinged on work on the Liffey. The Second World War broke out on Friday 1 September 1939, when at 4.55 a.m., the old German dreadnought *Schleswig-Holstein*, opened fire from the harbour of the Free City of Danzig with her 11-inch main armament on the Polish fortress of Westerplatt, just six miles away, while at the same time Hitler's army crossed the frontier. However, the German preparations for the war at sea had commenced on 16 August, when the Naval High Command sent telegrams in code to all commanders including Admiral Donitz, then head of the German submarine fleet, to report to Kiel for a 'Reunion'. Two days later sixteen ocean-going U-Boats departed to take up their stations in the Atlantic Ocean to the north, south and west of Ireland, covering the main shipping routes into the United Kingdom. On Sunday 3 September, Britain and France declared war after Germany refused to withdraw from Poland.

On that Sunday evening, at 4.30 p.m., the Type VII German submarine U-30 was on the surface south of Rockall to the north-west of Ireland, when smoke was sighted to the east. The submarine dived and in the gathering dusk, at 7 p.m., a ship was spotted on a converging course with the U-Boat. Seen through the periscope the vessel 'was large and blacked out [showing no navigation or steaming lights] and was zigzagging and appeared to be armed'. The submarine's captain, Lieutenant Commander Fritz Julius Lemp, concluded that she was a British Armed Merchant Cruiser and as such was subject to attack. At 7.40 p.m. he fired three torpedoes, only one of which struck. However, when the U-Boat surfaced, Lemp discovered he had made a terrible mistake and instead of sinking a naval auxiliary as he thought, he had in fact torpedoed the Donaldson Atlantic Liner *Athenia*, 13,580 tons gross, outward bound from Glasgow to New York with 1,103 passengers, including 311 Americans aboard. Three merchant vessels and three British destroyers raced to the scene following the liner's distress call and they picked up all but 118 persons, who included 28 Americans. Neutral Ireland became involved at once, as the Norwegian cargo ship *Knute Nelson* made for Galway with 430 survivors, who were transferred to the passenger tender *Cathair na Gaillimhe* and landed on Tuesday 5 September.[1] The United States ambassador to Britain, Joseph P. Kennedy, sent a delegation to Galway to assist his country's citizens. One of this party was his second eldest son, John Fitzgerald Kennedy, who twenty-one years later would be the first Irish-American to become president of the United States.

The sinking of the *Athenia* and the arrival of the survivors was headline news in all the Irish papers. The torpedoing without warning of this unarmed passenger vessel caused a huge political storm because the U-Boat's commander had not transmitted a signal to inform Admiral Donitz of his error, which would have given Berlin warning of his terrible mistake, but instead they were left completely in the dark. Technically the U-30's commander had been ordered to maintain radio silence, but in such extreme circumstances he should have used his wireless. This led to a cover-up by Germany and the U-Boat's war log was altered to conceal the sinking.[2]

The day before, Saturday 2 September 1939, members of both the houses of the Oireachtas had been recalled from their summer recess to meet in special session, 'for the purpose of considering such measures as may be proposed by the government for protecting the interests of the state in any emergency arising from the present international situation'. The Dáil debated and passed the final stages of these emergency bills, including the decision to declare the state neutral after midnight. At 2.30 a.m. these bills went to the upper house, the Seanad, which finally adjourned *sine die* at 4.50 a.m. on that fateful Sunday, having passed all the emergency legislation.[3]

A government statement issued on Sunday evening and quoted in the following morning's newspapers, outlined the provisions of the emergency legislation, entitled the 'Emergency Powers Order 1939', conferring special powers on members of the government which were 'necessary for dealing with the national emergency arising from the war which has broken out in Europe'. Sections of this legislation were of particular interest to the maritime sector as under the heading of 'Shipping' it stated: 'An Order has been made by the government, prohibiting the flying by Irish ships of any national colours other than the Irish national colours – namely, the tricolour green, white and orange. Every Irish ship is now to fly the said colours on all occasions on which they are required by law to fly the national colours.' The second paragraph said: 'The same order requires the sanction of the Minister for Industry and Commerce to every transfer of registry of a ship to and from an Irish port and also to every transaction involving the mortgage or change of ownership of an Irish ship, aircraft or part of an aircraft including chartering and letting on hire' (this Order No. 2 came into force on 7 September).[4]

The first result of these regulations was that British owners with ships registered in Irish ports transferred them to the UK registry, an action which the government was powerless to stop as most or all were outside their jurisdiction. It must be recalled that following the creation of the Irish Free State in 1922, this country was a member of the British Commonwealth of Nations and as such all Irish ships flew the British merchant marine 'Red Duster' as their ensign. Indeed there are recorded instances in the 1930s of the masters of Irish ships in British ports being charged by British Customs and being convicted in court for flying an improper ensign, i.e. the tricolour. The only vessel after 1922 legally wearing the tricolour as her ensign was the Fishery Protection cruiser *Muirchu*, which was joined in 1937 by the chartered and newly built trawler *Fort Rannock.*

The exodus of ships included all the cross-channel passenger and cargo vessels of the London Midland & Scottish Railway Company. While they had Dublin as their port of registry, they were manned from Holyhead and their crews at once refused to sail under a neutral flag. A second group of vessels to leave was a small whaling fleet, consisting of the factory ship *Sourabaya* and some catchers, operated by Charles Salvensen of Leith, which were registered in Dublin to take advantage of the Irish Free State whaling quota. The most important group of ships transferred the day before the shipping emergency rules came into force were seven motor oil tankers, each about 14,000 tons deadweight. These were named after Irish rivers with the prefix *Inver* and completed in 1938. These had been intended to transport oil to the refinery which Seán Lemass attempted to have built in Dublin port. Lord Inverforth had arranged to construct these vessels at the German yards of Bremer Vulcan and Howaldtswerke with German war reparation money. This fleet, totalling 97,000 tons deadweight, was owned by Inver Tankers Ltd of London, part of the Andrew Weir group of companies.

When the refinery project was put in abeyance, Lord Inverforth considered selling these ships to Japan, but the British government exerted strong pressure not to sell overseas because of the looming threat of war. The Irish authorities were even asked if they would requisition the ships for use by Britain, but they replied that it was against their policy to requisition the vessels, instead offering to transfer them to the British register. This transfer took place on 6 September 1939 and British files note that: 'The Éire government attached no conditions of any kind to the transfer of flag and were most helpful and gave every assistance in securing the use of the ships for His Majesty's government.' In hindsight, this was not the most sensible move, as during the conflict Ireland became totally dependent on tanker tonnage under British and Allied control to supply its petroleum needs.[5]

All of these Inver vessels were sunk during the hostilities, the first being the fully loaded *Inverliffey*, 9,456 GRT (gross registered tons), which was sunk by torpedo and gunfire from U-38 on 11 September. The commander of the submarine, Heinrich Liebe, at considerable risk to his submarine, towed the tanker's lifeboats clear of the blazing ship. This U-boat sank the Dublin trawler *Leukos* with a single shell off Tory Island six months later on 10 March 1940. Her disappearance and loss with all hands remained a mystery for over forty years.

The loss of the *Inverliffey* was the subject of questions in the Dáil on 27 September, when the number of ships registered in the state on 1 September 1939 was discussed. Seán MacEntee, TD, the Minister for Industry & Commerce said there were 123 Steamships of 98,000 GRT, and of these 11 vessels amounting to 18,968 tons had been removed from the register list since that date. Ten of these required ministerial approval. Also there had been 365 motor vessels amounting to 88,494 tons and of these 7 ships of 65,277 tons gross had been removed. All of these required the Minister's consent. The number of sailing vessels was 92 with a tonnage of 5,464 gross. There were 1,549 fishing vessels with unknown tonnage. The Minister reported that the ships transferred with government consent belonged to two companies: one which had been taken over by the British government for the prosecution

203

of the war and the other because the trade for which the vessels were originally constructed had not materialised.

Patrick McGilligan of Fine Gael asked the Minister for Industry and Commerce to state the number of Irish ships as defined in Emergency Powers (No. 2) Order and tonnage that had been sunk since 1 September and the circumstances of such sinking. The Minister replied that no ships had been lost and went on to say that an oil tanker, the *Inverliffey*, was sunk on 11 September. The registration of the vessel in Ireland had been closed on the 8 September and all the formalities in connection of the registration of the vessel in the United Kingdom had been complied with, in so far as they could be completed in respect of a vessel at sea. General Richard Mulcahy, TD, asked if, when the ship was sunk, she was flying the Irish flag and if representations had been made to the German government on this matter. The Minister replied that he had no information. This drew further opposition questions, including whether the master knew at the time of sinking of the change of registration? Further exchanges took place until Professor O'Sullivan asked the Taoiseach if he would answer the questions. Éamon de Valera replied that he thought enquires had been set on foot to ascertain the facts of the sinking. This debate concluded when Mr Esmonde (Fine Gael) asked if the Minister was aware that the British Ministry of Information categorically stated that the *Inverliffey* was flying the Irish flag and that the master protested to the commander of the submarine, that his ship was flying the Irish flag?[6]

It must be recalled at the time of writing over seventy years later that the Irish-owned merchant fleet was then small, with coastal, short sea traders and schooners, and no ocean-going ships. The neglect of the previous seventeen years of the maritime sector since the establishment of the Irish Free State and the lack of attention by successive governments to develop or even retain ocean-going merchant shipping would have very grave repercussions for our small neutral country. Even as late as 1935, the Limerick Steamship Company had sought assistance from de Valera's government to hold onto their two largest cargo vessels, the *Kilcredane* and *Knockfierna*, which were laid up off Cobh owing to the worldwide shipping slump, but without success.

The shipping sector in Ireland now became directly affected by events in Britain and overseas. As early as 27 September 1939, leader of the Labour party William Norton, TD, proposed in the Dáil that the government purchase a considerable amount of deep-sea tonnage before it became impossible because of war losses. The following day Patrick McGilligan repeated the same proposal in the House, but nothing was done, although even at that early stage the government of de Valera was concerned about possible shortages and one of their first moves was to encourage companies importing grain, tea and timber to come together and establish central purchasing agencies to import their requirements in bulk. The first blow to Irish imports came in November 1939, when the United States government ordered all American merchant vessels not to enter the 'War Zone', which was defined as east of a line drawn from Iceland to Northern Spain. This required that all cargoes carried in ships flying the 'Stars and Stripes' would have to be landed at Lisbon in Portugal for transhipment.

When the war broke out there were only three graving docks in the Irish state capable of accepting the large vessels of that time, but only two of these were in usable condition. The only working yard was the Ringsend Dockyard Company in Dublin, with its small facility inside the Grand Canal Basin on the south bank of the Liffey. Entry was restricted to small coasters and the largest ship which could be accommodated was under 148 feet in length overall and the capacity of their machinery shop was limited. The 412-foot long Dublin Port & Docks Board graving dock at Alexandra Basin was available, but without anyone to run it. The other graving docks were at Cobh and Limerick city. However, the dock at Rushbrook, with a length of 550 feet, was part of the former dockyard which had closed in the late 1920s and had not been used since that time. The dock in the Treaty city was owned by the Limerick Harbour Commissioners with a length of 428 feet, but again there was no local repair company operating there. The former Dublin Dockyard premises and machinery purchased by the Dublin Port & Docks Board for £15,000 in 1938 remained unoccupied and unused throughout 1939. Indeed at the AGM for that year of the Port Board held on 11 January 1940 and reported in the following day's *Irish Press*, the board chairman Captain Alan Gordon, re-elected for a second year said: 'I cannot hold out any hope of a re-start of this yard, meanwhile the machinery has been kept up and looked after.'

Despite these problems, the Irish facilities were then very much in the official mind of the British government according to files at the Kew National Archives. Those from 1940 to 1942 provide a most interesting background about ship-repair operations in the neutral state, with the uses of Dublin in particular as seen from the viewpoint of the British capital. They give an insight into the official government thinking of the time and reveal information about British and other non-Irish vessels repaired there. The first relevant document, dated 4 March 1940, is a letter written by Richard Ferguson, secretary of the Department of Industry & Commerce, and addressed to G.C. Duggan of the Ministry of Shipping in London, informing him that there was no change in the position at the Dublin Dockyard, as Industry & Commerce had been unable to find any commercial operator on either side of the channel to reopen the yard.[7] Ferguson went on to refer to the idle Rushbrook dockyard as being bought pre-war by John Lysaght Ltd of Newport, Monmouthshire, to manufacture galvanised metal sheets. Six days later Duggan replied, stating that Lysaghts, who purchased the yard in 1937 'have no direct interest in ship repair and that a report should be got from someone on the spot as a matter of urgency'. The same yard is mentioned in a letter from the Cunard White Star office in Belfast which stated: '… there are moves afoot to provide finance and support to Rushbrook and Passage West dry docks at present.' On 5 May 1940, there is an internal note from the Ministry of Shipping to Mr Powell at the Admiralty asking that 'some expert be sent to Rushbrook and Haulbowline to see what would be involved in this as an emergency ship-repair centre and the desire to see en route the facilities at Ringsend Dockyard and Dublin Dockyard closed, so as to complete the picture'.

The Irish newspapers of 1940 carry almost nothing about ship-repair facilities or the lack of same, although the *Irish Independent* on Monday 8 April ran a news item reporting that the Cork Chamber of Commerce had received a reply to their letter sent to the Department of Industry & Commerce, requesting that the derelict yard at Passage West be reopened as a national shipbuilding and repair centre. The letter from Dublin stated that the Minister was of the view that there was no prospect of any company being interested in any shipbuilding or repair yard in the country because of the record of such undertakings, but that he would persist in efforts to induce competent shipbuilding interests to discuss the matter. On June 4 the *Independent* carried another item: 'Dublin Dockyard to reopen soon?' where it referred to the previous night's meeting of Dublin Corporation, at which: 'Mr J. Larkin expressed the opinion that the Dublin Dockyard would reopen soon and provide work for 300 or 400 men.' Despite this, nothing happened for a number of months.

On Tuesday 2 October 1940, *The Irish Times* reported 'Dublin Ship Swept by Bullets', and printed a photograph showing the deck of the steam trawler *Kosmos* owned by the Dublin Steam Trawling Company. This trawler, under Skipper J. Leadbetter, was attacked by a German aircraft twelve miles south of Barra Head in the Outer Hebrides off the west coast of Scotland on Thursday 27 September. There were no casualties and the repairs costing £170 were carried out by the Ringsend Dockyard. The ship returned to the fishing grounds on the same day as the newspaper story was published. An official protest and claim for damages was lodged with the German government by the Irish Embassy in Berlin, which was met with the reply that the ship was within a war zone and therefore subject to attack. This was the tenth attack on neutral Irish vessels since the outbreak of hostilities.

The Dublin Dockyard Reopens

The first definite mention of re-activation of the Dublin Dockyard premises is found in *The Irish Times* of Tuesday 15 October. With the headline 'Dockyard to Start Work in a Few Days', the news item stated that the yard would start ship repairing work in the next few days and that the new Irish company which purchased the yard had been registered the previous day under the title Liffey Dockyard. On Friday 18 October, all the national newspapers carried news of the reopening, with headlines such as 'Dockyard Equal to Shipping Demands' (*Irish Independent*), 'Ready for All Repairs – Work Restarts at Dublin Shipyard' (*Irish Press*) and 'The Liffey Dockyard Preparations for the Reopening' (*The Irish Times*). The two most informative reports are those carried in the *Irish Press* and in *The Irish Times*. When the directors of Liffey Dockyard Ltd took formal possession of their newly acquired property, the reporters were shown over the dockyard by Captain Alan S. Gordon, chairman of Liffey Dockyard Ltd, and W.R. Murdoch, managing director of the new concern. *The Irish Times* records the latter saying: 'We can undertake all the repair work of Irish ships and six or seven times more. The equipment is adequate for any type of repair work and we can deal with repair jobs immediately with stocks already here. The machinery, if not the latest type, is such as to enable us to compete very satisfactorily. Under present circumstances we should be able to get the yard going with the minimum of difficulty and organised in such a way as to face competition when normal times are restored.' He added that the Port & Docks Board had kept the place in good condition and gave them credit for their foresight.

In the *Irish Press* Captain Gordon is reported as stating: 'Though the labour arrangements are not fully completed, they indicate that we shall have a satisfactory time in the yard. The prospects are bright, and in a short time we expect there will be plenty of work coming to the yard.' The paper went on to note: 'All efforts to restart the dockyard since Messrs Vickers Ireland closed in 1937 were without success until some months ago, when a group of Irishmen came together and in spite of many difficulties secured control of the yard.' The report continued that Captain Alan Gordon, who was largely responsible for establishing the new company, was chairman and managing director of Palgrave Murphy Ltd. *The Irish Times* commented that 'the new company was fortunate in securing the services of Mr Murdoch, who has much experience of shipbuilding work. He served his time in Harland & Wolff's, Belfast, and having taken a degree in engineering at London University went to his father's yard in Antwerp and when war broke out was doing a considerable business in ship repairing in that port. He was a senior partner in the firm Messrs Guthrie, Murdoch & Co., Antwerp, and did much repair work on the vessels owned by companies in which Captain Gordon is interested.' The *Irish Press* reported that another director, R.W. Synott, was present, along with J. Mallagh, engineer of the Port & Docks Board. *The Irish Times* noted that J. Lennox Marks was the manager of the new company.

The following week, on Tuesday 22 October, both the *Irish Press* and *The Irish Times* carried photographs of the Wexford-owned motor ship *Begerin* being repaired in the Alexandra Basin graving dock. The *Irish Press* also ran a small item on the same day under the heading: 'Busy Stocks at Ringsend Shipyard. Repairs have been completed to the Wexford-owned vessel *Edenvale* by the Ringsend

Dockyard (Dublin) Ltd. Also undergoing repair by the company at the Alexandra graving dock is the M/V *Begerin*, owned by Mr H. Wilson of Wexford'. The report went on to say: 'These are two of the many vessels which have been repaired by the company since its inception in 1912, the work embracing vessels ranging from colliers to 10,000 ton deep water cargo vessels.' The Ringsend yard directors had obviously invited the newspapers to see the work being done in their yard to counteract all the publicity generated by the reopening of the former Dublin Dockyard on the north bank of the Liffey.

A letter dated 12 October 1940 from Captain Alan S. Gordon, to the British Corporation of Shipping & Aircraft in Glasgow, confirmed that he hoped to have the Dublin dockyard opened quickly: 'We shall have men clearing and getting ready for work early next week, and we should be able to undertake repair work within a fortnight or three weeks.' He then goes to say that 'Mr Murdoch of Guthrie Murdoch & Co. of Antwerp, who had done very efficient work for us, is over here, and we have arranged that he will be in charge of the Dublin yard. The name of the yard will be Liffey Dockyard Ltd.'[8] The records in the Companies Office in Dublin show that the Liffey Dockyard came into existence on 14 October 1940 with an authorised capital of £75,000 in £1 shares. The first named directors were Alan S. Gordon, £1,000 (Palgrave Murphy), William Robert Murdoch, £1,000 (shipbuilder), Robert W. Sinnott, £1,000 (B & I SP Co.), James Stafford, £1,000 (Wexford Steamship Co.) and Raymond Augustine Burke £500 (shipbroker). The last named was a shipping agent from an old established family of agents in Belfast and Derry who came to Dublin just before the war and opened an office at 22 Eden Quay. Mr Burke had taken over the business of John Weatherall and Sons Ltd, a long-established Dublin firm of shipowners and agents, who owned a number of sailing ships at the end of the nineteenth century. That company had represented Greek shipowners in

Dublin, while Messrs Burke were the Greek owners' agents in Northern Ireland.

The other major subscribers to the new dockyard company were the Bank of Ireland with £2,750, the National Bank with £1,000 and Palgrave Murphy Ltd with £2,000. Two well-established British shipping companies also took shares: MacAndrews & Co. Ltd of Mincing Lane, London, with £2,000 and the United Baltic Corporation Ltd of London, also with £2,000. Both of these firms were associated with the Andrew Weir group and in addition there were other Irish shareholders.

The late Pat Walker, who was a fitter in the new yard, recalled that the first vessel to be dry docked by the new firm in 1940 was the *Haifa Trader*, which would be flying an Irish flag the next time it entered port.[9] It must be remembered that during the war the only source of steel plate and the marine engineering equipment needed for repairs was Britain and these items were in extremely short supply. They required first their release from stock or manufacture in Britain and then export permission from the Director of Merchant Ship Repairs (DMSR), before shipment to Dublin. A case had to be made to the DMSR in respect of each vessel requiring repairs. During a Dáil question time on Wednesday 11 December 1940, Seán MacEntee, the Minister for Industry & Commerce (Mr Lemass having been made the minister in charge of the new wartime Department of Supplies) told Alderman Alfie Byrne that 'the methods by which an increase in the number of Irish registered ships could best be effected have been under consideration for some considerable time.' He hoped to come to a conclusion at an early date. So far as shipbuilding was concerned, he had in mind continuously the desirability and possibility of reviving it. He noted that the Dublin Dockyard had at last reopened and 'the position elsewhere is under active consideration'.[10]

A memo dated 26 February from the director of the Trade Division in London to the DMSR quotes a letter from the Naval

Control Service Officer in Dublin, referring to a request for materials to carry out ship repairs in Dublin. The comment from the DMSR states that 'they had had contact with Mr Murdoch on the subject over a long period and that he was promised assistance with materials for approved jobs, on the condition that he must not take any labour from this side … So far as ordinary ship-repair materials are concerned, DMSR Materials and Priority Branch in Glasgow will attend to same on application from Murdoch.'[11] Shortly after this, the Admiralty took over direct control of all merchant ship repairs from the Ministry of War Transport. In a letter to Laurie Edwards at the DMSR dated 24 May 1941, J.R. Binmore, who was based in Belfast, stated:

> Visited Dublin yesterday and spent a few hours with Mr Murdoch the general manager, discussing the position. With regard to the repairs carried out there, and for which facilities for materials have been granted, the following applies:
>
> SS *Seringa*: Rather extensive hull damage. Repairs completed 19 March 1941.
>
> SS *Michaelios*: Reconditioning and repairs (boilers, machinery and hull) commenced 14 December 1940, completed 28 April 1941.
>
> SS *Miraka Polopapa*: Reconditioning and repairs (machinery and hull), started 5 December 1940, completed 8 February 1941.
>
> *Georgio G*: Machinery and hull repairs commenced 29 December 1940, completed 26 February 1941.
>
> SS *Dirphys*: Hull machinery and boiler repairs commenced 3 February 1941, completed 28 April 1941.
>
> SS *Culebra*: Started 29 January 1941, completing 24 May 1941.[12]

Mr Binmore also listed the extensive damage to the *Lady Connaught* (of the B & I Company), which had been mined in the River Mersey on St Stephen's Night and had 8 feet of water in the lower hold. She was patched up in Liverpool before being towed to Dublin for permanent repairs and conversion to a cattle-carrying vessel. That work commenced on 15 April, but was halted on 10 May pending a decision whether to replace her boilers. She was repaired and used as a livestock vessel for a while, but was later fitted out as a hospital carrier for the Normandy landings in 1944.

Reference is also made to the *Wild Rose*, 873 tons gross, on which repairs commenced on 18 May and were due to finish on 18 June. This Liverpool collier had been attacked by aircraft on 2 April, 12 miles south-east of the Tuskar Rock while on passage from Dublin to Cardiff. The Wexford-owned motor ship, *Kerlogue*, on a voyage to Cardiff from Wexford, answered the distress rockets of the Liverpool ship, rescued her crew, towed her to the Irish coast and beached her at Rosslare to prevent her sinking.[13] The *Kerlogue* was awarded £4,000 salvage money.

Mr Binmore also refers to a self-propelled discharge vessel owned by Ranks Ltd in Limerick, the *Garryowen*, 483 tons gross, used to lighten grain ships at the Beigh Castle anchorage in the lower Shannon. She was repaired in the local graving dock. Her tail shaft was drawn, stern bush replaced and some plates renewed, the work being carried out by labour from the Liffey Dockyard, with the damaged parts being sent to Dublin by rail, repaired and returned the same way to Limerick.

Binmore also mentioned that the yard was likely to deal with the *Cetvriti*, a Yugoslavian ship, for which purchase by the Irish Shipping Co. was being negotiated. Towards the end of the letter he quotes Mr Murdoch saying that he had between 350 to 420 men in his employ, a sufficient number considering the fact that the yard's capacity for repairs was limited by the availability of the dry dock, which was constantly in use. The letter concludes with Binmore's comment that the yard had difficulty in getting payment for the repairs made to the Greek ships mentioned. The charges amounted to £18,500, yet he had only received £9,400 and had just been informed by Mr Edmenson, the Ministry's representative in Belfast that 'the delays to the completion of the repairs to the *Culebra* may have been due to the incidence of financial considerations.'[14] Pat

Walker recalled being instructed by Hugh Lennox, assistant yard manager, to test the steering gear of the *Culebra* on 30 May 1941, the morning after the bombing of the North Strand in Dublin.

The interest of London in the Liffey Dockyard and also in Rushbrook, County Cork, was understandable. By December 1940 there was a huge backlog of repair work in UK shipyards of about two million tons, which was 13% of the whole British merchant fleet. By February 1941 there were 2,593 merchantmen under repair of which 1,585 ships were totally disabled. This serious situation resulted not only from war damage repairs, but also the extensive repairs needed to First World War standard cargo vessels which had been purchased from American lay-up fleets. These purchases had commenced after June 1940 and many of those ships were in a deplorable condition, but because of the high dollar costs in American yards, they were only patched up there and sailed to Britain for permanent repairs.[15]

More Difficulties For Neutral Shipping

We must also look at the wider picture of wartime shipping and the shortage of tonnage then being faced by Ireland and other neutral countries. On 14 June, the Limerick Steamship Company vessel *Maigue* was being broken up at Britain Quay, having gone aground off the south coast.[16] A sad aspect of Irish maritime affairs at that time was that, in spite of the dire shortage of vessels, there was no overall person such as a director of shipping, who could decide the best use of our tiny shipping resources at that critical time. The *Maigue* and at least five other vessels like her, which might have been repairable and could have gone into service, were broken up due to a lack of overall strategy.

Apart from British and Allied vessels bringing cargoes to Éire ports, there were other ships, which after discharge in an Irish port were unable to sail. In most cases this was caused either by their homelands joining the enemy Axis or being invaded by the enemy – these included vessels from Denmark, Estonia, Greece, Italy and Yugoslavia, most of which then hoisted the Irish ensign for the duration of the war, but needed major repairs before returning to sea. The first ship to be so trapped was the *Caterina Gerolimich*, an Italian steamer of 5,200 tons gross, owned by Gerolimich & Company of Trieste, which arrived in Dublin on 9 June 1940 from the River Plate. The next day, Monday 10 June, Italy declared war on Britain and France, which ensured the vessel remained tied up until Italy surrendered. The second vessel so trapped in Dublin was the Estonian steamer *Piret*, of 2,668 tons gross, owned by the Tallinn Shipping Company and built in 1902, which arrived in September 1940 and was unable to leave because of the invasion of Estonia by the Soviet Union.

Towards the end of 1940 matters became very serious on both the shipping and political fronts. Grain Importers Ltd, Dublin, one of the group purchasing companies established by the government, reported that they were unable to charter a single ship to carry grain other than those already organised. Three vessels had been sunk by U-boats en route to Ireland with cargoes of timber and grain.

It was not known publicly at the time that the Irish requirements for tonnage were being channelled through the British Ministry of Shipping charter office. The Irish government did this to oblige Britain, who complained that competition between them was pushing up the charter rates for neutral ships. In addition Éire got space on British ships and other vessels controlled by Britain and it is estimated that this facility was equivalent to the capacity of forty ships. However, in the late spring of 1940 the War Cabinet in London decided to put pressure on Dublin for not co-operating with the demands for storage and transhipment facilities at Irish ports as part of the Anglo-Irish Trade Agreement. Discussions on the problem had commenced in April 1940 and although an agreement had been reached with Britain on 19 August, it had been vetoed by de Valera in November, apparently because of his fear of German air attacks. On 6 December 1940, Chancellor of the Exchequer Sir Kingsley Wood, in response to memos from the prime minister concerning Irish agricultural imports, presented two plans to the War Cabinet. The first 'would make the [Irish] population feel uncomfortable in a few weeks' and the second would be 'economic war'.

In the eyes of Winston Churchill, neutral Ireland was the villain for not allowing the Royal Navy use of the Treaty anchorages handed back in 1938. Churchill sent a letter on 13 December 1940 to President Franklin D. Roosevelt of the United States, in which he bemoaned the denial of these ports in the fight in the north Atlantic against the U-boats. In scathing terms he wrote: 'In the meanwhile we cannot undertake to carry any longer 400,000 tons of feeding stuffs and fertilisers which we have hitherto conveyed to Éire through all the attacks of the enemy. We need this tonnage for our own supply and we do not need the food that Éire has been sending us … You will quite realise that our merchant seamen, as well as public opinion generally, take it much amiss that we should have to carry Irish supplies through air and U-boat attacks and subsidise them handsomely when de Valera is quite content to sit happily and see us strangled.'[17] De Valera later answered Churchill with a forthright speech in the Dáil, where he stated the position on neutrality with clarity and frankness.

Sir Kingsley Wood told the cabinet that Irish space on British controlled ships had been reduced and he proposed to tell the Ministry of Shipping not to give Éire any charter facilities at all. Earlier cargoes had been imported to Ireland on Greek vessels, but the Greeks and Norwegians were now to be told that they should not charter ships 'except to the allies or co-operators'. The result would be that 'Éire might get if she was very lucky, ten ships, which would give her 25% of her needs'. At a War Cabinet meeting on 2

January 1941, it was decided to go ahead with these sanctions and the chancellor added that 'the Ministry of Shipping will find itself unable to fix ships for Éire without, for the moment, making any official announcement. Later when the ministry had control of all available Norwegian and Greek ships, it would release Éire from her undertaking to charter through Britain. The Norwegians and Greeks would be told that they must not charter any of their free ships to Éire.' Some consolation was given by the cabinet in allowing Irish or neutral ships engaged in Irish trade to sail in British convoys.[18]

The New Year opened with further difficulties for the merchant ships of all neutral states, when on 1 January 1941 *The Irish Times* carried an official notice from the British trade commissioner in Dublin informing exporters from Éire that they must obtain a 'Navicert' or navigation certificate for shipments to certain countries, which would be issued by his office. That same paper the next day carried a follow-up news item on the 'Effect of the British Order' reporting that the majority of the countries listed were neutral apart from Greece, and that the United States and other countries in the western hemisphere were not included. It went on that 'the making of the order at the present time has no significance … It merely puts Éire in the same position as other neutral countries.' A 'Navicert' would not be required if the ship travelled via Britain. What this new law meant was that, for example, an Irish vessel on a voyage to Spain or Portugal had to load an outward coal cargo for Lisbon at a British port to avoid the need for a 'Navicert', where sailing instructions would be given showing the courses to be steered, prohibited areas to be avoided and the recognition signals for Allied warships when encountered. On the return passage from Lisbon an Irish ship would have to call at Fishguard in Wales for examination by a British navy boarding party. Vessels on Atlantic voyages would normally bunker at Ardrossan, Scotland, where they would join a convoy or receive their routing papers if sailing independently.

An example of the seriousness of the position at that time is contained in copies of letters from the secretary of Grain Importers (Éire) Ltd, A.S. Whitehead, dated 9 July and 15 August 1942, addressed to Liam Furlong of the Department of Supplies, which listed the number of ships lost on passage to Ireland, 'with full or part cargoes of wheat and/or maize'. These were all foreign and the schedule opens with the sinking of the *Germaine* on 15 December 1939 while loaded with 7,400 tons of maize. There were a further ten vessels sunk in 1940, including the Belfast steamer *Kenbane Head* carrying just over 1,000 tons of wheat in November. The last vessel listed is the *Penang*, sunk on the 6 February 1941 loaded with 3,193 tons of wheat. In all there were seventeen vessels sunk with the total loss of 43,097 tons of wheat, 37,303 tons of maize, 2,640 tons of pollard and 349 tons of bran, all of which this neutral state could ill afford.

Because of these events, it was driven home to the government that the shipping situation was now desperate and to survive, a deep-sea merchant marine fleet had to be established. A committee had been formed in 1940 to examine the problems associated with the operation of a fleet of merchant vessels and at the annual dinner of the Federation of Irish Manufacturers on 19 February 1941 the call was made again for the formation of a deep-sea fleet. On Monday 24 March *The Irish Times* announced news of the formation of Irish Shipping Ltd and that ships were to be acquired by the government for such a fleet. The previous Friday a meeting had been held in the Department of Supplies at Earlsfort Terrace, Dublin, chaired by John Leydon, at which the national shipping company known as Irish Shipping Ltd was officially established. John Leydon would become Chairman of Irish Shipping. The new enterprise would have a share capital of £200,000, with 51% held by the Minister for Finance and just over 43% held by Grain Importers Ltd, with the remaining percentage divided equally between the Limerick Steamship Company, Palgrave Murphy Ltd and the Wexford

Steamships Company, who each provided a director to sit on the board. The Minister for Finance took back all these shareholdings on behalf of the government in 1943.

The objectives of the new shipping company were: 'To acquire, operate and maintain a deep-sea merchant fleet in order that the country's economy and people could survive the course of the war.'[19] Urgency was the keyword and thirty vessels were seen as the minimum needed, if the pre-war levels of imported cargo were to be carried. As the new company did not have experience of operating ships, the management of any vessels taken over were placed with the established shipping companies of the day, who appointed directors to the board.

The main question, which had to be addressed, was how and where to obtain ships in the middle of a world war? Most states were reluctant to dispose of tonnage and Britain and the other warring nations had a total restriction on selling ships from their flags. However, eleven days before the Earlsfort Terrace meeting, agreement had been reached to buy the first vessel for the new Irish semi-state company. She was the *Vassilios Destounis*, a 29-year-old steamer of 3,282 tons gross for which Samuel Roycroft of Limerick Steamships, who would be a director of the new semi-state firm, had offered £120,000 through the Irish consul in Spain, although the figure of £142,000 is also mentioned.[20] She had been abandoned in the Bay of Biscay after an air attack off the north-west coast of Spain and brought into the port of Aviles by Spanish fishermen, who received £80,000 for their salvage efforts. Captain Matt Morgan from Wexford was flown to Spain via Lisbon to take the vessel over but when, together with the mate and chief engineer they went to Aviles, they discovered the ship had been moved to Vigo in Spain. When delivered to Irish Shipping Ltd on 9 April 1941, they found that the vessel was little more than a hulk, as everything not screwed down had been looted and the wireless had been sized by the Spanish authorities. This 6,100 tons deadweight vessel had been completed in October 1912 by Earl's Shipbuilding and Engineering Company Ltd, Hull, Yorkshire, as the *Withernsea* for W. Brown Atkinson & Co. Ltd, of that port. She was sold four years later in 1916 to Cardiff owners and again in 1918 to a West Harlepool company and once more in 1920 to Cardiff ownership. She remained under the British ensign until 1933, when she was bought by P.B. Destounis and renamed the *Vassilios Destounis*. She retained this name when sold in 1937 within Greece to P.E. Panis & Company, her owners when she was attacked.[21] She was renamed the *Irish Poplar* by her new owners.

A number of other 'Rust Bucket' vessels were acquired by the new company, either by charter or by purchase. All these ships needed repairs before they could be put back into seagoing service. The first of these, the *Cetvriti*, was found on 4 December 1940 drifting and abandoned off the coast in Dingle Bay by the patrol trawler *Fort Rannock*, who put aboard a salvage crew and took her into Knightstown, Valentia Island. The *Cetvriti* was a Yugoslavian steamer on passage from Thorshaven in the Faroe Islands to Spain with a cargo of 2,000 tons of dried fish, when she was attacked by a German aircraft and the crew abandoned her. Her salvage gave rise to a number of court cases, which had to be resolved before she could sail again. The first was reported in *The Irish Times* of Saturday 4 January 1941, under the heading: 'Salvage Crew on Larceny Charge'. The report claimed that four members of the boarding party were sent for trial at Tralee District Court on the previous day, where they were accused of stealing articles from the vessel. Evidence was given by two local boatmen from Valentia that they had seen suitcases, tins of meat, a wireless set, batteries, and other goods from the cargo ship being moved to the *Fort Rannock* in broad daylight. A garda sergeant and superintendent both spoke of finding property aboard the naval vessel and the army provost marshal for the Southern Command corroborated the superintendent's evidence. The district justice returned the ship's officers for trial on their own bail of £50 each. Three weeks later *The Irish Times* for Saturday 24 January reported that a court in Kerry had on the application of the state transferred the case to the Central Criminal Court. No record has been found of the outcome of this case. Perhaps it was held in camera because of the sensitive nature of the charges, or perhaps it was quietly dropped.

The next case involving the *Cetvriti* appeared in *The Irish Times* on Wednesday 5 March, under the heading 'Salvage of Yugoslav Ship' and it carried a completely different slant. The newspaper carried details of the £5,000 sum put up by the shipowners in settlement of the salvage claims against the vessel. Of the sum, £2,525 was awarded to the state for the services carried out by the *Fort Rannock*, while the remaining £2,475 was allocated for distribution among the officers and nineteen crew of the patrol vessel.

The Yugoslavian vessel was taken to Dublin in January 1941 and purchased on 15 May by Irish Shipping Ltd from the owners Parobrodarsko Drustvo Marovic. A vessel of 2,002 gross tonnage and 3,150 tons deadweight built in 1884 in Hamburg for the Hamburg-Amerikanische Packetfahrt AG, she was sold later to other German owners before hoisting the Yugoslavian flag in 1930. She was renamed the *Irish Beech* and her repairs, costing £38,000, were carried out by the Liffey Dockyard. A figure of 36 tons of steel required for the job was mentioned in a memo dated 24 September 1941 from Mr Binmore, the Ministry of War Transport surveyor in Belfast, who was in charge of releasing the steel to Dublin. He reported that the job was due to be completed on 11 October 1941. Later that month she sailed for Halifax, Nova Scotia, to load grain.

On 17 June 1941 another vessel taken over was the *Nomejulia* of Panama, which had been in Dublin for some months and was in the process of being sold to the Hammond Lane Foundry Company for breaking up. However, having been bought for

£67,500, she was found to be in very bad condition and 70% of her steelwork, including decks, was condemned. The owners at the time of purchase were the Cia Mar de Panama Ultramar.

By the middle of 1941, there is the first suggestion that vessels might be constructed in Dublin for Britain.[22] This information is contained in a letter dated 9 June thought to be from the Admiralty to G.C. Duggan, now of the British Ministry of War Transport, where it is stated: 'The Liffey Dockyard can build steel barges for us, as they are frequently compelled to lay off platers, riveters and caulkers.' The writer asked 'if this would suit you as these could be readily delivered to our own west coast ports as compared with towing them all the way round the coast when we are building same at Faversham?' Duggan noted in the margin: 'Seems a good idea, 160 or 200 ton barges would suit, six to begin with others afterwards. 10/6.'

The Irish Times for 5 September 1941 carries a front-page photograph of An Taoiseach Éamon de Valera, followed by Captain Alan Gordon, stepping aboard the second vessel purchased overseas by Irish Shipping Ltd and the first to appear in the Liffey, which had arrived on the last day of August. The headline read: 'Wheat for Éire, New Irish Ship reaches Dublin'. The report said: 'The first Irish ship to bring a cargo of grain from America to an Irish port since the outbreak of war has docked in Dublin. Mr de Valera and the Minister for Supplies [Seán Lemass] visited the ship discharging its cargo at Alexandra Basin. The cargo amounted to 6,188 tons of wheat.' This was the *Leda*, which had come from New York via Halifax. She had been bought for £200,000 from the Cia Leda de Vapores on 3 May 1941. Originally Danish owned, she had been taken over by the Chilean government and the Irish owners took possession of her in New York. On arrival in Dublin she was renamed the *Irish Elm* and placed under the management of Palgrave Murphy Ltd. She had been constructed in 1910 as the *Collingham* for Messrs Harris & Dixon Ltd, London, by the

Sunderland shipyard of J.L. Thompson & Sons Ltd. The 4,199-tons gross vessel remained in port for another seven months for repairs, as mentioned by Binmore in another memo: 'Repairs being to main engines and alterations to existing accommodation.'

Both *The Irish Times* and the *Irish Press* mentioned that before he left the port, de Valera went to a ship in the next berth, the *Irish Beech*, 'to inspect the survey work now in progress'. This appears to have been de Valera's first of two visits to the port during the war years. This second vessel was also under the management of Palgrave Murphy Ltd.

On 8 October, the *Irish Poplar* finally berthed from Lisbon with her cargo of grain and when dry docked by the Liffey Dockyard, she was found to be in poor condition. After repairs lasting two months she sailed for St John, New Brunswick, on 20 December 1941. Two weeks later, on 23 October, the *Irish Willow* entered Dublin from Cobh where she had been taken over by Captain Gordon of Palgrave Murphy on behalf of Irish Shipping. She was another Estonian vessel, formerly the *Otto*, whose crew and owners had refused to sail back to the Baltic after the invasion of Estonia by the USSR. However, in telling her story and that of other former Baltic vessels, which sailed under the Irish flag, we must go back to the beginning of that year when the first of a number of court cases for their possession commenced in Dublin.

THE USSR CLAIMS OWNERSHIP

The legal battle for the Estonian and Latvian flag vessels first appears in *The Irish Times* for Saturday 4 February 1941 under the heading: 'Four Estonian Ships Lying Idle – Proposal to use them for Irish Trade'. This reported that an application had been made to the Master of the High Court to extend the time for filing statements of claim for the possession of four ships. There were three actions brought by the Latvian Ambassador in London and the Consul General in Éire in respect of the SS *Ramava* of Riga, by the Honorary Vice Consul of Estonia in Éire, John McEvoy, on behalf of the *Otto* of Parnu and by John McEvoy and Captain John Veldi in relation to the SS *Mall* and SS *Piret* both of Tallinn. The cases were brought to seek directions from the court for the best course to pursue. In all these the Union of Soviet Socialist Republics (USSR) had claimed an interest in the ships arising from the alleged incorporation of the republics of Latvia and Estonia into the USSR, 'an action, which we regard as confiscatory and not recognised by the government of this country', according to Brereton Barry (for the shipowners). On Thursday 11 February, *The Irish Times* under the headline: 'Foreign Ships in Irish Waters – Negotiating for Charters', reported the next appearance in the High Court before the president, Mr Justice Hanna, where A.K. Overend, KC, contended on behalf of the Soviet authorities, who claimed to own these vessels, on the basis that the USSR was a sovereign independent state and that the courts in this country could not interfere. According to the report Mr Justice Hanna decided that 'the matter would have to be tried as he would not deal with it as a motion'.

A report of the hearing appeared in *The Irish Times* of Wednesday 30 April, under the headline: 'Foreign Ships in Éire – Application by the USSR' which gave a summary of the preceding day's case. Mr Overend, opening for the USSR, claimed that 'the Soviet Ambassador to Britain, Mr I. Masiky, had written on 9 August 1940 in reply to a verbal inquiry from Mr J. Dulanty, the High Commissioner for Éire in London, stating that two Estonian and one Latvian ship carrying timber would be allowed to call at ports in Éire'. The letter apparently said that the Soviet authorities had no objection to the vessels proceeding to Éire, providing that the government gave guarantees that after unloading they would obtain bunkers and food sufficient for the return voyage to a Soviet port. Overend submitted that Mr Dulanty had recognised that Mr

Masiky was the proper person to give instruction to the ships. In the next day's proceedings Mr Barry stated that the USSR were only claimants to vessels, over which they had not succeeded in establishing any control. At that hearing, the SS *Everoja* of Riga was included in the action.

In *The Irish Times* of Saturday 17 May the reserved judgement of Mr Justice Hanna was given. He had dismissed the claim of the USSR to the four ships and gave four reasons: 1. That the court had asked the government whether the USSR could be recognised as a sovereign independent authority over the states of Latvia and Estonia. The Minister for External Affairs intimated that the government of Éire did not recognise the USSR as the sovereign government of Latvia and Estonia; 2. That since the sovereignty of the USSR had not been established, the vessels were not the property of the USSR and the orders given by radio telegram to the various masters must be treated as being without legal authority; 3. That in fact the vessels were never at any time in the possession of the Latvian and Estonian governments or of the USSR, and remained at all times under the masters on behalf their respective private owners; 4. The immunity for state vessels did not apply to these vessels and for these reasons he dismissed the various motions by the USSR with costs.

The Soviet Union appealed Mr Justice Hanna's decision to the Supreme Court, where the four sitting judges dismissed the appeal and affirmed the order of the High Court, as reported in *The Irish Times* on 4 July 1941. However, this was not the last word, as *The Irish Times* headline on page one of Saturday 9 August 1941 proclaimed: 'Soviet Protest to Éire'. It reported: 'A most emphatic protest has been made by the Soviet Union to Éire against the decision of the Éire Supreme Court dismissing the USSR's claim to the ownership of two Latvian and three Estonian ships in Éire ports. It was made known yesterday that M. Maisky, the Soviet Ambassador in London has addressed a note to Mr J.W. Dulanty, the High Commissioner for Éire in London.' The note describes Mr Maisky's dismissal of the decision as 'illegal and detrimental to the interests of the USSR, and the Soviet reserves its right to take what measures it may deem necessary'. It continued: 'The Soviet government places full responsibility for the decision in question and their consequences on to the Éireann government, and reserves its right to draw the necessary conclusions and take what measures it may deem necessary including all claims for losses and damage sustained.' Nothing more was ever heard of this posturing, as the USSR had more important issues to deal with following the advances made by the Germans after their June invasion.

Only the three Estonian ships traded for Ireland during the war. The first taken over was the *Otto*, built in April 1918 by the Toledo Shipbuilding Company, Toledo, Ohio, for the US government as the *Lake Sunapee*. She was a vessel of 2,003 tons gross and 3,000 tons deadweight and was chartered for the duration of the war plus three months on 3 October 1941 from her owner K. Jurnas of Parnu by Irish Shipping Ltd. She was renamed the *Irish Willow* and placed under the management of Palgrave Murphy Ltd. After dry docking and extensive repairs in Dublin, she sailed on 7 December for St John, New Brunswick, to load grain, the same day that Japan attacked Pearl Harbour and the United States entered the war. While the Latvian ships are not part of our story, for the record the *Ramava* (2,100/1900) had gone to Britain on 28 August. The *Everoja*, 4,340 tons was torpedoed on 3 November 1941 by U-203, while on passage from Canada to Dublin with 6,400 tons of wheat.[23]

MORE CONCERNS IN LONDON

An interesting memo is stored in the Kew files, which apparently dates from late October/early November 1941. This is headed 'Éire and ship-repair facilities at Dublin and other Éire ports'. The opening paragraph notes that 'an application has been received from the agents of the ship and semi-officially from the Department of Supplies in Dublin for the release of 610 tons of ships' plates for the repair of the *Irish Hazel* (formerly the *Nomejulia*) now under the Irish flag and presently at Dublin. This is one of the old and inefficient ships which the Éire government has recently purchased.' The document continues with details of the Liffey Dockyard dry dock, together with that at Ringsend. It also mentions the Limerick dock as being little used, goes into a lot of detail about the facilities at Cobh and refers to the Rushbrook yard.[24] The memo noted: 'It has been suggested that the Éire government are considering taking over and equipping the Rushbrook yard, but it must be borne in mind they will have to seek the importation of the required repair machinery.'

The letter writer pondered: 'The Liffey yard has been of substantial assistance to the war effort and the question is whether in return for that assistance, or in order to ensure its continuance we should place at the disposal of Éire, not only steel for repairing British ships but also the steel necessary to carry out work on Éire ships. There is no source, except the United Kingdom, from which steel can, in practice, be drawn by Éire.' He concluded that 'the balance of advantage, the assistance we receive from the Dublin Dockyard facilities and now to be augmented by the Rushbrook yard, well repay the release of steel for repairs'. The letter notes that 92 tons of steel was sanctioned for the *Kerry Coast* engaged in the Irish Sea cattle trade and that work on that ship at the Dublin yard was expected to be finished at the end of November, while in the case of the *Lady Connaught*, an allocation of 100 tons of steel had been made. These two vessels, although owned by the B & I company, were under the British flag. The document ends with the very interesting statistic: 'In the period 1 October 1940 to 30 March 1941, seventeen UK ships were repaired in Dublin and during the twelve months ending 30 September 1941, thirty-four UK ships were repaired at that port. The total cost of the latter repairs is estimated at £50,000 sterling.'[25] All of these repairs were done at Liffey Dockyard.

The major repair work needed by the *Irish Hazel* generated a lot of correspondence between Belfast, Dublin and London. On 14 October A.N.C. Horn of the Marine Division of the Ministry of War Transport noted: 'Re request for release of 610 tons of steel for *Irish Hazel*, understand from our principal officer at Belfast, Mr Binmore, that steel not now required for some considerable time owing to the following circumstances. It is understood [she] is practically a wreck and would take Liffey Dockyard six months to repair and rebuild and in view of other work they have in hand, they do not feel disposed to take up their yard for that period. It is understood that ship will be repaired at Rushbrook, but before that can take place the yard will have to be put into commission and necessary plant imported. Éire government to form company to carry out this.'[26]

In a memo of 16 September Mr Binmore added: 'That they [MOWT] had refused steel for her repair to Liffey Dockyard, when she was in former ownership and on charter to Swiss interests.'

In London Mr T.C. Jenkins of the Ministry of War Transport noted on 17 October: 'Mr Leydon told me yesterday her repairs were postponed due to Liffey Dockyard being full and added if the yard was really capable of handling the job? He asked if the ship could be repaired on this side. I told him it was a difficult request, as our facilities were none too good for our own ships and these would be immobile for a long period and that the balance was not easy to strike.'[27]

Mr Horn, on a handwritten page dated 29 October, quoting the shipping journal *Fairplay* of 23 October, noted that a Panamanian steamer, the *Arena*, was reportedly being sold to the Irish government according to the New York press. This vessel caused letters to be exchanged between the two capitals. Mr Leydon writing on 14 November, referring to this ship, says he agreed with getting ships repaired abroad and that this policy was followed where circumstances permitted.[28] However, he concluded that the government had been sorely disappointed at the length of time repairs had taken in Philadelphia and that the ship had not yet sailed. This drew a reply from T.C. Jenkins, with an apology for not making himself clear about the *Arena*. He knew that the ship was being repaired in USA and stated 'we were anxious that she be fully repaired and not just patched up to get over here, so she would arrive and require no further work on this side'.

December 1941 saw no less than three more ships acquired overseas by Irish Shipping arrive in the Liffey. The first to tie up on 11 December was the *Irish Pine*, with 7,000 tons of grain from St John's, Newfoundland. She had been built in Seattle in 1919 as the *West Hamatte* of 5,621 tons gross for the US shipping board and had been chartered for £3,251 per month from the War Shipping Administration. They had initially refused to lend ships to Ireland on the instructions of the State Department, but President Roosevelt overturned the embargo and allowed the charter. She was taken over on 23 September 1941 at New Orleans and renamed. It is interesting that two previous ships offered by the Americans were turned down on the grounds that they were turbine propelled and thus too technical for the Irish yards to deal with. Less than a year later the *Pine* was sunk while on passage from Dublin to Boston and Tampa. She was torpedoed on 16 November 1942 by U-608, and sank in three minutes with the loss of all hands.

On St Stephen's Day 1941, the *Irish Larch* arrived from St John's, Newfoundland, via Reykjavik, where she had been forced to put in for repairs. She was a vessel of 3,192 tons gross, built in 1903 as the *Tregothan* for the Hain SS Co. Ltd of St Ives, Cornwall, and was the former *Haifa Trader* mentioned earlier of the Palestine Shipping & Trading Co., purchased for the sum of £85,000 on 28 July. Managed by the Wexford Steamships Company, she remained under repair until May 1942.

The last vessel purchased abroad to arrive was the *Arena,* which berthed on 28 December 1941 from Philadelphia, having finally sailed from there on 28 November.[29] She was another First World War American standard design ship, constructed in November 1917 by the Standard Shipbuilding Corporation, Shooter's Island, New York, for the US shipping board as the *Jupiter,* of 4,670 gross tonnage. Although she wasn't taken over until 23 September at a cost of £345,950 from the American port, the agreement to purchase the *Arena* had been reached two months earlier when she was lying in Durban. On arrival in Dublin she was renamed *Irish Plane* and placed under the management of Palgrave Murphy Ltd. In spite of the repairs already mentioned in the USA, she had to be put into the hands of the Liffey Dockyard for further work. The story of her purchase gives an idea of the worldwide searches that had to be made by the new company to obtain suitable ships, wherever and whenever they could be found.

SHIP-REPAIR BOTTLENECK

At the start of 1942 a major ship-repair bottleneck was developing in Dublin, because as we have seen no less than eight Irish Shipping vessels had arrived, or had been taken over, in the port since the middle of 1941, all of which required repairs and docking. While three of the ships, the *Poplar, Beech* and *Willow,* had sailed, five were still in port, with the *Elm,* the *Larch* and the *Hazel* needing major work. Moreover, in early January a further four vessels were in the process of being acquired by the new state company, while a fifth ship, the *Irish Oak* had been lying at St John, New Brunswick, since November 1941, with serious engine trouble. It must be remembered that the Liffey yard had been re-established as a commercial undertaking, not just for the repair of Irish tonnage, and that the yard was also carrying out a lot of work on British and Allied ships. The repair of such vessels on this side of the Irish Sea released space in British yards and freed berths for badly damaged merchantmen and warships.

The Ministry of War Transport must have agreed to repair the *Irish Hazel*, needing, as we have seen, 610 tons of steel. The *Hazel*, a vessel of 2,489 tons, had been built in November 1895 by R. Ropner & Son at Stockton on Tees as the *Barlby* for their own shipping company R. Ropner & Co. of West Hartlepool. For her repairs she was allocated to Baileys Dry Dock Co. Ltd and sailed for the Bristol Channel. However, when completed in November 1943, she was requisitioned by the Ministry, renamed the *Empire Don* and was only returned to Irish Shipping in September 1945. This may have been because as the *Nomejulia* the ship had been British registered since 1933 and had only hoisted the Panama flag in 1940 after war broke out, while retaining her manager in London. It is possible that she had changed flag without the permission of the British authorities and this caused her to be reclaimed. Another matter not generally realised is that during the war Irish ships, even though neutral, were considered British by the UK and as such are listed among the vessels lost by enemy action and inscribed on the British Merchant Navy war memorial at Tower Hill in London. The British authorities therefore may have felt quite justified in commandeering the ship.

Two days before the departure of the *Irish Hazel* from Dublin, agreements were signed to charter two more Estonian-owned ships trapped in Ireland. The first of these was the *Mall*, which berthed at the south quays on Sunday 25 January 1942 from Waterford, where she had been laid up since 1940. Placed under the management of the Wexford Steamships, she was renamed the *Irish Rose*. Four months later in May she left for Barry to be fitted with a new propeller and then proceeded to Cardiff to be 'wiped' for protection against magnetic mines.[30] She departed on 26 May, for St John, New Brunswick, where she loaded grain for Waterford. Owned by the Tallinn Shipping Company Ltd since 1930, she was another

American built vessel of 1,863 tons gross, constructed in July 1918 by the American Shipbuilding Corporation at Lorain, Ohio, for the US shipping board as the *Lake Harnley*.[31]

The second Estonian ship, taken over on 12 January, this time in Dublin, was the *Piret,* which had been laid up on the south quays since September 1940 and was also owned by the Tallinn Shipping Company. This 2,668 ton gross vessel was chartered for £945 per month, plus a lump sum of £7,500 for the duration of the war. She had been built by S.A. John Cockerill at their Hoboken yard at Antwerp in 1902 as a speculative venture and was named the *Princess Elisabeth.* However, when taken over by Irish Shipping she was found to be in very bad condition and in need of extensive repairs, as during the Russian Revolution she was blown up and sunk by Bolshevik forces, and later raised and repaired. The vessel was to be put in the hands of the Ringsend Dockyard, but they declined to carry out the repairs. Perhaps the scale of the job was too great, which was the deciding factor for Mr McMullan, the managing director of the dockyard. Also in early 1942, the schooner *Mary B. Mitchell* was in the hands of the Ringsend yard for underwater repairs. The *Irish Alder,* as she was now named, was handed over to the Liffey Dockyard in mid February, where she remained for two years. In January 1944 she sailed to Port Talbot to load 2,000 tons of coal on her first voyage for the company and had to be repaired again at Rushbrook before making her first passage to Canada on 17 February 1944.[32]

During January 1942 the *Irish Larch* was moored at the North Wall Extension with both masts removed and in early March she entered the graving dock and remained there until late April when her masts were re-stepped. Meanwhile the Ringsend Dockyard Company had the Wexford-owned but London-registered motor ship *Goldfinder* in their dock for the month of March. On 19 April the Wexford Steamships motor vessel *Kerlogue* entered the same dock.[33]

The *Irish Elm*, which had been in the hands of the Liffey yard since mid September 1941, sailed on 10 March 1942, about the same time as the *Irish Plane* left for the Clyde to load bunkers and to obtain British clearance. Having departed the Clyde on her outward passage to St John, New Brunswick, she ran aground on Tor Point, Cushendun, County Antrim, on 14 March and was not re-floated until 1 April. She returned to Dublin the following day and since the *Larch* still occupied the graving dock, the *Plane* was unable to go onto the blocks until the end of April and her bottom damage took until June to be repaired. An inquiry into this stranding of the *Plane* opened in the Four Courts on Thursday 4 February 1943, presided over by Mr McCann with Captains Hickman and Hanrahan as assessors, who requested that it be held in camera.[34]

The *Irish Larch* left Dublin on 1 May for County Cork, where she was the first vessel to use the graving dock at Rushbrook since the late 1920s. That yard had just been reopened as the Cork Dockyard Ltd, a subsidiary of the semi-state shipping company, which created extra repair capacity with full use of the 550-foot long graving dock. This yard remained as part of Irish Shipping until it was sold to the Dutch Verolme group at the end of the 1950s, when that company took over the yard and commenced building ships as the Verolme Cork Dockyard Ltd. Around the time the *Larch* left, another ship was bought in Dublin outright for £85,000 by Irish Shipping Ltd. She was the *Vicia*, of 2,502 tons, owned by A/B Transport Kristian Hansen of Finland and built in 1896 by Furness Withy & Co. Ltd, West Hartlepool, as the *Carlham* for the Thompson Steamshipping Co. Ltd of Sunderland. Although purchased on 20 April 1942, negotiations to buy the ship had commenced the previous July and by September 1941 she was laying at Quebec. Walter Kennedy records her for the first time in Dublin on 11 October 1941.[35] However, at this point the *Vicia* was detained under a warrant taken out by four of her officers and this order had to be lifted by the

High Court, before the ship could be purchased. On 27 January 1942, *The Irish Times* reported that the officers were only receiving two meals a day and disputed their dismissal. The matter was again mentioned in the same paper on Friday 17 April, when Mr Justice Hanna was asked to approve the sale of the ship, liberty for which had been granted by the Master of the High Court. The judge said the detention would continue, but it was later lifted.

On Monday 29 June, *The Irish Times* carried the report: 'Irish Vessel's Trial Run', stating that the *Irish Plane*, with Captain Hill Wilson as Master, made a trial trip in Dublin Bay with Mr de Valera aboard. Other passengers on that occasion were Frank Aiken, Minister for the Co-ordination of Defensive Measures, John Leydon, Chairman of Irish Shipping, J.J. McElligott, secretary of the Department of Finance and Captain Alan Gordon, a director of the Liffey Dockyard. The report noted that the ship carried a crew of thirty-four Irishmen.

At the beginning of July 1942, the eighth ship acquired overseas by Irish Shipping eventually arrived in Ireland and berthed on 6 July at Alexandra Quay, Dublin. This was the *Irish Oak*, which had been forced to put into St John, New Brunswick, the previous November. In April she had been towed to Boston, where her machinery was repaired by the Bethlehem Steel yard. She left Boston for Dublin on 16 June, but was forced to return, setting sail again four days later. The 5,588 ton gross vessel had been taken over from the US Reserve lay-up fleet at New Orleans the previous September, from where she sailed on the last day of that month, and had taken no less than seven months to make the voyage to Dublin. Built at San Pedro, California in 1919 as the *West Neris*, she was chartered for £3,245 per month from the US Maritime Commission. She was torpedoed in the Atlantic by U-607 on 15 May 1943, while on passage from Tampa to Dublin. Her crew were picked up four hours later by the *Irish Plane*, which returned to Cobh and landed the survivors.

SHIPBUILDING FOR BRITAIN?

The question of the construction of vessels for Britain in neutral Ireland comes to light for the first time in the middle of 1942. The only Irish government reference known is in a Department of External Affairs document: 'Discussions to Build Ships for Britain at Dublin and Rushbrook Dockyards'.[36] The slim folder contains just two pieces of paper, the first of which is a letter from the British diplomatic mission in Dublin, marked 'Secret' dated 17 July 1942 and addressed to F.H. Boland of the Department of External Affairs. Boland at that time was the assistant secretary of the department. The letter read:

> My Dear Boland,
> In confirmation of my conversation with you on the telephone this evening I write to let you know that we have received a telegram stating that the Admiralty have in mind the question of placing through a commercial agent in Dublin an order with a Dublin shipbuilding company for a small number of minesweeping trawlers. The Admiralty, however, are anxious to be assured that if this were done the trawlers will not be requisitioned in Éire. We have been asked to approach you informally with a view to ascertaining whether the Éire authorities would be prepared to give such an assurance.
> W.C. Hankinson

The second document marked 'Most Secret' is headed 'Extract from Mr Leydon's report to the Minister for Supplies on his discussions in London, July 1942. Par. 9':

> I raised the question of shipbuilding in the dockyards at Dublin and Rushbrook, explaining that I was doing so merely on an exploratory basis and I was not in a position to say what view Irish Ministers would take; you will remember that I discussed this with you before I went to London and I had also discussed it with Mr Boland of the Department of External Affairs. I said that I thought that it might be possible to make an arrangement under which if the British would

supply the materials, we might build ships on a fifty/fifty basis, but that we would want the first ship from each yard. They told me that, while the Ministry of War Transport has a very direct interest in this, control of shipbuilding is in fact exercised by Sir James Lithgow, who is a member of the board of Admiralty, but the Ministry of War Transport has a very close liaison with the Admiralty about this matter, and Mr Alderson, who is I gather Sir James Lithgow's deputy, discussed it with me over the telephone on two occasions.

Mr Jenkins told me privately before I left that he had mentioned the matter to his Minister who favoured the proposal, and I gathered from Mr Alderson that the Admiralty are also in favour of it, but we did not of course get down to any details. They raised the question about the type of vessel to be built and the availability of labour; they had in fact heard nothing about the possibility of shipbuilding at Rushbrook, but the managing director of the Liffey Dockyard had already been in touch with Sir James Lithgow about it. I told them there was a certain pool of skilled labour, which may not be fully occupied with ship repairs and it might be possible to train additional labour once the job is undertaken. I said that the labour at Rushbrook is rather 'green', but that I thought an effort might well be made with proper supervision to get them actually engaged in shipbuilding. I said the type of vessel we would favour for our own purposes would be ships of about 8,000 tons deadweight capacity; they had been thinking of cargo vessels of about 4,700 tons deadweight which would suit their purposes very well and could probably be built much more quickly. At a later stage Mr Alderson told me that the Admiralty had now begun to think of placing orders in the Liffey Dockyard for vessels he described as 'Puffers'; I gathered from Mr Jenkins that these are steam barges of less than 1,000 tons capacity and generally in the region of 500 tons. I said that the type of vessel to be built would be a matter for further consideration and it was agreed to leave the matter at that stage until we can see more clearly what the yard can do.

Mr Leydon knew all about the Irish industrial situation and it should be recalled that the largest ship ever built at the Alexandra Basin was the *Glenstal*, which was of similar tonnage to that quoted. As chairman of Irish Shipping Ltd he was well aware that the

Rushbrook yard had just reopened and docked its first ship since the 1920s and that the new workforce was not fully experienced. His proposal would mean that in return for constructing ships, Ireland would get modern tonnage for the national shipping fleet. On the margin of the letter is written: '28/7 no action'.

Information about both the thinking and the political considerations which came into play at this time can be gained from a number of sources kept in files in the National Archives at Kew.[37] The first is a letter dated 25 June from Sir James Lithgow to Mr Duggan, in which he states: 'In conversation with Murdoch of Liffey Dockyard who thinks he has the capacity to build ships. So far as I can see from the material situation, we could well afford to let him have steel and machinery, if he can supply labour. I had in mind to get Murdoch here and suggest that he look for an order for one 4,700 vessel on private account or account of his own government and we confine ourselves to giving him facilities for the material. This raises the question of high politics and one I would like to get some guidance on before I go into the matter.'

The next British reference is a letter dated 30 June, from Mr Duggan to Sir E.J. Foley and copied to T.G. Jenkins, one of those mentioned in Leydon's report. Duggan mentions the possibility of the Liffey Dockyard building 'a number of 4,700 ton vessels on private account for the account of the Éire government, the Admiralty giving facilities as regards steel and provision for the machinery'. In his next paragraph he records: 'We had opened discussions unofficially with the Éire government about Liffey Dockyard being reopened and building coastal vessels for the Ministry. Nothing came of this scheme because private interests acquired the yard as a repair yard and have developed it satisfactorily … As you know facilities are being given for ship-repair material to be released to the yard, the whole being controlled through the principal officer at Belfast who is in direct touch with the Liffey Dockyard Company and occasionally inspects it to see what work is going on.' His third paragraph speculates: 'If we could control the shipping output of the yard, there are certainly advantages in getting additional vessels built there, but I cannot see the Éire government allowing vessels to be built there which will not be used for the purposes of Éire trade.' He concludes that if the scheme is to be developed there must be discussion at a higher plane on the policy, which the Ministry and Admiralty should aim for.

The next three pages of this file contain written notes contributed by various people on the steps to be followed. The main thrust of the comments is that since both departments involved cannot move themselves, a position paper should be prepared and submitted to the Economic Policy Committee for Éire for a decision. This would allow some bargaining leeway for the Admiralty with Dublin.[38] Another Kew memo on 20 July to L. Morris, marine sea division of the Ministry of War Transport points out: 'if we supply materials for two ships in order to obtain one, in considering this point, no doubt you will consider whether additional vessels for the Éire flag might be charted and what relief if any to British merchant shipping would be achieved by increasing the size of the Éire fleet'. Following this, a letter written from the Military Branch of the Admiralty dated 25 July to N.E. Costar at the Dominions Office, throws an interesting light on international diplomatic relations. It states, 'we were anxious to place orders for merchant vessels in Éire' and mentions the semi-official discussions with Mr Leydon. The letter goes on to note that 'the Éire government would probably insist that for every vessel built for us, a vessel would be built for the Éire flag', and suggests that orders be placed for puffers. It continues: 'We should be glad of advice whether it is desirable to obtain any assurance from the Éire government that the vessels will not be requisitioned. We do not, of course, propose to delay placing the orders on this account ...We should welcome any advice how hard a bargain we should try and drive should Éire ask for materials for her own ships, i.e. do you attach political importance to Éire getting ships, and have we carte blanche to get as much as we can and give as little as we can.'[39]

There is another interesting letter on the matter dated 30 July from Mr Ferguson at Industry & Commerce to G.F. Braddock, the UK Trade Commissioner in Dublin, which shows the Irish side anxious to increase their fleet. The letter suggests that 8,000 deadweight ton capacity ships could be constructed for the Irish while at the same time the Liffey yard could be simultaneously building ships of less capacity. It goes on to say that the best way to make progress on this issue would be if a British expert could visit the Liffey yard and possibly Cork as well to assess the situation. Ferguson adds: 'We have just received a note from the Cork dockyard, that they had in mind to lay down two slipways, each capable of taking a 400-foot ship or thereabouts.' He concluded that the Rushbrook dock would probably be free to repair British ships from the middle of August.[40]

The next document shows that the question of shipbuilding in Éire had been referred to the highest level.

War Cabinet – Economic Policy towards Éire, Secret, 14 August 1942. Copy No. 33. Note by Minister of War Transport.

The Éire government have raised both with the Ministry and the Merchant Shipbuilding Branch of the Admiralty, the possibility of use of shipyards in Éire for building merchant ships. The prime interest of the government of Éire is to secure ocean-going ships for their own use. They must depend on this country for the materials including complete engines and equipment and suggestion tentatively put forward that ships built in Éire should be shared equally … It seems to me that arrangements on these lines would be unduly favourable to Éire. Their contribution is the use of their yards and labour. Our contribution, in the shape of fabrication of machines and complete engines is far greater than Éire's. I think we should do our best to secure that ships should be built in Éire yards for our account – we of course making proper payment for the services rendered by Éire shipyards and we should try to persuade Éire government that benefit which they would receive in finance and finding employment for Irish workers would amply repay them for facilities placed at our disposal ...

I understand some doubt whether Éire yards have technical capability of undertaking shipbuilding of ocean-going ships. There has to be a proposal that they should build puffers and their capacity should be judged on the result of the experiment. For my part I do not think that it is worthwhile supplying materials to Éire yards to build these small types, which are not in urgent demand. If the conclusion of the Merchant Shipping Branch of the Admiralty, after further investigation, is that Éire yards should not be entrusted with the building of ocean-going tonnage, I would not see any objection to their undertaking the building of a better class of coaster, say the 2/3,000 tons D.W. class, this activity would make a much needed contribution to our needs than building ocean-going tonnage.

L. [probably Lord Leathers, who had taken over as the Minister of War Transport]

The final major document concerning this issue, is an unsigned memo dated 25 August 1942, which states:

I attended a meeting at the Admiralty this morning, at which alternative proposals of building trawlers in Éire was discussed. Sir John Lithgow and other representatives of Merchant Shipbuilding Department of the Admiralty and Admiral Preston, Head of Small Ships Pool Department of Admiralty, were present. It appears Admiralty had already made considerable progress with proposal to build trawlers in Liffey Dockyard using as intermediary Sir A. Lewis, who has been involved in connection with building trawlers in Portugal. The vessels would be built as ordinary fishing type and the necessary additions to make them suitable for minesweeping etc. would be done in this country. The DNC [Director of Naval Construction] has plans and the size 140 feet is same as the 320 ton deadweight coaster which is being built in a number of yards in this country. The demand for trawlers is continuous as sinkings are ever present and the Admiralty have to draw on the remains of the fishing fleet. In order to avoid this continuous drain, they ordered a number of trawlers to be built in yards allocated to the navy. To the extent that they can get trawlers built in Éire it will enable the naval yards to return to other naval craft. I stated I believed the Minister probably will not argue the case for 320 D.W. Coaster against trawlers but it would be necessary to be satisfied that Dublin and Cork dockyard could not take bigger ships e.g. 4,700 D.W. vessels. Sir John Lithgow stated he would not advise giving an order for any bigger type of ship and he was in agreement with Sir Amos Ayre, if this were done that the ship would be a stand-by on which work would be done when ship repairs were not absorbing men. On the other hand, if small craft were ordered, the yard would concentrate on the work. In order to give the yard a real incentive to get going in shipbuilding there would be an order for three trawlers for each yard, if the proposal was to go ahead.

The general view of the meeting was that trawlers would afford the most suitable building programme for the two yards and it would be left to the naval side of the Admiralty through the intermediary of Sir A. Lewis. The Admiralty will discuss with Dominions Office. I stated that no definite action should be taken until I had informed the Minister of the views of the meeting in order that he might come to a final decision in regard to alternative of merchant [ships]. The Admiralty asked that the matter be treated as one of urgency.[41]

Two further documents conclude this episode in wartime Anglo-Irish relations. The first is a letter dated 19 September 1942 addressed to W.C. Hankinson, the secretary of the diplomatic mission in Dublin, probably from the Dominions Office, under which Irish affairs fell. It stated:

We are now able to let you know what has been decided regarding the building in Éire of ships for this country. It is not proposed to go ahead for the moment with plans for building coasters or seagoing ships, as it is thought desirable in the first place to test the capabilities of the yards concerned on less ambitious types. It has been agreed between the Admiralty and the Ministry of War Transport that the first order be placed for trawlers and not for puffers. They are earmarked for naval service but in construction they will be in all respects commercial vessels and will have no warlike fittings of any kind. At present the

Admiralty have definite plans only for the Dublin yard, but they are eager to utilise Éire's shipbuilding capacity to the utmost for vessels of the fishing trawler type, and they have in mind to place orders in Cork should things go well with first venture. There are two points which they would like to have cleared up. First, the question of requisitioning and export licences. You say in your letter of 29 July that Boland has given an oral assurance that the trawlers, if permission to build them is not withheld, they will not be requisitioned. This is of course a point to which the Admiralty attach the greatest importance – second there is the question whether it is necessary to give these orders commercial cover. They have, however, made tentative arrangements for commercial cover with Sir Andrew Lewis, an Aberdeen trawler owner, for the first orders to be placed with the Dublin yard. We should now be grateful if the whole matter could be further discussed with the Éire authorities on the basis of this letter and of paragraph 2 of my letter of 29 August.

N.E. Archer.[42]

Mr Hankinson replied to Archer on 26 September: 'Sir John Maffey [the British representative in Dublin] discussed the matter with Braddock and me and it was decided that the best plan would be that Braddock would discuss the matter further with Ferguson in the first instance. He told him the United Kingdom authorities could not agree to the suggestion that a proportion of the ships built here from materials supplied from the United Kingdom should be retained by this country. Ferguson said that he would submit our proposals to those concerned, but was decidedly pessimistic about the outcome.' This ended months of British discussions to obtain extra shipbuilding capacity in Dublin and Cork at the least possible cost to or drain on their own wartime resources. It shows that John Leydon was well able to stand up to the British pressures and was one of the outstanding civil servants of that era. Nine years later, Sir Walter Hankinson was appointed British Ambassador in Dublin and presented his credentials on Thursday 1 November 1951.

On 1 September 1942, the *Irish Fir* was noted at Alexandra

Quay discharging grain.[43] She was the tenth vessel to be taken over by the semi-state shipping company and was on her second visit to the port. Built by the German shipyard of Bremer Vulkan in 1920 as the *Agnetapark* for the Dutch Halcyon Line, the 1,472-ton vessel was sold to Chile in 1929 and became the *Margara*. Negotiations with her owners Rafael Torres y Cia to buy this ship had begun in April 1941, while the vessel was still in Chile. However, because of difficulties with her purchase, she sailed to the United States and the port of Norfolk, Virginia, where she was bought for £82,000 on 14 October 1941. Two days later she left for Limerick, retaining her original name, but before she got far she had to return to Norfolk for repairs. After sailing she suffered two more breakdowns, on 17 and 19 November, and was forced to put into Halifax on 23 November for further repairs. She eventually sailed for Limerick on 2 February 1942, where she arrived on the last day of that month. She was placed under the management of Palgrave Murphy Ltd. It was quickly discovered that she was not suitable for the North Atlantic run because of her small coal bunker capacity and it was decided to use her on the short sea routes to Britain. On her first voyage she broke down once more and had to be towed into Milford Haven, before returning to Dublin with her coal cargo. She proceeded to Rushbrook, where from 16 April she underwent repairs, including an increase in her bunker capacity to allow her to cross the Atlantic. Two months later she took coal from Port Talbot to Lisbon, where the grain cargo mentioned above was loaded.

On 23 September 1942, *The Irish Times* reported: 'New turf barges ready, completed ahead of schedule. Two out of a fleet of twenty barges ordered by the Department of Industry & Commerce will be handed over to Mr Lemass at Ringsend Dockyard tomorrow. They are 61 feet by 12 feet 6 inches by 5 feet 6 inches capable of carrying 40 tons of turf.' Two days later the paper reported the handover, when Mr Lemass and R.C. Ferguson, secretary of the department, were met by G. Brock, chairman of the dockyard and

A.V. Alexander. The report stated: 'The twenty barges were being built at Arklow, Carlow and Dublin and would be able to carry 30,000 tons of turf annually.' In the Dáil, Mr Lemass moved a Supplementary Estimate, which included £25,000 for thirty horse-drawn barges of which eight had already been delivered.[44]

The new year of 1943 was only a day old, when on 2 January the *Irish Independent* reported a labour dispute concerning a claim made by the Ship Constructors & Shipwrights Association on behalf of eleven shipwrights employed by the Ringsend Dockyard Company. Mr Alexander of the dockyard company asked that, if an order was made, any wages to be paid should not be retrospective. J. O'Brien of the association said he desired that wages be brought up to the level of those on the Clyde. There is no note of how this issue was resolved.

On the last day of January the Lighthouse tender *Alexandra* was at Sir John Rogerson's Quay with her mainmast ashore being repaired by the Ringsend yard. By Saturday 21 February her mainmast had been re-steeped. The Commissioners small tender *Ierne,* which had been built to carry construction materials for the building of the Fastnet Lighthouse was alongside. On Friday 26 February the *Irish Independent* carried a fine photograph of the three-masted schooner *Mary B. Mitchell* under sail. The accompanying caption stated: 'The vessel was being reconditioned at Ringsend Dockyard for Captain A. Dowd, Principal of the Irish Nautical College, who had resigned his position, bought the ship, which will carry a crew of eleven, all Irish, for the charter trade.'

Early in March 1943 there was another dockyard dispute, this time over heating, but the problem seems to have been quickly resolved. *The Irish Times* reported on Friday 5 March that: 'Dockyard Strike Ends – About 30 Fitters and Burners on strike at Liffey Dockyard since last Saturday owing to alleged failure of the company to supply heating in the turners shed, returned to work yesterday.' At this time the *Irish Elm* was in the graving dock.

On Sunday 27 March another Irish Shipping vessel discharged her cargo at Alexandra Quay on her first visit to Dublin.[45] This was the *Irish Ash* formerly the *Mathilde Maersk*, unloading wheat and general cargo from St John at the end of her first voyage for the semi-state company. Built in 1921 by Yarrow & Company Ltd, Glasgow, for Danish owners who named her the *Haderslev*, she was sold in 1924 to the A.P. Moller group and renamed in 1932. The 2,088 tons vessel was purchased on 27 August 1942 at Limerick, where she had been laid up since 1940 after Denmark was invaded. Having been taken over a month later she went to Rushbrook for repairs and sailed for Port Talbot for refuelling on 21 January 1943, broke down and eventually sailed for St John on the last day of that month. She was placed under the management of the Limerick Steamship Company.[46]

In May two more vessels came under the Irish flag in Dublin. The first was the *Gaizka*, purchased by the Limerick Steamship Company Ltd, which was renamed the *Monaleen* and underwent repairs at the Liffey yard. She was the only ship bought during the Second World War by an Irish company other than Irish Shipping Ltd. When purchased in 1943, this 637-ton gross ship was owned in Malta by Ortu Zara and registered in Panama and was of very particular design with a most interesting history. Completed after the Great War as the *Kilmersdon*, she was one of twenty-five vessels built by Smiths Dock Ltd on the River Wear for the British navy as anti-submarine escorts. Eighty-five in total were ordered from various yards and these were the corvettes of the 1914–18 war. They were built with a straight stem and stern to confuse a U-boat commander, as seen from under water it would be difficult to determine in what direction the vessel was going. Thirty-seven of these were commissioned into the Royal Navy as the Kil class and given Scottish or Irish place names such as *Kilbride* or *Kildare*. They had a length of 182 feet, a beam of 30 feet and their 1,400 HP engines gave them a speed of 13 knots as patrol vessels. In January

1920 fifty were sold, including the *Kilmersdon*, and converted into cargo vessels to take advantage of the postwar shipping boom, which did not last. To create greater cargo space one boiler was removed. The remaining single boiler produced less power, which made them bad steamers.[47] The 1949 *Shipping Handbook* issued by the Department of Industry & Commerce gives the engine of the *Monaleen* as developing only 600 IHP. However, she gave her Limerick owners seven years of service before she was scrapped in Dublin at Ringsend in 1950.

At the end of May 1943, the *Caterina Gerolimich*, which had been trapped since 1940, was towed into Alexandra Basin by the port tugs *Coliemore* and *Ben Eadar* from her lay-up berth downriver just inside the eastern breakwater. This place, then known to the people of Ringsend as Bengazi, was a desolate reclaimed area inhabited only by rabbits and nesting terns. There are two incidents worth recounting about this vessel during her time in this out of the way place. While she was out of sight of the public, she was certainly not out of mind of the authorities, who kept a close eye on her. According to Johnnie Donnelly from Ringsend, some time before joining the Marine Service he and two mates were at the Ringsend slipway one day, when they were approached and asked by a woman if she could be ferried over to the Italian vessel. When the lads said this was not possible, she asked them to take a letter to the ship, which they did for half a crown. However, about two days later, when a special branch car arrived at the slip and the garda officers asked about a letter being carried to the Italian ship, nobody knew anything![48]

The second event concerning this vessel was much more dramatic. In July 1940 the authorities introduced a port control service at twelve harbours in the state. This meant that all incoming ships had to stop outside the port entrance until a naval boarding party went out to check their papers. If these were in order the master was given the correct flag hoist by day or light signal by night to be displayed, which allowed the vessel to proceed into port without being fired on by a shore artillery battery. On berthing she would be boarded again and her defensive weapons would be disabled and her wireless sealed for the duration of her stay. Captain Thomas McKenna, the commanding officer of the Naval Service from 1956 to 1973, wrote about Dublin's port in this period. He recorded: 'A rather hair-raising incident occurred one day when a ship arrived and before we could board her and secure her armament she fired two rounds from her 12-pounder gun at an Italian ship, the *Caterina Gerolimich* – luckily they missed, but caused some consternation!'[49]

In May 1943 the Italian ship was put into the graving dock for survey. The vessel remained in the dock for a month undergoing extensive repairs and on 19 June she was chartered by Irish Shipping Ltd and put under the management of the Wexford Steamship Company. A vessel of 5,430 tons, launched in December 1912 by Cantire San Roco at Trieste, she was registered in Rome and owned by Imprese Nav. Commerciale Soc. Anon. She was the fifteenth and last ship to be acquired by Irish Shipping and was renamed the *Irish Cedar*. The vessel was granted a Navicert by the British as a *quid pro quo* for their seizure of the *Irish Hazel*, which allowed her to trade.

The absolute necessity of a Navicert for neutral shipping is illustrated by the case of the *Kilkenny*. The Irish Department of Supplies wanted to put the B & I motor ship *Kilkenny* onto the Lisbon trade route, she being one of only two modern vessels in the Irish merchant fleet (the other was the *Menapia*). However, the British Ministry of War Transport refused to provide her with a Navicert, presumably on the grounds that she was more useful to the war effort in carrying livestock to feed the people on the 'home front'. Moreover, while the British & Irish Steam Packet Company was nominally an Irish enterprise, it had actually been completely controlled from Liverpool since the 1920s. Without the Navicert the *Kilkenny* was forced to continue doing what the British wanted her to.

At the beginning of September, the *Irish Cedar* was alongside the south quays, resplendent in fresh paint under her new name. She was later moved to the North Wall and sailed on her first voyage under the Irish ensign in October. The *Irish Spruce*, moored on the south quay, was at the same time preparing for sea, loading stores and coal blocks as bunkers before departing for the Rushbrook dockyard, where she would remain under repair until April 1945. Further down that quay, at the entrance to the River Dodder, the trawler *Tom Moore*, owned by the Dublin Trawling Ice & Cold Storage Company Ltd, had come out of the Ringsend dry dock on 8 October. The steam collier *Oak* owned by the Newry & Kilkeel Steamship Co. Ltd occupied the same facility for a considerable period in December and only left the basin on Saturday 15 January 1944. On the north bank of the river, as 1943 closed, the Liffey yard still had the *Irish Alder* under repair in the cross berth in Alexandra Basin and by December the *Irish Elm* was occupying the large graving dock.[50]

As the new year of 1944 opened, the motor vessel *Kilkenny* was at Alexandra Quay and in the graving dock on 8 January, while the *Irish Alder* had sailed. At the end of the month the three-masted schooner *Mary B. Mitchell*, built in 1892, was in the Grand Canal Basin dry dock and she would be back in dock again on 13 May. She was followed on 19 February by the Light vessel *Guillemot* and in early March by another Arklow schooner, the *Windermere*, constructed in 1890. At that time these small sailing vessels were engaged in the carriage of wood from small ports as far away as County Donegal to Dublin for fuel. The Cork-owned coaster, *The Lady Belle*, occupied this dock on 10 June.

From the end of April 1944, all sailings from Ireland to Lisbon were suspended for security before the D-Day landings, which took place on 6 June, although transatlantic traffic was not affected.

THE FINAL WAR YEARS

By the middle of 1944 steps were being taken to address what would be the changed face of the post-war Irish merchant shipping industry. On 12 July the *Irish Press* carried in its issue an article headed 'Sea Aspirants'. This gave news of a competition for three scholarships in both nautical training and marine engineering offered by Irish Shipping Ltd, which would be based at the Technical School, Galway and the Crawford Municipal Institute Cork. There would be a subsistence grant of £50 for those who had to leave home and £10 for those living near a training school. This scheme evolved into the Irish Shipping cadetship programme, which lasted until the liquidation of the semi-state company forty years later in November 1984. Indeed it continued for a further two years under the auspices of Irish Marine Services, formed by ex-employees of that company.

In Dublin no major repairs could be undertaken aboard large vessels between June and November of 1944 because of a strike at the Liffey Dockyard over the employment of one man. News of this only became public on 4 October when the *Irish Press* reported:

> The sixteen-week-old inter-union dispute, which is holding up ship repairs at the Liffey Dockyard, where nearly fifty are on strike, was the subject of a letter from the Department of Industry & Commerce, read at last night's meeting of the Dublin Trades Union Council. The letter stated that the dispute was due to the Society of Boilermakers and Iron Shipbuilders objecting to a certain member of the Irish Engineering & Industrial Union being employed as a boilerman at Liffey Dockyard. The partial stoppage at Liffey Dockyard is interfering with the repairing of ships required urgently for importing necessary commodities in the present emergency. The Minister regards it as a grave reflection on the trade union movement in this country that a dispute between two unions on a matter in which the employers have no responsibility, should lead to a stoppage in an industry which is most essential to the country's well being ... it was either for the

Council or the Irish Trade Union Congress to take immediate steps to end this deadlock between the two unions catering for the same trade. The letter said the Minister would welcome an indication that drastic steps in this direction were been taken. Councillor James Larkin presiding said there had been constant conflict since the yard opened and management was responsible. The agreement that management would recruit all employees through the unions had not been kept. If the unions were united they could settle this matter in an hour ... It was decided to ask the Minister to call a conference of representatives of the two unions, the management of the dockyard and the trades council executive.

The next mention of the strike was carried in *The Irish Times* on 28 November: 'The five-month-old strike caused by an inter-union dispute was settled yesterday, when twenty workers at the Liffey Dockyard returned to work.'

Shipbuilding was in also the news for other reasons in November. It was the subject of a parliamentary question, as reported in *The Irish Times* of 3 November, under the heading: 'Dáil Query on Éire Shipbuilding Needs'. This article recorded that the question of building ships for Éire in Belfast was to be raised in the Dáil by J. Larkin, 'who will ask the Minister for Industry & Commerce, if in view of the recent statement of the chairman of Irish Shipping Ltd that it would be necessary to maintain an Irish mercantile marine after the war, was he was prepared to enter into discussions with the government of Northern Ireland with the object of having ships built for Éire in Northern Ireland. Mr Larkin will suggest that by doing so, employment will be provided for Northern Ireland workers after the war and it would promote the development of goodwill and economic relations between northern Ireland and southern Ireland.' No further reference to this question has been found.

However, John de Courcy Ireland reported a related news item which he stated as having sourced from the *London Sunday Graphic* of 19 November 1944: 'News from Ireland. Gesture of friendship by Éire to Ulster, which will transcend all diplomatic overtures, will shortly be made, I hear. It is that the national Irish fleets, both of warship and merchant ships, shall be built in Belfast shipyards. Following my disclosure of tentative feelers, the question of thus forging a link between the north and south has been receiving serious consideration of both Parliaments. A deputation of Ulster Nationalists will shortly visit Dublin to seek Premier de Valera's personal support for the project.'[51]

This is a most bizarre story and the passage that Dr Ireland quotes could not be found in the November edition of the *Graphic* or indeed in the October and December editions. Also it is strange that no author or even pen name is given as the source for the story. The control of ship construction was still a matter for the Admiralty in 1944 and the building of Irish warships and merchant vessels in a British yards was definitely a non-runner. Interestingly, however, John Higgins, Public Relations Manager for twenty years with Irish Shipping Ltd, has said that when their building programme commenced after the war, Seán Lemass, TD, Minister for Industry & Commerce instructed the company to get ships built in Belfast whatever the cost. However, when Harland & Wolff were approached to construct ISL vessels, the answer from Laganside was always the same – that they were not in a position to tender.[52]

As the last year of the war opened, the *Irish Plane* was noted in the graving dock on 17 January and she was still being attended to by the Liffey yard alongside the Alexandra Quay a month later, while on Saturday 3 March the *Irish Poplar* was in the graving dock.[53]

On 4 May 1945 the German surrender on the Western Front was signed at General Bernard Montgomery's headquarters. On Sunday 29 May, Walter Kennedy noted 'a derelict vessel with grey hull, no funnel, masts or bridge, moored at the riverside of the North Wall Extension.' The following day's paper identified the ship as the *Kerry Coast*, sunk in a collision in the Mersey eighteen months earlier and now re-floated and brought to Dublin. She was to be refitted, sold to H.P. Lenaghan of Belfast and renamed *Bangor Bay*.[54] On the last day of the month the *Irish Independent*, under the headline 'Year of idleness ends', in reference to the slow year at the Liffey yard, noted that the *Irish Plane*, after thirteen months in dockyard hands was due to sail transatlantic on the following Sunday. That same day the *Irish Fir* was at Alexandra Quay with her funnel removed.

During June 1945, shipping or rather the lack of it made news in the papers. On 8 June the *Irish Independent* carried a story: 'Eight ships to start Lisbon Service' reporting that 70,000 tons of supplies for Éire were awaiting transport in Portugal and that the eight vessels could lift between them 7,500 tons every three weeks. However, four days later the *Irish Press* reported that Navicerts had not arrived for the *Menapia*, *City of Dublin* and *City of Antwerp* and four other Lisbon-bound ships, and that their departure had fallen into abeyance. The Ministry of War Transport in London was still keeping tight control over Irish merchant shipping.

On 19 June the *Irish Independent* noted that the value of shipping would be demonstrated during the forthcoming Maritime Exhibition organised by the Maritime Institute of Ireland, to be held in the Mansion House Dublin between 3 and 11 August. Three days later, in its Dáil Report, the same newspaper reported that 'shipping was the big problem and one large ship was out of commission for about six months due to an inter-union dispute at the Dublin Dockyard.' What the dispute was about is unknown.

The morning after the opening of the Maritime Exhibition the *Irish Independent* reported the speech of the Minister for Defence, Oscar Traynor, TD, opening the event in which he noted Ireland's reliance on shipping: 'The history of the past few years has demonstrated clearly our dependence on ships and how internationally the economy of our life is related to the sea.'

As 1945 drew to a close, the first of the vessels chartered by Irish Shipping Ltd was handed back to her owners. This was the *Irish Cedar* and the *Irish Independent* reported her departure from Cork on 1 November bound for Naples with a cargo of relief supplies for Italy. Aboard were twenty-four of her original thirty-two crew members, with Captain Gore-Hickman as master and four other Irish officers.

On 13 December, a photograph appeared in the *Irish Independent* showing the *Kerry Coast* being reconstructed in Alexandra Basin. The full story of this ship deserves mention. The *Kerry Coast*, 1,407 tons, was one of three sister ships owned by Coast Lines, all built by the Caledon Shipbuilding & Engineering Company in 1919. She was outward bound from Liverpool to Waterford with a general cargo including barley and salt on 11 March 1944 when off the landing stage in the River Mersey, she collided with the Norwegian motor vessel *Mosdale*. Holed in the engine room, she drifted upriver and in danger of sinking, the crew was taken off and the ship was beached on the Birkenhead side of the Mersey, near the Cammell Laird shipyard. On 20 May she was refloated and moved further inshore. The ship was declared 'a constructive total loss' and her underwriters probably made a settlement on the policy to her owners; the insurers would then sell the wreck for what they could obtain.[55]

The *Kerry Coast* would have been very well known to one of the directors of the Liffey Dockyard, R.W. Sinnott, who was also the general manager of the B & I company, which was a member of the Coast Lines group. In any case B & I stepped in and purchased the fully repaired vessel, which was renamed the *Kerry*, a name she had borne earlier. Once taken over she was allocated to the Burns & Laird Line of Glasgow and in 1947 was transferred to the B & I company and registered in Dublin. Her two sister ships, the *Kildare* and *Meath*, which also operated from Dublin, flew the 'Red Duster'.

It is worth recording that during the dark days of the Emergency, from 1941 to 1945, the vessels of Irish Shipping Ltd carried 712,000 tons of wheat, 178,000 tons of coal, 63,000 tons of phosphate, 24,000 tons of tobacco, 19,000 tons of newsprint, 10,000 tons of timber and other general cargo which totalled 105,000 tons. Regrettably there are no figures available for the cargo tonnage carried by other Irish merchant ships belonging to companies such as the Limerick Steamship Company, Palgrave Murphy Ltd and Wexford Steamships Ltd, which traded mainly to Spain and Portugal, or for the Arklow-owned schooners and the Irish flag vessels of the B & I Steam Packet Company Ltd. The Dublin Gas Company ships were engaged in supplying coal to the company's plant at Grand Canal Basin, Dublin, with Thomas Heiton's colliers, *The Lady Belle* of Messrs Suttons, Cork, and the *Margaret Lockington* of S.J. Lockington from Dundalk also carrying coal. All of these once household-name companies are long gone. The Dublin yards kept most of them sailing, which allowed this neutral country to exist at a time of serious economic shortages.

Armoured Car Steel

It is worth mentioning that as well as its crucial service of ship repairs, the Liffey yard assisted in the defence of neutral Ireland in another way. At the outbreak of war in 1939 military GHQ quickly realised that there was a serious shortage of armoured fighting vehicles for the army. There were only eighteen armoured cars available in total. By the end of June 1940, after the Germans had overrun Belgium, the Netherlands and France, Hitler now controlled the west European coast. The threat of the invasion of Britain became very real and beyond that the invasion of Ireland. An army panel was set up to consider whether armoured cars could be built locally. Although excluded from those discussions, Col Joe Lawless, Director of the Cavalry Corps, drew up a design for an armoured body mounted on a lorry chassis. He went to Messrs Thomas Thompson, the engineering company in Carlow, about fabricating such a vehicle and approached Henry Ford in Cork for a chassis. However, there was the still the matter of steel for the armour, which of course was in very short supply.

While the Carlow works had some 50 tons of steel lying on the quays at Montreal in Canada ready for shipment, the Department of Supplies, which controlled all essential cargos carried in Irish ships would not give it priority clearance. Early in January 1941, Col Lawless and Col Devlin from GHQ visited the Liffey Dockyard where they found half-inch steel plate suitable for their requirements. 'Yard not inclined to facilitate the officers to extent of selling the required amount of steel. A Mr Thomas said he needed this for ship repair work and would not let it go except forced to do so by government order.' Col Lawless wrote: 'By 24 February 1941 Messrs Thompson were trying to get Dublin Dockyard to agree to exchange ½" plate for ⁵⁄₁₆" plate weight for weight. Also Commandant Aubrey Mayne from the base workshops went to County Donegal and saw the wreck of a ship held by Mr Frame [Hammond Lane Metal Company] at Lough Swilly. Sufficient ½" plate about 40 tons available to do 17 hulls.' The ship was probably the British SS *Pandion*, 1,944 tons gross, which was bombed in the Atlantic on 28 January 1941 and was put ashore in Lough Swilly. According to Art Magennis, a commandant in the Cavalry Corps in the 1960s, he was told by Col Stapleton that the Ford armoured cars were built with steel from the Liffey Dockyard.[56]

CHAPTER 7

THE POST-SECOND WORLD WAR YEARS

The shipping and repair scene in Ireland at the end of the Second World War was very different from that in 1918. For one thing, the state, while still a member of the British Commonwealth, now had its own economic policies. Moreover, because it had been neutral during the conflict, Ireland was denied the right to purchase any surplus American standard war built tonnage including the 10,000-ton deadweight Liberty ships or the faster turbine-propelled Victory ships and Jeep class ships. The latter were very suitable for timber transport from the Baltic and a number were bought both by Glen & Company of Glasgow and the Head Line of Belfast, both regular callers to Irish ports pre-war that now resumed their trades. These American ships could have been useful interim replacements for the old ships of Irish Shipping Ltd, now that the company was to be a permanent part of Ireland's merchant marine fleet. Another downside was that the bonanza of wartime ship repair work was over. There was no longer any need for British vessels to come to Cork or Dublin for repairs and, because of the country's neutrality, the removal of armament and wartime fittings from merchant ships could not take place in Irish yards.

In general over the post-war years, work was slow and the yards were kept going by repair jobs. One type of work that did become available was the conversion of suitable classes of warships into merchant vessels. On 6 May 1946, both the *Irish Independent* and *Irish Press* carried reports and photographs showing a tank landing craft berthed at the lead in-jetty at the Alexandra Basin graving dock, which had arrived for conversion into a merchant vessel. This was the *Segundo*, owned by the Anglo Swiss Maritime Company of London. However, the vessel sailed without being converted.

On 4 October the *Irish Press* carried a picture of the Liverpool collier *Molfere Rose* owned by Richard Hughes & Co. beached on the mud at the entrance to the River Dodder. She was discharging steam coal for Coras Iompair Éireann (CIE) at the North Wall quay at the Point Depot, when she sprang a leak and had to be towed across the river to prevent her sinking. Her repairs necessitated going into the graving dock. In June 1947 the Aran Islands steamer *Dun Aengus* struck rocks at Inismore and partly sank. A few days later the salvage vessel *Ranger* of the Liverpool & Glasgow Salvage Association refloated the thirty-nine-year-old vessel, now operated by CIE. According to the *Irish Press*: 'The seven small holes were plugged with cement and she was to be repaired by Dublin Dockyard.'[1]

The only yard in the state to undertake warship conversion work, was Cork Dockyard Ltd at Rushbrook, which converted one Flower-class corvette into a cargo ship for use in the Mediterranean. This was the *Andria*, owned by the Compañía Marítima Mensabe under the Panama flag and completed in April 1947 for a Greek shipowner. She was fitted with accommodation for forty first-class, twenty second-class and sixteen third-class passengers, with a small hold for 20 tons of cargo.[2]

On 3 January 1948, *The Irish Times* reported that 'shipwrights had returned to work at the Liffey Dockyard, after a two-month strike, which only involved thirteen men', although it gives no information about what the strike had been about. It also recorded that work had resumed on the *Shamrock* and that the *Veraguas*, the former *Irish Willow* which had been renamed on her return to her owners, had arrived two days earlier for voyage repairs. The year 1948 also saw the delivery of the first ships of the post-war reconstruction programme for Irish Shipping Ltd from English yards. Towards the end of that year we see the first mention of shipbuilding in Dublin, when on 3 November *The Irish Times* reported that a delegation from the Dublin Trades Council had met officials from the Department of Industry & Commerce: 'At the previous night's meeting J. Collins, a member of the Council, said that a Departmental official informed the delegation that the prospects of securing orders for the Dublin shipyard were remote. The deputation asked that the Minister use his influence to secure more repair work for the yard.'

At the end of March 1949 the *Irish Press* reported that the steamer *Irish Fir* had arrived in the Liffey Dockyard in tow of the tug *Empire Aid* from Rushbrook, where she had been lying for a considerable time. The ship had been bought by Palgrave Murphy Ltd and her reconditioning would take four months.[3] This work included the construction of livestock pens for the carriage of cattle on outward sailings to the continent, as the main exports from the state in those days were from the agriculture sector. These pens were then dismantled to load general cargo for the homeward voyage to Ireland. The ship was renamed the *Delgany* and later *City of Amsterdam*, and served the Palgrave group for another ten years, before being scrapped in 1959 at Ringsend.

Towards the end of May the question of shipbuilding being resumed at Dublin was raised at two important venues on successive days. According to the *Irish Press* on Thursday 26 May, in the previous day's Dáil proceedings in the debate on industry, Mr Lemass said: 'Those in the industry were anxious to undertake shipbuilding on a competitive basis, and only required steel supplies. They felt this would be forthcoming if there were government representations to Britain.' The article went on to say that Mr Lemass 'did not think they should try to build an industry on the Belfast scale, but skilled workers could not be kept employed on ship repair only and shipbuilding should be kept going. If there was to be an addition to the Irish shipping fleet, the ships should be built in Irish yards, where vessels of 5,000 tons could be constructed. If there was any question of additional cost to Irish Shipping Ltd, the government should consider whether they could take action to relieve it. There was a rumour that Irish Shipping was losing money and he hoped that the Minister would contradict it.' It was the time of the Inter Party government, which had taken office in 1948, and Mr Lemass was addressing his remarks to his successor Dan Morrissey of Fine Gael, who held the Industry & Commerce portfolio. On Friday 27 May the same newspaper under the heading 'Docks Board to hear Shipbuilding Group' reported that the Dublin Port & Docks Board had decided at a meeting held the previous day to receive a deputation from the shipyard group of the Dublin Trades Council to discuss shipbuilding in the city. Messrs Bruton, Moore, Rehill, Sinnott, Twohig and Captain Gordon were to meet them – R.W. Sinnott and Captain Gordon were directors of the Liffey Dockyard. In the same article the newspaper reported: 'The matter of shipbuilding was raised in the Dáil on Wednesday by Mr Larkin [Labour], who alleged that Irish Shipping Ltd, a state subsidised company, had passed over Dublin dockyards [for work needed on their ships] despite services during the war and that he had asked for an inquiry into the placing of contracts by Irish Shipping.'

In May 1950, Rex McGall, in his Dublin port feature in the *Irish Press*, reported that tenders for a new 630-foot long graving dock costing £750,000, which would take five years to construct, would close on 27 June and that derricks were being erected for the building of a new Irish Lights' vessel.[4] During 1950 Hugh Lennox, the general manager of the Liffey Dockyard, was made a director with an allocation of 500 shares, while John Gordon, son of Captain Gordon, was appointed to the board on the death of his father. On Saturday 24 February 1951, the *Irish Press* carried a picture of the dry dock contract being signed. The same newspaper on Wednesday 24 March carried the story: 'Resumption of Shipbuilding Welcomed. The resumption of shipbuilding in the city and the construction of the new graving dock, were described by delegates to the annual meeting of the Dublin Trades Council, as the greatest things that have happened in trade union circles in thirty years. Tributes were paid to the late Jim Larkin and W.F. Bond, the Port & Docks Engineer, and the shipbuilding group for having work resumed.'

In the middle of 1951 *The Irish Times* carried a photograph taken at the Liffey Dockyard showing a vessel on the stocks with the caption 'Soon to be in service' even though the ship had only a few frames erected.[5] On Saturday 1 September 1951, the same newspaper carried a photograph showing 'three platers' helpers working on the hull plating of the new Irish Lights Service steamer now nearing completion at Liffey Dockyard'. The accompanying story stated: 'The work now progressing on the construction of three vessels at the Liffey Dockyard, North Wall, Dublin, represents the first stage of an enterprise that may eventually give the Republic a place in the world shipbuilding industry. There is an ample supply of skilled workers. The number now employed is 450, of whom 300 are in the skilled categories.' It went on to say that the world shortage of steel because of armament production was the only impediment to a more rapid realisation of the Republic's shipbuilding aspirations.[6]

Hugh Lennox was quoted: 'Like shipbuilders everywhere steel is the main problem, but it is dribbling in, enough for a fair start anyhow.' He also noted that the latest increase in steel prices would mean an increase of £20,000 in the cost of a 9,500-ton vessel: 'Although hampered by this shortage, this dockyard has completed 75% of the shell of the 1,100-ton twin-screw service tender, ordered by the Commissioners of Irish Lights. When she is launched at the end of this year she will be named the *Isolda* after a vessel which was lost during the war. By her side on the company's three building berths, the keel blocks are already laid down for a single screw diesel collier for Irish Shipping Ltd.' However, it turned out that his forecast for the completion of the *Isolda* was over-optimistic, as the vessel did not enter the water for another twelve months. Later that week the first mention was made in *The Irish Times* of Irish oil tankers, in a report on a meeting of the Maritime Institute in Dublin. It was stated that a letter had been received from Mr Lemass, who was once again Minister for Industry and Commerce, claiming that the government had under active consideration the provision of Irish-owned oil tankers. Also that month Irish seamen, who had been lobbying for a raise, accepted proposals from the shipowners for an extra £3 10s per month and a 48-hour working week.

As the New Year opened, on the 8 January 1952 *The Irish Times* displayed on the front page a picture of the Irish Lights' vessel, showing work proceeding on the upper deck and stating that it was the first ship 'laid down' since the B & I boat *Kilkenny* in 1938. Steel was still in very short supply, but this was the case universally with *The Irish Times* of 25 April reporting on the situation in Belfast, where Sir Frederick Ribbeck, speaking after the launch of the 17,000 ton *Braemar Castle* at the Harland & Wolff yard, stated that there was not enough work in Belfast and that the yard was only receiving 60 per cent of their steel needs. In September, Rex MacGall, in his MacLir column in the *Irish Press*, reported that the new coaster laid down for Irish Shipping Ltd in the Liffey Dockyard had been had been delayed by the shortage of steel.

FIRST SHIP LAUNCHED IN FIFTEEN YEARS

At 13.00 hours at high water on Saturday 20 September to the sound of tug sirens and ship's whistles, the cheers of yard-workers and invited shipyard guests, the hull of No. 171, the *Isolda* slipped down the ways into Alexandra Basin from the Liffey Dockyard Ltd. The new lighthouse tender was named by Mrs Webb, wife of Captain J.H. Webb, the vice-chairman of the Commissioners of Irish Lights and a retired harbour master of Dublin. Having been brought to rest by the drag chains, she was taken in tow by the Port & Docks tugs *Ben Eadar* and *Coliemore* and brought round the North Wall Extension to the 100-ton crane, where her machinery was later installed.

In researching this event in the Dublin newspapers over fifty-seven years later, it is interesting to compare the emphasis given to this event in the newspapers. No one paper reported all the details of the ceremony, ship or speeches. The Irish Independent, on 22 September, apart from a short item of the launching ceremony, devoted most of its coverage to the Gresham Hotel, with quotations from speeches made by the Minister and the general manager, and concluded with a list of those who attended, together with a photograph of the ship. Seán Lemass stated in his speech that in this case 'the steel for the ship was provided at the British home price – a very exceptional concession' and pointed out that the position created for their dockyards and for all Irish firms requiring imported steel in their manufacturing process was one of acute difficulty. Lemass went on to say that 'the existence of adequate ship-repairing facilities at the main ports was a matter of prime importance and although a ship-repairing firm did not necessarily also undertake shipbuilding, it was generally recognised to be desirable, to ensure continuity of employment for skilled shipyard workers that the ship-repairing yards should also be capable of undertaking shipbuilding and should have a reasonable prospect of securing regular orders. The resumption of shipbuilding work in recent years was undertaken despite very formidable handicaps, particularly in securing steel at prices which made it possible for them to compete with yards outside the country with any prospect of success. It appeared to be British policy for the time being to sell steel for export to this country at prices substantially higher than those charged to their own manufacturers. The higher British export prices were in line with those at which steel could be purchased from other European exporters. Such a situation could not and would not continue indefinitely and there were already signs that it was passing.

He went on to draw attention to the fact that it was possible to import coal from the USA and get it delivered at Irish ports at an all-in cost including freight of about £1 per ton cheaper than British coal. It was a tribute to the Liffey Dockyard Company and to its workers that they succeeded in continuing to build ships to a considerable degree.

In reply Hugh Lennox, general manager of the yard noted 'the recent substantial increase in steel costs, which did not affect their British competitors, coupled with the ever-rising wage differential, must militate against them. Therefore more than ever before, if shipbuilding and ship repairing were to expand and thrive, there must be closer liaison between labour and management in the common aim of increasing production. When the merchant fleet was sufficient in tonnage to cater for the country's immediate needs, a policy of constructing at home at least one vessel, say every two years, would lay the foundations for an industry that would provide adequate maintenance facilities with trained personnel. The Liffey Dockyard had recently installed new plant and equipment costing £80,000, whereby they hoped to increase their efficiency and productivity by the introduction of the most modern engineering techniques.'

He concluded that the *Isolda* was a 'thoroughly modern vessel with all the latest navigational aids, such as radar and radio-telephone installed. Luxurious accommodation would be afforded to both officers and crew.' The *Isolda* was a twin-screw steel lightship tender built to Lloyd's highest class and to the special requirements of the Commissioners of Irish Lights.

On the other hand *The Irish Times* on the same day focused on the port and on the history of ship construction on the river, giving the names of the current directors of the Liffey Dockyard – Messrs R.A. Burke, James Stafford, R.W. Sinnott (chairman) and John Gordon. Hugh Lennox in an interview with that paper's correspondent is quoted as saying: 'We would have had the *Isolda* handed over a year ago but for the steel problem. Fortunately we got British steel – at the British internal price – but it came in small consignments and before the price for overseas was increased by over 100%.' He added that for his own firm 'it would be a wise policy if it were possible to buy subsidised steel from the government, so as to turn out a ship here every two years. If necessary we could build a 400-footer here, of 5,000 tons, but that would mean taking up the space used for the other berth.'

That paper also provided the main dimensions and statistics of the *Isolda*, begun on 28 November 1950 – length 234 feet, moulded breadth 38 feet, a moulded depth 17 feet, and a maximum draft of 12 feet 9 inches. She had two sets of totally enclosed steam reciprocating engines, supplied by Messrs Lobnitz & Co. of Renfrew, Scotland, each developing 750 HP, driving two four-bladed propellers giving a service speed of 12 knots. Steam was raised in two single-ended Scotch boilers supplied by Messrs Barclay, Curle & Co. of Glasgow. The ship was 1,100 tons gross and her loaded displacement was 1,952 tons. She carried two 26-foot lifeboats, two 25-foot motor cutters, one pulling cutter and a sailing dingy and had accommodation for officers on the main deck amidships and double berth cabins for ratings aft.

The *Irish Press* from 22 September played the political card, quoting another part of Lemass' remarks at the lunch that shipbuilding was essential to economic aims 'not merely because of the contribution it could make to the national output and to the provision of employment, but also to the realisation of wider economic aims. The development of an Irish merchant fleet and the encouragement of other countries to ship necessary raw materials direct to us, are accepted aims of national policy. The purpose is to reverse the former position in which most goods reached this country in cross-channel vessels after transhipment at British ports.' The paper also quoted R.A. Burke declaring: 'If steel at competitive costs with British shipyards could be added to the present Coal & Cattle Pact, it would be a great help to the shipbuilding industry here and enable it to remain on a competitive basis.' The paper also gave the cost of the *Isolda* as £259,000 and noted that she had bunker capacity of 250 tons of fuel oil sufficient to permit 3,000 miles cruising without replenishment.

(L. to R.) Mr Andrew Clarkin and Mrs Clarkin with three directors of the Liffey Dockyard, W.J. Sinnott (chairman), John Gordon and Raymond Burke, photographed at the Gresham Hotel after the launch of the *Isolda*.

Following the launch in September, *The Irish Times*, on 2 October, carried a photograph showing work continuing on the main deck of the *Isolda*. Under the heading 'Slow Deliveries Hit Shipyards', the *Irish Independent* on the 5 December carried the report: '"A

Dublin shipyard, which had a contract for the building of a collier is experiencing certain slowness in the delivery of steel," Mr Lemass told Alderman A. Byrne (Ind.) at Question Time in the Dáil. He was also informed in regard to two ships for which tenders were recently invited by the Commissioners of Irish Lights that no Irish firm tendered. The inability to tender competitively was due to the fact that the necessary steel would only be supplied to shipyards here at a price substantially higher than that at which steel was available to outside competitors. He had gone to Britain and discussed the matter with the President of the Board of Trade without success.'

In December, *The Irish Times* carried a report of the Cork Harbour board meeting the previous day 'when a reply from the General Manager of the Liffey Dockyard was read regarding the board's protest against the transfer from Cork to Dublin of the Greek steamer *Nereus* for repairs. The letter stated repairs were approved by Mr Carson, the underwriter's surveyor on Saturday 6 December, who requested a price for carrying out the heavy weather damage repairs to this vessel and we submitted a figure of £1,750 and a time of eight days.' The letter went on to point out that the vessel had arrived in Cork on 4 December and that Cork dockyard quoted a price of £3,000 and three weeks to do the job. When Carson complained about these figures the price was reduced to £2,800 and then to £2,000; a figure of £1,850 was finally submitted when it was realised there would be competition for the job. The letter concluded by saying that the ship's owners were prepared to go to the Bristol Channel.[7] In the end, Dublin was awarded the job.

On 31 March 1953, *The Irish Times* published an article about the *Isolda*, which stated that the ship was undergoing trials that day. The interesting thing is that one of the pictures showed the ship's stern with her name but no port of registry. For the significance of this omission we must go back to the wartime loss of her predecessor, the *Isolda* of 1928, which had been sunk in 1940 by German aircraft despite being registered in Dublin. Following that attack, the remaining two Irish Lights vessels were transferred to Liverpool registry and armed. Efforts were made to have the new ship also put under Dublin registry in 1953, but without success, and it was registered in Liverpool. It would take another twenty-nine years before the Commissioners put their ships under the Tricolour almost overnight, after the tragedy of Bloody Sunday and a threat that the ships would be blown up by the IRA.

The next morning *The Irish Times* carried three small paragraphs headed '13 Hour Test for the *Isolda*'. The report went on to say: 'TSS *Isolda* spent just over 13 hours undergoing her sea trials in Dublin Bay. She left Alexandra Basin at 7.30 a.m. and did not dock again until 8.45 p.m. Technicians and representatives of the builders and the Commissioners, who were on board during the trials, said they were satisfied with her performance.' The final sea trials of the ship took place on 19 May and the following day the three Dublin papers carried single page advertising features, with news of the event and that the new tender had been officially handed over to the Commissioners of Irish Lights at midnight. It must be noted that the *Isolda* went on sea trials flying the Irish Tricolour, as the vessel was still in the hands of the builders, and the blue house flag of the dockyard also flew from the mainmast.

The main ship repair news in Dublin for 1953 was the damage caused to a naval vessel early that year. A photograph was published on the front page of *The Irish Times* for 28 February, showing the distorted bow and twisted forecastle plates of the corvette LÉ *Maev (02)* in Dublin. The caption stated that damage had been sustained the previous day. It is believed that when the corvette was berthing at the top of Alexandra Basin, the bridge rang down on the telegraph to go astern but the engine room misinterpreted the signal and put the engine ahead. When the bridge rang down again for emergency full astern, the engine room response was to open the steam valve for emergency full ahead with the result that the ship collided with the cross berth at right angles with considerable force. The ship was some time in the hands of the Liffey yard for repairs.

Questions were asked in the Dáil about this incident and a naval board of inquiry was held at Haulbowline. News of this eventually appeared ten months later in the *Irish Independent* in December 1953, noting: 'Court Martial finding held at Cork in October into the collision in the early morning of 27 February has been promulgated, and the acting engineer officer, a warrant engineer, was found guilty of a breach of standing orders, which required him to be in the engine room when entering or leaving harbour and at all other times when engine movements were being exercised from the bridge. He was reduced in rank to chief petty officer.'[8] According to Tom McGinty the captain of the corvette told the inquiry that the ship was not manned according to establishment and he was short a first lieutenant, a second engineer and two engine room artificers. As a result the captain was the only officer on the bridge and the engine room was similarly undermanned. The court expressed concern at the shortage in the ship's complement, which was a contributory factor to the accident.[9]

THE DUN LAOGHAIRE SHIPYARD

As 1954 opened, a small boatyard on the West Pier at Dun Laoghaire, the Dalkey Shipyard Ltd, must be mentioned. The yard, situated at the shore end of the pier just opposite the clubhouse of the present-day Dun Laoghaire Motor Yacht Club, constructed a number of small steel craft for the Turkish government. It first came to public notice on 19 February 1954, when the Dublin newspapers published a photograph of a small tug, the *Mersin 1*, being launched the previous day. *The Irish Times* gives the most detailed report on the yard, stating that there would be six tugboats and one diving vessel built there, and that the £50,000 contract was secured in the face of international competition. These vessels were constructed to Lloyd's Register of Shipping rules and the requirements of the Turkish ministry, and were the first steel craft built by the company. All the tugs displaced 16 tons and were propelled by a 62 HP diesel engine, while the diving vessel displaced 10 tons.

The *Mersin 1* was christened by Mrs Hardman, wife of the managing director J.H. Hardman. The vessel had a length of 40 feet, a beam of 11 feet and a draft of 4 feet 6 inches. The launching was attended by Bey Orhan Atliman of the Turkish ministry, who came from Holland where he was supervising the construction of other harbour boats for the port of Mersin. The contract was expected to be completed the following August and the following year pictures appeared in the national newspapers in April showing one of the tugs being lifted aboard the *City of Ghent* by the 100-ton crane at the North Wall Extension. The Dun Laoghaire firm was a yacht and boat building yard, which afterwards apparently tried to obtain other foreign contracts for steel craft, but without success. It closed down within two years of this. Nowadays the site is a car scrap yard. It is interesting that the London consulting engineer to the Turkish government, S. Hopkins, was quoted in the papers as saying that it was a wonderful opportunity for Ireland to obtain further work from Turkey, as Turkey would then be paying Ireland for work which would offset the £800,000 sterling of prime products Ireland had bought in the two years previously from Turkey.

More Ships from the Liffey Dockyard

The second vessel to be launched from the Liffey Dockyard slid down the ways in bright sunshine just after 12 noon on Saturday 28 August 1954. This was the *Irish Fern* (ON 400118), Yard No. 172, and constructed to the order of Irish Shipping Ltd. The vessel was named by Mrs Seán T. O'Kelly, wife of the President of Ireland.

Before naming, the ship was blessed by the Very Rev. Father J. Marnane, parish priest of the Church of St Laurence O'Toole, Seville Place. On arrival the presidential party was received by J.J. Stafford, chairman of Irish Shipping, and R.W. Sinnott, chairman of the builders.[10]

Irish Fern (Yard No. 172): this was the first Irish-built vessel constructed for the semi-state shipping company, Irish Shipping Ltd., Dublin.

The new vessel was a single screw motor collier or small bulk carrier of 1,113 tons gross and 1,375 tons deadweight. She measured 205 feet between perpendiculars and 218 feet overall in length, with moulded breadth 35 feet, and a moulded depth of 15 feet to the main deck. Her propelling engine was a British Polar Atlas 6 cylinder two-stroke single acting diesel developing 960 BHP, giving the ship a speed of about 11 knots. The captain and deck officers were accommodated in the mid-ships house under the bridge, while the engineers and crew had their quarters aft, all in single cabins. MacGregor single pull steel covers were fitted on the two hatches, one in the forward well and the other on the raised quarterdeck. The ship was the second of two short sea vessels ordered by the company, which up to that point had only operated deep sea cargo vessels. Her sister ship, the *Irish Heather*, had been completed exactly two years previously at Goole on the east coast of England. The company ordered these two vessels to break into the cross-channel bulk trade by carrying coal cargoes for other Irish state companies. Initially the two vessels were engaged in carrying steam coal cargos for CIE and to ESB power stations.[11]

At a luncheon in the Gresham Hotel after the launch, Hugh Lennox, director and general manager of the yard, said: 'The launch of the *Irish Fern* marked another step in the programme laid down by the Liffey Dockyard in their efforts to revive the shipbuilding industry in Dublin. The initiation of the venture took place under the most adverse conditions – shortage of essential raw materials, differential export steel prices and a shortage of skilled tradesmen in many of the crafts. So far our experience, especially from a financial aspect, has not been encouraging: in fact the advisability of persevering with this branch of the industry could well be questioned.' He went on to say that the absence of shipbuilding in Dublin for so many years had been responsible for the decline in the number of skilled men and that at least one ship per year must be built in order to re-establish the necessary labour force, while at the same time ensuring continuity of work. The company was grateful to Irish Shipping Ltd for placing the order for the *Irish Fern* with the Liffey Dockyard at additional cost to themselves, which helped in reducing that expense over which they had no control. However, Lennox also believed that the prospects for the future were bright: 'In addition to the launching of the *Irish Fern*, they had a self propelled steam hopper barge for the Dublin Port & Docks Board, two floating gates for the new graving dock and the replacement steamer for the Galway-Aran Island service, which had been ordered by CIE.' He concluded by congratulating Irish Shipping for their part in building up an Irish mercantile marine industry.[12]

The chairman of Irish Shipping, J.J. Stafford, in reply said that while the *Irish Fern* was not a big ship, 'it was the first ship to be launched by our company from an Irish yard and the first ship to be launched by the Liffey Dockyard for an Irish company'. He said that speed in production was essential and added that negotiations were proceeding between Irish Shipping and the Liffey Dockyard for the construction of another vessel, provided a reasonable delivery date was adhered to, together with a fixed price – both of these conditions were obtainable elsewhere. An Tánaiste and Minister for Industry and Commerce, William Norton, TD, congratulated Irish Shipping and the Irish workers on the day's achievements and said that he hoped the launching would only be the forerunner of many similar ceremonies in the years ahead.

The *Irish Fern* carried out her sea trials just over three months later, on Wednesday 1 December. On Friday of the following week the ship was in the news again in *The Irish Times* of 10 December under the heading 'Ship Beats Storm On Maiden Trip', reporting that the vessel, which arrived in Dublin from Cardiff in Wales with her first cargo of coal, had encountered gale force conditions on the return voyage to Ireland, but had come through without damage.

The *Irish Fern* remained in service with Irish Shipping for ten years, until she was sold to John Stewart & Co. Shipping Ltd of Glasgow and renamed the *Yewtree*. These Scottish owners were operators of small bulk carriers in the Irish Sea trade. After another ten years she was sold in 1974 to the Arcepey Shipping Co. SA, Panama, and changed her name to *Al Hassan*. In 1976 she was sold to the Laconia Marine Co. Ltd, Cyprus, and was renamed the *Andreas*.

Despite Lennox's optimism at the launch of the *Irish Fern*, the headlines in the papers of Monday 20 June 1955, following the launch of the third vessel from the Liffey yard, were 'Aid for Shipbuilding Industry Urged' (*Irish Independent*) and 'Manager Calls For Guarantee of Full Day's Work' (*The Irish Times*). Steam hopper *Number Ten* (ON 400130), Yard No. 173, ordered by the Dublin Port & Docks Board, took to the water in bright sunshine at noon on Saturday 18 June, following naming by Mrs Stephen McKenzie, wife of the chairman of the board. Speaking at the reception in the yard canteen, Hugh Lennox said: 'They were most anxious to continue shipbuilding and they were fully conscious that their costs were higher than they would like them to be, but with price differentials to be paid for, steel and other essential materials, together with higher wages and transport, it was very difficult for private enterprise to overcome these disadvantages without some form of government aid. Before any other increases were granted, some form of guarantee should be forthcoming to ensure that the working day was eight hours work not five or six, which was the average for shipbuilding and other industries.'[13]

Number Ten (Yard No. 173): a 1,700 tons deadweight steam hopper launched on 18 June 1955 for the Dublin Port & Docks Board. She was used in the harbour carrying dredged spoil out to the Kish Bank and dumping it there.

Mr McKenzie, Chairman of the Port Board, who was also a prominent Dublin coal importer, made reference to the demarcation of labour when he said: 'He understood that most [workers] were members of British Unions and the Liffey Dockyard was being expected to carry on its work under the same conditions as British and foreign yards with years of experience and profits in the industry. He would suggest to the workers that they should co-operate more and work together in the interest of shipbuilding in Ireland.' *The Irish Times*, in a fuller report of this speaker, quotes him saying: 'I regret that we in Ireland are not shipping minded. Our tonnage today is a mere 79,000 tons; in the past this country had a great tradition in shipping and as far back as 1849 there was a tonnage of 250,000 tons representing 2,000 ships. If we had the same interest today, our mercantile fleet would be 2,000,000 tons.' McKenzie concluded that they were pushing ahead with the new graving dock, which would enable repairs to be carried out in Dublin and hoped the dock would be opened next June, but warned: 'We will not get repair work unless we are able to carry it out at competitive rates.'

The main particulars of *Number Ten* were length BP 175 feet; beam moulded 34 feet; depth moulded 15 feet 4 inches, deadweight 1,700 tons and her hopper capacity was 1,000 tons on a mean draft of 13 feet 6 inches. The sixteen bottom doors for discharging the spoil were operated via chains by two Clarke Chapman steam winches on deck, one forward and one aft of the hopper. Her propelling machinery was a triple expansion engine developing 800 IHP driving a single screw at 115 RPM giving a speed of 9½ knots. Steam was supplied from a single multi-tube oil-fired boiler. Day cabins for the master and engineer were provided aft, with the remainder of the crew accommodated forward. Because of some dispute, final payment for the vessel was not made by the board until 1962, according to the port archives.

The year 1956 opened with a strike at the Alexandra Basin yard, when the boilermakers walked out following an attempt by the management to impose overtime working and to dismiss sixty-two men who refused to comply with the directive. They were also angry about an effort by the company to employ new men, whose contract would include overtime. In *The Irish Times* of 10 January, their union claimed the strike was unofficial, but it seems the yard withdrew the attempt.

On Saturday 21 July 1956, the Liffey Company launched its fourth ship, the *Irish Fir*, No. 176 (ON 400177) and the second constructed for Irish Shipping Ltd. She was named by Mrs William Norton, wife of An Tánaiste and leader of the Labour Party, and entered the water in bright sunshine at noon.[14] She was one of three sister ships ordered by these owners for the Great Lakes trade; the other two, the *Rose* and the *Willow*, were built in Scotland by the Ailsa yard at Troon, Ayrshire. An interesting aspect about construction of these vessels was that the two Scottish ships obtained charters to operate on the St Lawrence River, while the Irish-built vessel was precluded from running in Canadian waters, as Ireland was no longer part of the Commonwealth.[15] The speeches at the Gresham Hotel luncheon by Mr Norton, TD, and S. McKenzie, chairman of the Dublin Port & Docks Board, were concerned mainly with the progress of Irish Shipping Ltd – the profits, progress and number of new ships that were being delivered to them that year. Interestingly Hugh Lennox stated that this was the second ship the Liffey Dockyard had built for Irish Shipping on a fixed price contract and noted that they had suffered a loss of £15,000 on their first one, a deficit which they had to cover from their own resources. He said that the new vessel would be finished ahead of time and was glad to announce that orders had been received for a new sludge vessel for Dublin Corporation and a grab and suction dredger for Limerick Harbour Commissioners.[16]

The *Irish Fir* was a between-deck general cargo vessel with a special timber carrying load line. Her length overall was 258 feet 6 inches, breadth 38 feet 6 inches and depth to main deck 15 feet 6 inches. Her deadweight was 1,941 tons and her gross tonnage was 1,752 tons. Her propelling machinery was a British Polar Atlas 9 cylinder single acting diesel engine, developing 1,700 BHP, giving a speed of 12 knots. She had a raised forecastle with the bridge and accommodation placed aft for ease of cargo handling. A single cabin was provided for every member of the crew of twenty-four and separate recreation rooms were arranged for both officers and seamen. There were two cargo holds, with three hatches served by four 5-ton derricks at numbers one and two, with two 3-ton derricks provided at number three hatch, all operated by electric winches. An electric anchor windlass and electric hydraulic steering were also installed, together with the full range of aids to navigation, including radar, gyro compass, echo sounder and direction-finding aerial. The *Irish Fir* ran trials on Thursday 20 December and was handed over on the last day of the month. She was the last of five new vessels delivered to Irish Shipping that year. However, she did not leave Dublin for Parkington on the Manchester Ship canal to load until Wednesday 9 January 1957, because of a dispute between crew members working in the engine room and the owners.[17]

The *Irish Fir* remained with Irish Shipping for twelve years until she was sold in January 1969 to Arta Shipping of Liberia and renamed *Arta*. In 1972 she was purchased by the Edelweiss Shipping Company Ltd, Cyprus, retaining her name. In 1977 she changed owners for the last time to the Edelweiss Compania Naveria S.A., Greece, and took the name *Kotronas Bay*. On 1 January 1978 she arrived at Cartagena, Spain, in tow, having sustained major engine damage which was too severe to repair economically and she was sold to D. Jose Navarro Frances who commenced demolition in June of that year.[18]

During the remainder of 1956 work also proceeded with the construction of Yard Nos 174 and 175, the two steel caisson gates for the Dublin Port & Docks Board to be installed in the new graving dock, then nearing completion alongside the existing dry dock. In November it was announced that the Liffey Dockyard was to build its biggest ever ship, a motor vessel for the British and Irish Steam Packet Company. The ship, 289 feet long, would carry 750 cattle and 500 to 600 sheep. Her Sulzer diesel engine would develop 2,500 HP at 150 RPM, giving a trial speed of 13.5 knots.[19] It is interesting to look back and see at the time, while the Dublin yard had a healthy order book, the newspapers were reporting large lay-offs in Belfast. In August alone there were 600 tradesmen dismissed from eight unions at Harland & Wolff Ltd.[20]

The year 1957 saw the biggest boost for ship repair in Dublin for almost 100 years, when the new graving dock was completed. The new dock, designed by Nicholas O'Dwyer, BE, MInst, CEI, and built by the Irish Construction Company Ltd, had a length of 637 feet and a width of 95 feet. While the dock was not officially opened until July, the first ship to enter was fittingly the Dublin-built motor ship *Kilkenny*, which on 16 March took the blocks in the inner section, followed by the coaster *River Fisher* owned by James Fisher & Company of Barrow-in-Furness in the outer section. The £1,400,000 dock was officially declared open by President Seán T. O'Kelly at noon on Thursday 27 June when the Shell oil tanker *Narica* broke the white ribbon stretched across the entrance. The tanker, owned by the Anglo-Saxon Petroleum Company (Shell) of London, had got under way from the lead-in jetty when Mr O'Kelly came aboard and the presidential standard was broken out on the foremast. Hundreds of dockers and yard workers cheered and ships in port sounded their sirens. Two hours later the dock was empty and the *Narica*'s repairs began, which were to last three weeks. All the guests, including members of the diplomatic corps, the Lord Mayor of Dublin, Robert Briscoe, TD, Seán Lemass, TD, the Minister for Industry & Commerce, and others went to luncheon in the Gresham Hotel. Mr O'Kelly congratulated the Port & Docks Board and its officials for their achievement. Mr Lemass said the availability of the new dock would result in the expansion of the shipbuilding and ship-repairing industries, which was one of the main targets of government policy. The dock would attract work into the port, but this was not likely to remunerate directly the capital expenditure and for that reason the government had decided to make a grant of £500,000 towards its cost. C.M. Vignoles, Managing Director of Shell Mex and B.P. Ltd, said he was proud that the ship used for the official opening was a Shell tanker. He also pointed out that in addition to the tanker *Irish Holly*, which his company had on charter, they had taken the 18,000-ton tanker being built for Irish Shipping Ltd on charter.[21]

On the last Saturday of October 1957 the Liffey Dockyard launched the *Naom Eanna* (ON 400048), Yard No. 176, for CIE, the state transport company, for use on the Galway to the Aran Islands route. The new ship, named by Mrs Letitia Courtney, wife of the chairman of CIE, was ordered as a replacement for the *Dun Aengus* built in the same yard in 1912 for the Galway Bay Steamboat Company. That firm had been taken over as part of the nationalisation of road and rail transport in the state by the government in 1944. The new passenger and cargo ship had an overall length of 136 feet, a breadth of 25 feet 6 inches, a depth of 19 feet, a gross of 483 tons and a speed of just over eleven knots. She had two decks – a continuous upper deck with the bridge and a boat deck on top of the deckhouse situated towards the stern. This contained three passenger saloons, a ladies room, a sick-bay and tea pantry with a bar in the forward saloon. The hold forward of the accommodation was served by a 3-ton derrick with the upper 'tween deck fitted to carry livestock. When the ship was not able to berth at Kilronan on Inis Mór, the cattle would be towed by currach out to the vessel and then be lifted aboard by the derrick. Speaking at the following lunch, T.C. Courtney, chairman of CIE, said that amount spent on the new ship, which cost £150,000, would not be covered by the operating of the service and there would be a deficit of about £10,000 annually.[22] The vessel, which was designed by Messrs Graham & Woolnough, Naval Architects of Glasgow, ran her trials in April 1958. Three days prior to her launch the yard laid the keel for a new B & I livestock vessel.[23]

The keel plate for Yard No. 180, the *Meath*, being placed in position on 23 November 1957.

The *Naom Eanna* remained in service until 1987, when during her annual survey and overhaul at the yard then operated by the Alexandra Engineering Company, departmental surveyors refused to renew her passenger certificate because she did not meet the latest safety regulations. She was laid up while it was decided what was to happen to her and she was later sold to the Alexandra Engineering Company, which was a subsidiary of Arklow Engineering. Finally in 1989 she was sold on to the Irish Nautical Trust for a reputed £20,000 and was towed from Sir John Rogerson's Quay into the Grand Canal Basin alongside their headquarters. There she remains at the time of writing as a clubhouse for wind surfers and canoe users.

The next vessel to enter the water from the Liffey Dockyard was the *Seamrog 11* built for the Corporation of Dublin to carry sewage sludge from the Main Drainage Works tanks at Ringsend out into Dublin bay, where it was dumped off Howth Head and the Kish Bank. She was also a replacement vessel, this time for the *Shamrock*, built in the same yard in 1908. The new ship was launched on June 1958. Also in that year Richard F. Burke was co-opted as a director of the yard on the death of his father.

Seamrog 11 (Yard No. 176) was launched in June 1958 for the Corporation of Dublin. Retired in 1988 as too small, she now forms part of the breakwater at the marina at Carlingford, County Louth.

'NOT EVEN A PARASOL'

At the luncheon following the launch of the next vessel from the dockyard on 24 February 1959, which was the dredger *Curraghour II*, constructed for the Limerick Harbour Commissioners and christened by Mrs W.M. Maguire, wife of the chairman of the Harbour Board, general manager of the Liffey Dockyard, Hugh Lennox, spoke on behalf of the builders, stating: 'These were not very sunny days in the world of shipbuilding. Any yard that was provided with an umbrella against financial downpours could be regarded as extremely favoured. So far as that was concerned the Liffey Dockyard had not even a parasol, but they had the confidence of those owners for whom they had built and launched ships since the company was formed, in respect of which no complaint had ever come back to them.' On behalf of the commissioners, Mr Maguire thanked the Liffey Dockyard Ltd, for the splendid work and for the expeditious manner in which they had executed the order. He also took the opportunity to make a plea for the port of Limerick: 'There is a tremendous revolution today in shipping circles and not withstanding this, I feel that Limerick should not be forgotten. We are the last port on the western seaboard outside the underdeveloped areas, which is a distinct disadvantage. I hope, now that the Minister has fulfilled his obligation to Cork, that he will give a little attention to Limerick and the Shannon.' He concluded that since the Minister had taken away the grain ships from Limerick, something should be done to replace them.[24]

The new vessel was a combined grab and suction hopper dredger, which replaced her previous namesake *Curraghour* dating from 1910. She had a deadweight capacity of 440 tons, with a length of 141 feet, a beam of 32 feet and a depth of 13 feet. She was propelled by a 'Father and Son' arrangement of two British Polar diesel engines of unequal power developing 434 HP. These engines were connected to the single screw via a modern wheel drive gearbox. The vessel ran trials on 13 June but seemingly there was a delay in delivery as she did not depart for Limerick until 16–17 October 1959. At the time of writing the *Curraghour II* is still in service, but she was re-engined in 1998 with a single Caterpillar 800 HP 4 stroke single acting diesel engine. She also received a new Ruston 30RB crane in 1990.

On 1 July 1959, Dr Ryan, the Minister for Finance, moved an amendment to the finance bill then going through the Dáil, which agreed provisions and relief from income tax and corporation profits tax in respect of repairs to Irish-owned ships carried out by shipyards in the state, which had previously applied only to foreign-owned vessels repaired here. The Minister said he had received representations that shipyards here could repair foreign ships more cheaply than they could repair Irish vessels.[25]

The second launch of 1959 from the Liffey yard took place on 4 November, when a cargo and livestock motor ship was christened by Mrs Lemass, wife of Seán Lemass, TD, who was at that point An Taoiseach. There is a very interesting background to this event. All the prior B & I company launchings were carried out by the wife of a director of that company. The choice of Mrs Lemass came about because secret talks about the purchase of the B & I Line were taking place between the Irish government and Coast Lines who were the owners of the Irish company. These negotiations had begun in 1957 and letters were hand-delivered from the head office in Liverpool to the master of the night passenger vessel to Dublin in the nearby Princess Dock. Having crossed the Irish Sea in the captain's safe, on arrival at the North Wall they were brought ashore to the managing director's office and then taken by company messenger to the Department of Industry & Commerce in Kildare Street for Mr Lemass. This same procedure was used for the return correspondence to Liverpool.[26]

The new vessel, named *Meath* (ON 400281), Yard No. 180, was the largest built under the original Liffey Dockyard company. She was a shelter deck vessel of 1,800 tons gross and measured 289 feet in length, with a beam of 42 feet and a loaded draft of 16 feet. At the lunch held in the Gresham Hotel the Minister for Industry & Commerce, Jack Lynch, said: 'He brought congratulations from An Taoiseach Mr Lemass, who was unavoidably absent and also his own appreciation and admiration for the general manager, staff, technicians and skilled workers, who had for many years been producing ships of a very excellent quality'. On behalf of the yard Mr Lennox said: 'Were it not for the loyal, generous and continued support in the survey, overhaul and repair work of every class on their fleet given to them by B & I, the dockyard could hardly have continued to exist.' He concluded his speech saying that 'since 1952, when the *Isolda* was built, the berths at the Liffey Dockyard had been occupied, but today they were idle. He hoped that in these sad circumstances the Minister for Industry & Commerce would do something by guiding their way a vessel or two of modest dimensions.' The next major speaker was Captain A.R.S. Nutting, OBE, chairman of the British & Irish Steam Packet Company (and of the Coast Lines Group), who said: 'The new vessel could have been constructed no doubt elsewhere at a lower cost and in a shorter time but the company had decided that encouragement of the industry in Ireland was an important consideration.' He continued: 'The B & I. Steam Packet company paid the Liffey Dockyard approximately £45,000 per annum in repairs to vessels. As an indication of the rise in the cost of building new tonnage, the *Kilkenny* in 1937 cost £90,000 while the *Meath* cost well over £500,000. Freights had not increased in anything like the same ratio and he could only trust that the vessel would secure her full share of increasing trade between this country and Britain.'

The new vessel underwent her trials in Dublin Bay on 10 May 1960 and made her maiden voyage to Liverpool with a full cargo of 850 head of livestock on the 24 May.[27]

In June, the Liffey Dockyard was busy with the B & I vessels *Kilkenny* and *Wicklow*, which were in for their annual overhauls, while SS *Guinness*, which 'had been in for three weeks being converted from coal to oil fuel should be on trials within a few days'.[28] Eight days later the *Irish Independent* reported in its 'On the Waterfront' feature that the tanker *Irish Holly* was due for her annual overhaul and was expected to remain ten to fourteen days. The same column later carried news that work on the new Cork harbour ferry boat would begin within two weeks with the keel laying of the ship.[29] James Lennox the yard manager was appointed a director of the Liffey Dockyard on 2 June 1960 – he was a brother of Hugh Lennox, the general manager.

The 1960s and a First for Cork

In December 1960 the Cork Harbour Commissioners received permission to raise a loan of £250,000 towards the cost of building new passenger tenders.[30] Early in April the Dublin newspapers were reporting difficulties with the naming of the Cork tenders, which were to be called *Blarna* and *Cill Airne*, with Irish on the stern and English on the bow. The Minister for Transport & Power objected, noting that the Mercantile Marine Act of 1955 ordained that the name of a vessel be on each side of her bows with the same name in the same language, plus port of registry on her stern. The Commissioners got round the matter by having the correct form of name in Irish on the bow and stern, with the English version on the bridge.[31]

On Tuesday 2 May 1961, the first of these two passenger tenders for the Cork Harbour Commissioners was launched into Alexandra Basin, Dublin, having been christened *Blarna* by Mrs John Horgan, wife of the chairman of CHC. The new ship (ON 400262 and Yard No. 181) measured 151 feet 9 inches in length, beam 39 feet and depth 12 feet 6 inches and had a gross of 500 tons. The ship was designed by Messrs Graham & Woolnough of Liverpool with a passenger gangway on either side aft of the funnel with three saloons, a smoke room and a tea bar with upholstered seating on three decks. The propelling machinery consisted of two 8-cylinder Crossley diesel motors giving a cruising speed of 12.5 knots.

The Minister for Transport & Power, Erskine Childers, TD, who spoke at the luncheon in the Gresham Hotel, said the government had provided half of the cost of this vessel and would also provide half of the cost of the second tender under construction (£250,000).

He went on to say that the government 'recognised the importance of the tourist trade in providing suitable facilities at major landing points such as Cobh. In 1960, 10,663 passengers arrived and 8,841 departed from Cobh, while the total tonnage of vessels using Cork and Cobh was 4,030,250 tons.' Hugh Lennox then spoke, saying that 'it was pretty well known in these times that shipbuilders in Ireland and across the channel are very reluctant to quote fixed prices for new construction.' On the same day as the launch, Robert Murdoch, one of the original founders of the yard in 1940, disposed of his shares to Messrs Sinnott, Stafford, Lennox and Heard.

The *Blarna* ran her trials on 21 September 1961 and at the end of that year the newspapers reported that a strike at the Liffey Dockyard had ended after two days of talks at the Mansion House. This was a dispute over retrospective pay involving four riggers and the 400 other workers refused to pass their picket. It was agreed that the dispute was to go to arbitration and the Seamen's Union of Ireland pickets would be withdrawn and the four riggers would resume immediately. On the following Monday there would be a full resumption of work and a five-day forty-two hour week would come into operation.[32]

It is worth mentioning that at this time the newly established Dutch Verolme Cork Dockyard in Rushbrook had just launched its first new ship into the waters of the River Lee on 5 December 1961. This was the motor bulk carrier *Irish Rowan* constructed for Irish Shipping Ltd, which was christened by Mrs de Valera, wife of President Éamon de Valera. That yard went on to construct vessels for the B & I, Naval Service, Irish Shipping, many foreign companies and Arklow Shipping Ltd before closing in 1984.

The second passenger tender for Cork, the *Cill Airne* (ON 400266 and Yard No. 182), slid down the ways in Dublin on Tuesday 20 February 1962. The launching ceremony was performed by Mrs T.F. Doyle, wife of the new chairman of the Cork Harbour Commissioners, following the blessing of the new ship by Fr W.

Lillis, parish priest of St Laurence O'Toole's church. As the vessel entered the water shipyard workers cheered and ships in port sounded their sirens. At the post-launch luncheon the Minister for Industry & Commerce, Jack Lynch, paid tribute to the efficiency of the Liffey Dockyard. Hugh Lennox noted that the ship was the tenth built in the yard and he believed that both Cork tenders would give many years of safe, sound, economical and satisfactory service. On a less up-beat note he concluded that the company was left without a keel laid and he hoped that 'our berths will not be empty for too long'.[33] However, as it turned out the *Cill Airne* was to be the last vessel constructed in the yard under the ownership of the directors who had reopened the facility two decades earlier. The new vessel ran trials on 2 May 1962.

In October the trade unions and organised labour were expressing concern about the lack of work at the Liffey yard. *The Irish Times* reported that 'Irish Shipping and British Railways were mentioned at the meeting of the Dublin Council of Trade Unions during a discussion on redundancy at the Liffey Dockyard'. During this meeting T.D. Watt of the Workers Union of Ireland said: 'After a study of the problem, Irish Shipping is one of the principal offenders in this matter. There has never been less work since it opened in 1941.' He noted that no construction or repair work of any note was being carried out in the yard at present and listed recent examples of Irish Shipping's disgraceful attitude: 'The *Irish Oak* was due to be surveyed and overhauled at the dockyard but the job was transferred to Glasgow, while the *Irish Blackthorn* had travelled from Sweden to Verolme Rotterdam, when it could have been sent to Dublin or Cork. The *Irish Holly* was scheduled for a big job and Liffey Dockyard was not even asked to tender, the work eventually being done in Liverpool. British Rail had never given work to Liffey, having traded out of the port for many years.' It was decided to raise the matter at the council's next meeting between their executive and management of the Liffey Dockyard.[34]

In reality, at that time work was generally scarce in the shipbuilding industry and later that week it was announced that more Belfast shipyard men were to lose their jobs, with another 620 to be paid off in mid November.[35] A few days later *The Irish Times* carried news that there was an alarming increase in the number of ships laid up, with the Chamber of Shipping reporting 520 British ships laid up, which was 4% of the UK fleet.[36]

EMPTY BERTHS

In Belfast, on 1 November 1962, 50,000 workers marched to the Stormont parliament buildings to protest at rising unemployment and the Northern Ireland government's failure to halt the worsening economic situation. At the end of the year Irish Shipping announced that because of the unsatisfactory trends in world shipping the *Irish Spruce* was to be laid up in Dublin until the spring of 1963. This slump in shipbuilding was also highlighted in the first annual report of the Shipping Finance Corporation for 1961. This subsidiary of the Industrial Credit Corporation was established to provide finance and encourage owners to place orders in Ireland. This company was probably created on the initiative of the Dutch-owned Verolme yard, to match similar schemes operating on the continent in providing finance.

The following year there was more bad news on the international shipbuilding scene, with a front page photograph in the *Irish Press* on 10 January 1962, showing empty berths at the Abercorn yard of Harland & Wolff Ltd in Belfast for the first time in twenty-five years. For most of that year there is no mention of shipbuilding in Dublin. However, on 1 September *The Irish Times* reported on the world slump in shipping stating that there was limited work for the Irish shipbuilding and repairing industry and that the shipyards in the Republic were experiencing mixed fortunes. They noted a slackness at Liffey Dockyard, but a spokesman claimed this was not causing undue concern as this type of lull came in cycles.

On Saturday 1 December the national newspapers carried headlines 'Objection to Statement on Tug Tender' (*Irish Press*) and 'Dublin Shipyard Firm Replies' (*The Irish Times*). These related to a decision by the Dublin Port & Docks Board to place a contract for a new tug with an English company and not with the local yard. At their meeting on Thursday 29 November, according to *The Irish Times*, the decision was criticised by Thomas Watts, a Port & Docks Board member, who said there was unemployment at the Liffey Dockyard and he, as a member of the Irish Congress of Trade Unions, thought that the contract should have gone to the Liffey Dockyard. He was reassured at the meeting by D.A. Hegarty, General Manager of the Board, that the contract's specifications had been adhered to by the company whose tender had been accepted, inferring that the Liffey yard had failed to do so. The tender of Richard Dunston Ltd, Hessle, Yorkshire, was for £142,207, while that of the Liffey Dockyard Ltd was £192,660. The following day Hugh Lennox of the Liffey Dockyard responded to Mr Hegarty, saying that they had looked again at their tender and were quite satisfied with their quote. He also criticised as 'unfavourable and damaging' the comments made by Mr Hegarty. The newspaper reports of the exchanges between the yard and the board are too long to be quoted in full, but in summary the dockyard contended that they were not given an itemised list of the machinery and equipment to be supplied on the tug in the tender documents they received from the Port Board, while from the opposing side Lennox quoted the London consultants of the Port Board who had said that 'the specifications are predominantly for guidance and the tender may submit variations consisting of any alternative power or other arrangements which he considers may advantages [*sic*] whether technical or economic'.

Mr Hegarty then quoted the price differential of £50,000 and made reference to the wage content in the two quotes. He said the board could have paid the English workers the wages expected by the men at the Liffey Dockyard to build the vessel and still shown a saving of £2,000. In his response Mr Lennox said: 'The board was quite entitled to place its contracts with whomever and wherever they pleased and we do not feel that if the DP&B desired to place this particular elsewhere, opportunity of doing so should not have been seized upon to make comments on [this] company's tender … Mr Hegarty's comments were all the more surprising, when one remembered that they emanated from people who had placed themselves in the forefront of the crusade to put Irish industry to meet the impact [*sic*] of the Common Market as successfully as possible.' Mr Lennox concluded that 'the yard was prepared to meet with officials of the Departments of Industry and Transport & Power if and when they so desire' about the terms of the contract, which still went to England.

The year 1963 opened with the *Irish Press* on 3 January carrying a story that the Workers Union of Ireland had complained to the Minister for Industry & Commerce, Jack Lynch, and the General Manager of Irish Shipping Ltd, L.S. Furlong, about the sending of the *Irish Maple* to the Clyde for repairs. The shipping company responded by saying that the *Maple* and her three sister ships were being converted by a yard in Glasgow under contract into closed shelter deck ships and since she was the last of the class, the opportunity was being taken to have this work done. This seems to be the only reference in the newspapers that year to the Dublin yard. In 1964 there is also a lack of shipbuilding news, except for what seems to have been a rancorous debate in the Dáil chamber as reported in the *Irish Independent* in June of that year, when James Dillon, TD, leader of Fine Gael, complained about the amount of subsidies given to Verolme's Cork Dockyard at Rushbrook, for the construction of vessels for overseas companies. Some of these companies were alleged by Mr Dillon to have Cornelius Verolme as a substantial shareholder. The debate ranged over two days, with

Jack Lynch, the Minister for Industry & Commerce from Cork, robustly defending the payments.[37]

The next year, 1965, passed without any news concerning shipbuilding on the Liffey until Christmas time, when on 24 December *The Irish Times* carried a report of a statement made by Deputy Martin Corry of the Labour Party the previous day. The TD said British & Irish Steam Packet ships were being sent to Scottish or Northern Ireland shipyards for repair and overhaul to the exclusion of shipyards in the Republic. He noted that some months previously the Dáil had agreed to the use of a large sum of tax-payers money to enable the government to take over the B & I line and that before this large sums had been used to establish Irish Shipping Limited, yet the government would not give him information about the repair of Irish Shipping vessels. He asked if it was too much to ask, that twenty-six vessels be kept in this country for annual overhauls, so that at least £20,000-worth of work would be kept in the country? He continued: 'I am reliably informed if overhaul and repair was guaranteed to our Irish dockyards, constant employment for an extra 100 [men] would be available. I don't think I am asking too much in inviting the directors of the B & I and Irish Shipping to meet the directors of both Verolme and Liffey dockyards in conference, to hammer out ways and means of having these ships serviced in our dockyards and keep both the money and employment at home.'

The TD's statement prompted a letter to the editor of *The Irish Times* from Hugh Lennox published on 30 December 1965, in which he pointed out that Mr Corry was mistaken in an implication that the Liffey Dockyard was government subsidised: 'Such good fortune never came the way of this yard, notwithstanding sustained efforts to that end.'

The Liffey yard continued in business, but shipbuilding and ship repair did not feature in any Dublin newspaper headlines for the next two years, except for a small item in the *Irish Independent* on 30 December 1966 about a collision in the Liffey between the Norwegian vessel *Skofoss* of 1,090 tons and the British ship *Hillswick* of 382 tons. The British vessel was being repaired, while the Norwegian had sailed for Llandulas in North Wales presumably to load a cargo of stone.

John Gordon sold his 565 shares in the company to Hugh Lennox on 1 August 1965.

THE LIFFEY YARD CHANGES HANDS

Just as the first quarter of 1968 was ending on 29 March, the three Dublin papers carried news that the Liffey Dockyard had changed hands. The *Irish Independent* carried by far the most comprehensive report:

> The transaction was concluded after talks lasting only a couple of hours in the Gresham Hotel Dublin yesterday. It was described by a spokesman for the new owners, as a straightforward cash deal with no strings. The new owner, 47-year-old Archibald Desmond Kelly, a Scotsman of Irish descent, is joint owner together with his wife of the Ardrossan Dockyard in Ayrshire. He commented, 'We are here to support Ireland. We want no guarantees of any kind from the Irish government. We came to discuss a straightforward deal without any conditions of support from the government.' With the purchase completed, the board of directors of the former Liffey Dockyard Ltd resigned. A new company with Mr Kelly as chairman will be formed. J. Ronald Millar, financial adviser to Mr Kelly's group of companies, told a news conference that the new company would concentrate on increasing the turnover and ship repairing business at the dockyard. He hoped that the employment figure of 250 at the yard would eventually be increased. The first thing they hoped to do was to establish goodwill with Irish shipowners, the workers and the trade unions. Hugh Lennox, former Director of the Liffey Dockyard emphasised that the company had not been losing money and was not in any kind of financial difficulties.

The next paragraph was headed 'To Build Ships?' and in it Mr Millar hinted that shipbuilding at the Dublin yard in the future was not out of the question. He said: 'There will be continued development; maybe given the right markets and conditions we might begin building ships there. You never know. The Liffey Dockyard covers an area of seven and a half acres and can take ships up to 18,000 tons. It is bigger than the Ardrossan yard … one would complement the other.' The report continued: 'The new deal would mean that Mr Kelly's group would now be able to accept accounts which they had to forego in the past. Negotiations with Mr Kelly's company began about six months ago, but it was only in the last few weeks that they reached the conclusive stage.' It concluded by saying that after the Second World War, Mr Kelly had entered business and built up his group of companies from scratch, which now employed 350 people. He was born in Greenock, but his father was a native of Dungannon, County Tyrone. Following the takeover, the board of the Liffey Dockyard Company, Hugh Lennox, James J. Stafford, R.D. Heard and R.F. Burke, resigned, but Hugh Lennox continued in an advisory capacity. The reasons for the sale of the yard were not known, but the report speculated that it was probably due to the fact that some of the directors were no longer involved in shipping. Mr Stafford of Wexford Steamships, no longer owned ships, while Mr Heard, who would have been a nominee of the British & Irish Steam Packet Company, which had taken over by the Irish government three years previously, was also was out of the shipping business.

A very interesting footnote to this 1968 deal came to light in 2005, during an interview I had with Denis McMillian from Glasgow. A 'Black Squad' member, who had started work as a boy in the Harland & Wolff yard at Govan in 1938 and later worked at the Fairfield yard on the Clyde, he came back to Ireland during the Glasgow Fair holiday in 1954. When the steamer *Lairdshill* berthed at the North Wall Quay in Dublin, he was met at the gangway by a mate Archie McDonald, who had worked with him in Glasgow and told him that there was a job for him in the Liffey yard. Denis McMillian took up the offer and worked in Dublin for many years. However, in 1968 when going over to Glasgow for his holidays, he passed through Ardrossan and decided to look at Kelly's operation there. It did not equate with the publicity stories being published in Dublin, and he went on to say that Mr Kelly was considered by many hands in the yard to be a 'scrap merchant' and that he would simply strip the Liffey yard.

Despite this fear, the yard continued in business. In August 1968 during the civil war in Nigeria between the Federal Government and the breakaway province of Biafra, people in Ireland were very concerned about the suffering that was being inflicted on the Ibo inhabitants of that area. Early that month newspapers reported that the Irish Biafra Aid fund was to purchase a 600-ton freighter from a Dutch company, the *Colmcille*, which would carry supplies from Europe to the island of São Tomé off the African coast, from where they would be transhipped. However the ship, which was due to leave on her first voyage on 28 August, developed a machinery problem and had to be repaired by the Liffey Dockyard. She sailed on 6 September with her first master Captain O'Shea of Irish Shipping Ltd and for the following fourteen months the small vessel sailed from ports in Ireland and Europe to Libreville and São Tomé with an Irish crew.

Although no actual shipbuilding was taking place in Dublin, on 27 October 1968 *The Irish Times* reported that on the previous day in the Dáil the Minister for Transport & Power, Erskine Childers, TD, had introduced a bill to provide grants for shipbuilding, 'The Shipbuilding Investment Grants Bill'. This was intended to provide capital for new ships of more than 100 tons gross registered under part 11 of the Merchant Marine Act 1955. The capital sum was not to exceed 25 per cent of approved capital expenditure after April 1967. As it turned out, this bill did not provide any assistance to the Liffey Dockyard, as it came too late and was intended for funding overseas vessels.

In December 1969 the new Liffey Dockyard owners launched what was to be the last vessel to be constructed on the Alexandra Basin slipways. She was a small grab hopper dredger intended for inland waterways use on the River Shannon and built to the order of the Office of Public Works in Dublin. The new vessel cost £40,000 and was financed jointly by the Commissioners of Public Works and Bord Fáilte. She was named *Coill an Eo* by Mrs A.D. Kelly, wife of the chairman of the builders. The *Irish Independent* on 10 December reported: 'The ship was designed to specific requirements including limited draught, beam and length with low headroom to enable her to pass from the tidal waters of the Shannon to the fresh water portion above Ardnacrusha.' The report went on to say that the *Coill an Eo* would carry out maintenance and improvement works on the Shannon, mainly on the Killaloe-Lanesbro' reach and including Lough Ree and Lough Derg. Speaking after the launch Dr T.J. O'Driscoll, Director General of Bord Fáilte, suggested that 'the time may come, if the Office of Public Works can find the money, to link the Barrow, Shannon and Erne North and South we would then have one of the greatest inland water complexes in Europe'. The *Irish Times* also carried a short report of the launch on that day and reported two speeches by Noel Lemass, TD, the parliamentary secretary to the Minister for Finance. One of these, at the launch reception, stated that the dockyard and the Dublin Port & Docks Board should resolve their differences over the lease for the yard premises. This drew a response from Denis Hegarty of the Port & Docks Board, who said that the dockyard needed to come up with a development plan.

Mr Kelly retained ownership of the Liffey Dockyard for most of the 1970s and during that time the most interesting job undertaken was the fabrication of a completely new bow visor for the B & I line car ferry *Munster (1)*, which was fitted in place in the large graving dock in February 1974. Towards the end of the decade the Ardrossan Dockyard Company was bought out by the Laird group of Birkenhead and London who appointed a new, all British, board of directors consisting of J.A. Gardiner (chairman), M.S. Murray (managing), R.W. Melville (secretary) and J.H. Taylor (general manager).

New visor being swung aboard into position at the bow of the M/V *Munster* in number 2 dry dock Dublin during 1974. She was the first roll on/roll off car ferry to come into service with the B & I Line and the door was fabricated by Liffey Dockyard to replace the original, which had been damaged in a collision.

In 1978 Liffey Dockyard informed its customers and suppliers by letter on 13 March that: 'The board of directors had decided to cease trading on completion of the contracts now on hand. The assets, including the premises at the Liffey Dockyard, have been disposed of to Solarship (Ireland) Ltd, a recently established ship-repairing company with the Laird Group Ltd.' The same envelope also contained a letter from the new company, saying that 'as and from today they would operate in the premises of the Liffey Dockyard as ship repairers and general engineers, having acquired that company's assets and facilities'. However, Solarship (Ireland) Ltd would appear only to have been the operating firm. The company's return, dated 23 August 1983, gives Laird Hotels Ltd, 10 James Street, London SW1 (formerly Ardrossan Dockyard) as the owners. The English group may have already pulled out at this time, as filings with the Companies Registration Office may take place months or years later.

Solarship ceased in 1981 and was followed by B & R Ship Repairs. Their largest job was the repair of coastal minesweeper LÉ *Fola CM12*, which incurred damage at Arklow while being taken out of the water following a collapse of the syncro lift platform. Arklow featured again when the next operators of the Dublin yard, Alexandra Engineering, were formed on 30 November 1981. This was the trading name of Arklow Engineering Ltd. Their largest job was the overhaul of a Russian freezer fish carrier, and the firm was eventually dissolved on 22 August 1985.

The next owner was Liffey Marine Ltd, formed on 27 August 1985, with directors William Laurence Greene, secretary, and Patrick Joseph O'Callaghan. Their largest job was the overhaul, refurbishment and major engine repairs to the passenger ferry *Cruise Muhibah*, 8,093 tons gross, which had been bought in Malaysia by an Danish Irish company set up for the purpose of chartering the vessel to the B & I Line. Taken over in Singapore in December 1989, she was so rat infested that she went to Indonesia to be fumigated. She passed through the Suez Canal on 20 January 1990 and berthed in Dublin at 19.30 hrs on 5 February after being hove-to in the Bay of Biscay by force 11 gales. The vessel had to be fumigated again as the infestation was so bad. Two and a half months later she sailed for sea trials on 25 April as the *Munster (2)*. This repair contract was estimated to have been worth between £350,000 and £500,000, and the ship remained on charter to the B & I Line for two years. Liffey Marine was dissolved on 24 November 1995.

The German-owned bulk carrier *Regina Oldendorff* entering No. 2 graving dock on Good Friday 1996. This vessel and her sister *Rixta Olendorff*, both of 26,000 tonnes deadweight, were the largest ships ever to dry dock in Dublin.

The Dublin Dry Dock Company Ltd was formed on 8 August 1995. The directors were Peter Schmidt and his wife Loretta. The former, a German national, had been active in ship repair in the Persian Gulf and had reportedly sold his interests there. In 1997 another firm, Dublin Ship Repairs, merged with the German's company. In 1998 the Dublin Dry Dock Company was placed in receivership and its assets were offered for sale. In the short time operating the company had re-instated the gates of No. 1 dry dock, which had been out of commission since 1989. These were repaired and in August 1997 the mini bulk carrier *Arklow Meadow* was the first vessel to enter the dock. Early in 1996 the company overhauled the bulk carrier sister ships *Regina Oldendorff* and *Rixta Oldendorff* each 28,000 deadweight. They are largest vessels ever to enter No. 2 graving dock with a clearance of just 18 feet at the entrance gates (9 feet on each side). The Dublin Dry Dock Company was eventually dissolved on 3 December 2002.

The next company to operate the facility was Harris Pye Dry Docks Ltd, established on 6 January 1998. The directors were Anthony Jones, secretary, Michael Victor Dawson and Christopher Trigg. All were Irish citizens with addresses in the UK. The firm only lasted about three years, but was not officially dissolved until 1 March 2006. The last ship repairing firm to operate on the 1864 site was Dublin Graving Docks Ltd established on 5 March 2002. The directors are John O'Brien, James Tyrrell, Michael Kennedy and Patrick Corcoran (secretary), the three latter all associated with Arklow Shipping Ltd. While this company still exists at the time of writing, it no longer operates from the 1864 site. It is grouped around the head of No. 2 graving dock, as all the remaining structures on the old shipyard site were demolished in 2007 to make way for container storage and a new access road to the roll-on/roll-off ferry ramp on the basin side of the North Wall Extension. The No. 1 graving dock was filled in with sand in 2008, while the seaward side was also filled and reclaimed in 2009.

Nothing now remains of 143 years of shipbuilding on the River Liffey.

ENDNOTES

CHAPTER 1

1 It should be noted that his craft were designed before the discovery by later explorers of the Polynesian outrigger canoes which had lateral supports for stability.

2 Gilligan, H.A., *A History of the Port of Dublin* (Gill & Macmillan Ltd, 1988) p. 247.

3 In 1991 a replica of Petty's craft was built at the Irish Nautical Trust premises at Grand Canal Basin, Ringsend, for Hal Sisk as part of a FÁS youth training scheme.

4 Gilligan, H.A., *A History of the Port of Dublin* (Gill & Macmillan Ltd, 1988) p. 247.

5 *Faulkner's Dublin Journal*, 24 December 1751.

6 *Exshaw's Gentleman's and London Magazine* (1778) p. 536.

7 Hammond, Joseph W., 'Georges Quay and Rogerson's Quay in the 18th Century', *Dublin Historical Record*, Vol. 2, No. 2, Dec. 1942–Feb. 1943 pp. 41–54.

8 British Admiralty survey of manpower, 1804.

9 *Ibid.*

10 *Ibid.*

11 Letter from the late Joe Clarke, a Dubliner from North King St, to the author in 2004. In 1997 he wrote two volumes of the definitive history of shipbuilding on the north-east coast of England. Clarke, J.F., *Building Ships on the North-East Coast: a labour of love, risk and pain*, Part 1 *c*. 1640-1914 and Part 2 *c*. 1914-1980 (Bewick Press, 1997).

12 Gilligan, H.A., *A History of the Port of Dublin* (Gill & Macmillan Ltd, 1988) p. 247.

13 Delaney, Ruth, *The Grand Canal of Ireland* (David & Charles PLC, 1973) pp. 120 & 260.

14 His findings are available in a pamphlet in the National Library of Ireland, ref. PO21, as is another, from 1846, to the Canal Company about plans for the graving docks and plant in Ringsend Basin, which were not carried out.

15 Commissioners of Irish Lights List, 2001, compiled by M.P.L. Costello.

16 Gilligan, H.A., *A History of the Port of Dublin* (Gill & Macmillan Ltd, 1988) p. 247.

17 The Official Number is the number allocated to a ship by the government, much like a car registration.

18 Irish, Bill, *Shipbuilding in Waterford, 1820-1882: a historical, technical and pictorial study* (Wordwell, 2001).

19 *Illustrated London News*, 5 March 1864, p. 237.

20 *The Irish Times*, 20 February 1864.

21 Anderson, E.B., *Sailing Ships of Ireland* (Morris and Company, 1951) p. 266.

22 Gilligan, H.A., *A History of the Port of Dublin* (Gill & Macmillan Ltd, 1988) p. 247.

23 Recorded in *Sea Breezes* magazine, May 1936, p. 269.

24 Fenton, Roy & Clarkson, John (eds), *British Shipping Fleets* (Ships in Focus series, Preston, 2000) p. 82.

25 Delaney, Ruth, *The Grand Canal of Ireland* (David & Charles PLC, 1973) pp. 120 & 160.

26 *The Irish Times*, 11 July 1869.

27 *The Irish Times*, 22 November 1870. A Gazette was the official Government paper for contracts and official announcements.

28 D'Arcy, Gerald, *A Portrait of the Grand Canal* (Transport Research Associates, 1969) pp. 70–1.

29 Information supplied by the late Joe Clarke.

30 O'Mahony, C., *The Maritime Gateway to Cork: a history of the outports of Passage West and Monkstown 1754– 1942* (Tower Books, 1986) p. 33.

31 Joe Clarke, letter, 2005.

32 Information taken by kind permission of the speaker from James Scannell's lecture 'A Dublin Victorian Industrial Gas Accident'.

33 A 6 rate port means a small port of no importance.

Chapter 2

1 Smellie, John, *Shipbuilding and repairing in Dublin: A record of work carried out by the Dublin Dockyard Co. 1901–1923* (McCorquodale & Co. Ltd, 1924), p. 48.

2 *Ibid.*, p. 54.

3 *Ibid.*, pp. 54–6.

4 *Ibid.*, pp. 31–6.

5 *Ibid.*, p. 60.

6 *Ibid.*, pp. 61–2.

7 *Ibid.*, p. 78.

8   *Ibid.*, p. 79.

9   Author's interview with George Rock in 2004. Mr Rock was born in No. 7 Fairfield Avenue in 1923, when his father worked in the shipyard.

10   Smellie, John, *Shipbuilding and repairing in Dublin: A record of work carried out by the Dublin Dockyard Co. 1901-1923* (McCorquodale & Co. Ltd, 1924) p. 80.

11   *Freeman's Journal,* 7 May 1903.

12   Smellie, John, *Shipbuilding and repairing in Dublin: A record of work carried out by the Dublin Dockyard Co. 1901-1923* (McCorquodale & Co. Ltd, 1924) p. 111.

13   *Ibid.*, p. 121.

14   *Belfast Newsletter*, 7 October 1911, 9 October 1911, 12 October 1911, 13 October 1911, 10 November 1911 and 22 November 1911.

15   *Syren & Shipping*, 18 September 1907.

16   *Shipbuilder*, 1908, Vol. 3, No. 18, p. 167.

17   Smellie, John, *Shipbuilding and repairing in Dublin: A record of work carried out by the Dublin Dockyard Co. 1901-1923* (McCorquodale & Co. Ltd, 1924) p. 113 The Howden's forced draught system allowed air to be blown into the furnace to increase combustion temperature.

18   The log is held in the British National Archives at Kew, ADM 52/4406.

19   Findlater, Alex, *Findlaters: The Story of a Dublin Merchant Family 1774–2001* (A & A Farmar, 2001) p. 280.

20   A deep sweep is where a long steel wire was towed behind an anti-submarine trawler, which had explosive charges fixed on it to blow up any submerged object that it struck.

21   Personal letter to the author from G.M. Gwynn Jones of Holyhead, 10 October 2007.

22   Smellie, John, *Shipbuilding and repairing in Dublin: A record of work carried out by the Dublin Dockyard Co. 1901-1923* (McCorquodale & Co. Ltd, 1924) p. 111.

23   *Ibid.*, p. 81.

24   Cox, Ronald C., 'The Grand Old Man of Irish Engineering', paper delivered on 5 Oct 1998 to a joint meeting of the Institute of Engineers of Ireland and Heritage Society.

25   *Shipbuilder*, October 1914, pp. 248 & 254.

26   Smellie, John, *Shipbuilding and repairing in Dublin: A record of work carried out by the Dublin Dockyard Co. 1901-1923* (McCorquodale & Co. Ltd, 1924) pp. 139–40.

27   *Ibid.*, pp. 140–1.

28   *Shipbuilder*, February 1915, p. 138.

29   Smellie, John, *Shipbuilding and repairing in Dublin: A record of work carried*

     out by the Dublin Dockyard Co. 1901-1923 (McCorquodale & Co. Ltd, 1924) pp. 151–65.

30 *Shipbuilder*, February 1915, p. 138.

31 *Ibid.*, August 1915, p. 41.

32 Smellie, John, *Shipbuilding and repairing in Dublin: A record of work carried out by the Dublin Dockyard Co. 1901-1923* (McCorquodale & Co. Ltd, 1924) p. 144.

33 *Ibid.*, pp. 145–50.

34 *Shipbuilder*, June 1916, p. 138.

35 *Ibid.*, p. 308.

36 Smellie, John, *Shipbuilding and repairing in Dublin: A record of work carried out by the Dublin Dockyard Co. 1901–1923* (McCorquodale & Co. Ltd, 1924) p. 140.

37 *Shipbuilder*, February 1917, p. 85 & March 1917, p. 125.

38 *Ibid.*, April 1917, p. 135.

39 *Dublin Commercial Year Book*, 1917, p. 158.

40 *Shipbuilder*, June 1917, p. 290 & December, p. 217.

41 *Ibid.*, November 1918, p. 173.

42 *Ibid.*, October 1919, p. 348.

43 Smellie, John, *Shipbuilding and repairing in Dublin: A record of work carried out by the Dublin Dockyard Co. 1901–1923* (McCorquodale & Co. Ltd, 1924) p. 170.

44 *Ibid.*, pp. 170–2.

45 *Ibid.*, p. 171.

46 *Shipbuilder*, June 1920, p. 458.

47 *Ibid.*, August 1920, p. 75.

48 *Ibid.*, September 1920, p. 130.

49 Smellie, John, *Shipbuilding and repairing in Dublin: A record of work carried out by the Dublin Dockyard Co. 1901-1923* (McCorquodale & Co. Ltd, 1924) p. 115.

50 Harvey, W.J., *Head Line: G. Heyn & Sons Ltd* (World Ship Society, 1990) p. 28.

51 Smellie, John, *Shipbuilding and repairing in Dublin: A record of work carried out by the Dublin Dockyard Co. 1901-1923* (McCorquodale & Co. Ltd, 1924) pp. 162–3.

52 *Shipbuilder*, April 1921, p. 258; May 1921, p. 398.

53 Smellie, John, *Shipbuilding and repairing in Dublin: A record of work carried out by the Dublin Dockyard Co. 1901-1923* (McCorquodale & Co. Ltd, 1924) p. 120.

54 *Shipbuilder*, January 1922, p. 75.

55 Smellie, John, *Shipbuilding and repairing in Dublin: A record of work carried*

out by the Dublin Dockyard Co. 1901–1923 (McCorquodale & Co. Ltd, 1924) pp. 172–3.

56   Ibid., p. 162.

57   Ibid., p. 173.

58   Ibid., p. 174.

59   Ibid., p. 163.

60   Ibid., pp. 163–4.

61   Ibid., p. 175.

62   Shipbuilder, February 1923, p. 139; Smellie, John, Shipbuilding and repairing in Dublin: A record of work carried out by the Dublin Dockyard Co. 1901–1923 (McCorquodale & Co. Ltd, 1924) p. 175.

63   Smellie, John, Shipbuilding and repairing in Dublin: A record of work carried out by the Dublin Dockyard Co. 1901–1923 (McCorquodale & Co. Ltd, 1924), p. 177.

64   Shipbuilder, March 1923, p. 195.

65   Each ship that a yard contracted to construct was given a Yard No. or reference no., which covered documents, coasts and materials needed for her building.

66   Shipbuilder, October 1923, p. 193.

Chapter 3

1   Twigg, Arthur M., Union Steamships Remembered, 1920–1958 (Campbell River, 1997).

2   Smellie, John, Shipbuilding and repairing in Dublin: A record of work carried out by the Dublin Dockyard Co. 1901–1923 (McCorquodale & Co. Ltd, 1924) p. 113.

3   MacPherson, K. & Burgess, J., The Ships of Canada's Naval Forces 1910–1981 (Collins & Sons, 1981).

Chapter 4

1   Delaney, Ruth, The Grand Canal of Ireland (David & Charles PLC, 1973) p. 177.

2   Shipbuilder, November 1916, p. 186.

3   Ibid., December 1917, p. 217 & January 1918, p. 49.

4   Ibid., May 1918, p. 257.

5   Being sold on the stocks meant that before the ship was completed she was offered for sale to a third party.

6   Shipbuilder, June 1921, p. 440.

7   *Ibid.*, December 1921, p. 336.
8   *Ibid.*, March 1922, p. 96.
9   *Ibid.*, August 1923, p. 83.

Chapter 5

1   *Shipbuilder*, November 1923, p. 83.
2   The Vickers Ltd Archives are held by Cambridge University Library.
3   Vickers Ltd Archives in Cambridge University Library, Ref. 1565, pp. 278–279.
4   *Ibid.*, October 1923, p. 291.
5   *Ibid.*, December 1923, p. 309.
6   *Ibid.*, 19 December 1924, p. 34.
7   *Ibid.*, 27 February 1925, pp. 44–5.
8   F. Strickland letter to V.F.G Pritchett, 24 October 1958, Vickers Ltd Archives in Cambridge University Library.
9   King, S.M., *The Port of Wanganui and the City of Wanganui*, unpublished thesis. By courtesy of Penny Allen, Wanganui Archives.
10 *Syren & Shipping*, issue 3, November 1926.
11 A davit is a crane-like device, usually one of a pair, for suspending or lowering equipment, for example a lifeboat.
12 Dick, H.W. and S.A. Kentwell, *Sold East: Traders, Tramps and Tugs of Chinese Waters* (Nautical Association of Australia Inc., 1991).
13 Vickers Ltd Archives in Cambridge University Library, Ref. 773, p. 112.
14 *Ibid.*, Ref. 825, p. 134.
15 *Shipbuilder*, No. 66, vol 17.
16 *The Shipbuilding & Shipping Record*, 26 March 1936, p. 399.
17 Vickers Ltd Archives in Cambridge University Library, Book 13, Ref. 1508, p. 198.
18 *Ibid.*, Ref. 1656, p. 6.
19 *Ibid.*, Ref. 1685, p. 18.
20 Files from the Department of An Taoiseach, Ref. S10471.
21 Vickers Ltd Archives in Cambridge University Library, Ref. 1708, p. 27.
22 This number of 200 is substantially less than the 500 shares originally held by the Irish directors, it is possible that 300 shares had already been taken back.
23 Vickers Ltd Archives in Cambridge University Library, Ref. 1740, p. 40 and Ref. 1758, p. 46.
24 *Ibid.*, Ref. 1853, p. 82.

CHAPTER 6

1 Blair, Clay, *Hitler's U-Boat War: The Hunters 1939-1942* (Volume 1) (New edition Weidenfeld & Nicolson, 2000) pp. 66–7.

2 *Ibid.*, p. 70.

3 *The Irish Times*, 4 September 1939; Share, B., *The Emergency: Neutral Ireland, 1939-45* (Gill & Macmillan, 1978).

4 *The Irish Times*, 4 September 1939.

5 Carroll, J., *Ireland in the War Years, 1939-45* (David & Charles PLC, 1975) pp. 79 & 90.

6 Dáil Debates, Vol. 77, 1–27 September 1939.

7 National Archives, Kew, File MT9 3374, letter of 4 March 1940.

8 *Ibid.*, letter from Captain Gordon to Glasgow.

9 Interview with Pat Walker in 2004.

10 Dáil Debate report, 11 December 1940.

11 National Archives, Kew, File MT9 3374.

12 *Ibid.*

13 Fenton, Roy P., *Mersey Rovers: the coastal tramp shipowners of Liverpool and the Mersey* (World Ship Society, 1997) p. 107.

14 National Archives, Kew, File MT9 3374.

15 Slader, John, *The Fourth Service: Merchantmen at War 1939–1945* (Brick Tower Press, 1995) p. 180.

16 Kennedy, Walter, *Shipping in Dublin Port 1939–1945* (The Pentland Press, 1998) p. 12.

17 Carroll, Joseph T., *Ireland in the War Years* (David and Charles, 1975) pp. 79–80.

18 *Ibid.* p. 82.

19 *The Irish Times*, 24 March 1941.

20 Spong, H.C., *Irish Shipping Ltd 1941–1982* (World Ship Society, 1982) p. 25.

21 *Ibid.*, p. 9.

22 National Archives, Kew, File MT 3684.

23 Kennedy, Walter, *Shipping at Dublin Port 1939–1945* (The Pentland Press, 1998) pp. 38 & 45.

24 National Archives, Kew, File MT9 3374.

25 *Ibid.*, File MT9 3774.

26 *Ibid.*

27 National Archives, Kew, File MT 3684.

28 Spong, H.C., *Irish Shipping Ltd 1941–1982* (World Ship Society, 1982) p. 31.

29 Letters between Leydon Dublin and T.C. Jenkins, MOWT, London, 14 and 18 November 1941.

30 Spong, H.C., *Irish Shipping Ltd 1941–1982* (World Ship Society, 1982) p. 31.

31 Wiping involved fitting magnetic cable around the ship to create an electrical field to deter magnetic mines. Kennedy, Walter, *Shipping at Dublin Port 1939–1945* (The Pentland Press, 1998) p. 50.

32 *Irish Independent*, 5 February 1943.

33 Kennedy, Walter, *Shipping at Dublin Port 1939–1945* (The Pentland Press, 1998) pp. 42, 50 & 54.

34 *The Irish Times*, 4 February 1943.

35 Kennedy, Walter, *Shipping at Dublin Port 1939–1945* (The Pentland Press, 1998) pages 42, 50 & 54.

36 Irish National Archives, Dublin.

37 National Archives, Kew, MT9 3684.

38 *Ibid.*, File M/9371/W.

39 *Ibid.*, MT9 3684.

40 *Ibid.*

41 *Ibid.*

42 *Ibid.*

43 Kennedy, Walter, *Shipping at Dublin Port 1939–1945* (The Pentland Press, 1998) p. 60.

44 *The Irish Times*, 11 December 1942.

45 Kennedy, Walter, *Shipping at Dublin Port 1939–1945* (The Pentland Press, 1998) p. 70.

46 Spong, H.C., *Irish Shipping Ltd 1941–1982* (World Ship Society, 1982) p. 32.

47 Fenton, Roy P., *Mersey Rovers: the coastal tramp shipowners of Liverpool and the Mersey* (World Ship Society, 1997) p. 67.

48 Author's interview with Johnnie Donnelly, 23 April 2003.

49 McKenna, T., 'Appendix 2: Port Control and Examination Service, Competent Port Authorities', *An Cosantoir*, April 1973, p. 133.

50 Kennedy, Walter, *Shipping at Dublin Port 1939–1945* (The Pentland Press, 1998) pp. 77, 79 & 82.

51 de Courcy Ireland, John, *Ireland and the Irish in Maritime History* (Glendale 1986), p. 345.

52 Interview with the author.

53 Kennedy, Walter, *Shipping at Dublin Port 1939–1945* (The Pentland Press, 1998) pp. 109 & 111.

54 *Ibid.*, p. 117.

55 Fenton, Roy P., interview with author, 2005.

56 Interview with the author in August 2008, who got this information from papers of Colonel Joseph Lawless dating from 1944 in his possession. In the early 1960s the army were shipping some of these vehicles to the Congo in support of the United Nations deployment there. As alterations were made to make them suitable for service in Africa, tests were also carried out in the

Glen of Imaal on their armour. These showed that when ordinary .303 Lee
Enfield bullets were fired, they did not penetrate, but when armour piercing
rounds were used these were not stopped. However, the Fords still went.

CHAPTER 7

1   *Irish Press*, 6 June 1947.
2   *Cork Examiner*, 12 April 1947.
3   *Irish Press*, 29 March 1949.
4   *Ibid.*, 29 May 1950.
5   *The Irish Times*, 5 June 1951.
6   Éire had left the Commonwealth in April 1949 and was now the Republic
    of Ireland.
7   *The Irish Times*, 23 December 1952.
8   *Irish Independent*, 21 December 1953.
9   McGinty, Tom, *The Irish Navy: a story of courage and tenacity* (Kerryman,
    1995) p. 141.
10 *Irish Independent* and *The Irish Times*, 30 August 1954.
11 Interview with John Higgins, PRO Irish Shipping Ltd, June 2004.
12 *Irish Independent*, 30 September 1954.
13 *Irish Press* and *Irish Independent* 20 June 1955.
14 *The Irish Times*, 23 July 1956.
15 Interview with Capt. Bob MacMahon, 1988.
16 *The Irish Times*, 23 July 1956.
17 *The Irish Times*, 9 January 1957.
18 Interview with John Higgins, PRO Irish Shipping Ltd, June 2004.
19 *The Irish Times*, 22 November 1956.
20 *Ibid.*, 25 November 1956.
21 *Shell-BP News*, August 1957, no. 120, p. 11.
22 *Irish Independent* and *The Irish Times*, 28 October 1957.
23 *The Irish Times*, 24 October 1957.
24 *Irish Independent*, 22 May 1959.
25 *Ibid.*, 2 July 1959.
26 Interview in 2000 with Capt. John Devany, Marine Superintendent, B & I,
    1965–1984.
27 *Irish Independent*, 18 & 24 May 1960.
28 *Ibid.*, 16 June 1960.
29 *Ibid.*, 24 June 1960.
30 *Ibid.*, 13 December 1960.
31 *Ibid.*, 3 April 1961.
32 *Ibid.* and *Irish Press*, 2 December 1961.

33 *Irish Independent*, 22 February 1962.
34 *Ibid.*, 10 October 1962.
35 *Ibid.*, 13 October 1962.
36 *The Irish Times*, 16 October 1962.
37 *Irish Independent*, 10 July 1964.

GLOSSARY

Ballast: The additional weight carried in a ship to give her stability and provide a satisfactory trim fore and aft. In larger ships this was done by taking water on board into tanks, or loading stone or gravel temporarily on board into the holds.

Boat Deck: A deck on a ship where lifeboats are kept.

Commission and Commissioned: Document by which officers hold their accredited status as naval officers issued by the Head of State. Or a warrant that is issued by a state appointing a vessel as warship of that nation. Can mean 'in use'.

Daymark: A wooden diamond or ball shape hoisted up the mast of a light vessel, which identifies a particular danger to passing ships.

Depth moulded: The vertical distance measured from the top of the keel to the underside of the upper deck at the side.

Draft or Draught: The depth of water that a ship is drawing. A loaded ship will sit deeper in the water than a ship which is half loaded or empty.

Dry or Graving Dock: An enclosed dock closed at the seaward end by gates, which when shut keep out the sea, allowing the water inside to be pumped out. This allows the under water hull of the ship to be inspected and repaired.

Elevator: A series of linked buckets lifting coal or cargo to a height and discharging the contents onto a chute.

Length overall: The extreme length of the ship measured from the tip of the bow above the water line to the stern again above the waterline.

Length BP (between perpendiculars): Length of the ship measured from each end of the keel between two vertical lines.

Lloyd's: An association of underwriters or insurers in London, which has been in existence since 1601.

Lloyd's Register of Shipping: Established by Lloyd's insurers in 1760 this is a publication that lays down rules regarding a ship's structure, depending on her length, beam, depth and draft and type of cargoes to be carried, and also the type of equipment fitted on board. If a ship is compliant with the rules, she is issued with the classification 100 A1. The underwriters asked to insure the vessel thus know that she will be found worthy of insurance cover.

Moulded depth: Measurement from weather deck to the keel along the line of the hull.

Poop deck: the aft and highest deck of a ship.

Red Ensign: Flag flown by all merchant ships registered in the United Kingdom.

Red Duster: Sailors slang term for the Red Ensign.

Screw: A propeller.

Self trimming: A ship may able to adjust her position in the sea by pumping water from one tank to another, so that she sits correctly in the sea.

Tonnage Gross: The volume of all the enclosed spaces on a ship.

Tonnage Nett: The measurement of the cargo earning capacity divided by 100 to give metric tonnes.

Tonnage Deadweight: The total weight of the cargo carried plus fuel and stores.

Tonnage Displacement: Used for naval vessels, the total amount of water displaced by the ship.

Topgallant forecastle: The space beneath the short raised deck forward, known by this name in sailing ships, usually seen in smaller ships.

White Ensign: The flag flown by a British warship.

Yard Number: Each order received by a yard to either build or repair a ship is allocated a job or yard number which refers to all work and materials used and the costs of installing machinery and equipment.

INDEX

Coast Lines Ltd 33, 103, 178, 253, 282, 283
Cobh (see also Queenstown) 7, 19, 205, 223, 227, 234, 285
Coill an Eo, the 294
Coliemore, the 246, 262
Collingham, the 222
Colmcille, the 293
Commissioners of Irish Lights 29, 58, 87, 100, 121, 153, 154, 173, 174, 175, 244, 259, 260, 261, 262, 263, 266, 267
Commission on Tidal Harbours 14
Congested Districts Board 58, 77, 78, 89
Constance, the 79
Cork Harbour Commissioners 284, 285
Cork Steamship Company 19
Countess Corinne, the 175
Countess of Dublin, the 33
Countess of Erne, the 28, 29, 30
Courtney Clarke 12, 13, 14
Craigavon, the 146, 148
Crawford, Robert 90, 249
Cruise Muhibah, the 296
Curlew, the 63
Curraghour, the 88, 281
Curraghour II, the 280, 281

D

Dalkey Shipyard Ltd 268
Dargan, William 15
David Rowan & Company 77, 110, 112, 122, 140
Dawson, Arthur Trevor 158, 160, 163
Dawson, James 12
Delgany, the 258
Department of Agriculture and Technical Instruction for Ireland 76, 78, 85
Department of Finance 194, 234
Department of Industry & Commerce 155, 194, 196, 197, 206, 207, 243, 246, 249, 258, 282
Depthfinder, the 180
de Valera, Éamon 82, 181, 204, 205, 216, 222, 223, 234, 251, 285
Director of Merchant Ship Repairs 211, 212
Dodder, the 28, 29, 30, 49, 50

Donefield, D. 41
Dorset of Ireland, the 9
Doyle & Company 68
Doyle, Alderman Vincent 57, 60
Doyle, Alderman William 53, 54
Drake, Francis 9
Drogheda 23, 37, 40, 174, 188
Drogheda Steam Packet Company 40
Duane, P., Capt. 82, 83
Dublin & Drogheda Railway 16
Dublin & Kingstown Company 16, 28
Dublin & Wicklow Railway 25
Dublin and Kingstown Steam Packet Company 25
Dublin Chamber of Commerce 53
Dublin Corporation 53, 55, 58, 71, 154, 207, 275
Dublin Distillery 82
Dublin Dockyard Company 14, 41, 65, 66, 69, 71, 72, 74, 79, 80, 85, 90, 92, 96, 97, 99, 100, 101, 103, 104, 105, 109, 110, 111, 112, 114, 115, 119, 121, 123, 124, 126, 129, 130, 131, 132, 133, 134, 135, 140, 144, 150, 153, 157, 158, 159, 160, 162, 163, 165, 179, 180, 182, 183, 185, 186, 188, 189, 191, 193, 194, 195, 196, 197, 206, 207, 208, 210, 211, 227, 237, 252, 255, 257, 263, 292
Dublin Dockyard War Munitions Company 101
Dublin Dry Dock Company Ltd 297, 298
Dublin General Steam Shipping Company 102
Dublin Glasgow Line 58
Dublin Port & Docks Board 15, 22, 37, 38, 39, 40, 48, 50, 53, 54, 55, 58, 59, 63, 64, 65, 66, 67, 68, 69, 70, 72, 73, 91, 92, 97, 98, 99, 100, 102, 103, 105, 109, 118, 122, 123, 125, 126, 127, 128, 129, 145, 154, 157, 158, 160, 164, 179, 180, 185, 186, 193, 194, 195, 196, 205, 206, 209, 259, 260, 262, 271, 272, 273, 275, 276, 277, 288, 294
Dublin Shipbuilders Ltd 113, 143, 145, 147, 149, 150, 151, 152
Dublin Society of Shipwrights 42